REVISION WORKBOOK

Company Law

Second Edition

EDITOR: SUSAN BARBER
LLB, Barrister, PgD, MILT

OLD BAILEY PRESS

OLD BAILEY PRESS
at Holborn College, Woolwich Road,
Charlton, London, SE7 8LN

First published 1997
Second edition 2002

ISBN 1 85836 369 1

British Library Cataloguing-in-Publication.

A CIP Catalogue record for this book is available from the British Library.

Printed and bound in Great Britain.

Contents

Acknowledgement

Some questions used are taken or adapted from past University of London LLB (External) Degree examination papers and our thanks are extended to the University of London for their kind permission to use and publish the questions.

Caveat

The answers given are not approved or sanctioned by the University of London and are entirely our responsibility.

They are not intended as 'Model Answers', but rather as Suggested Solutions.

The answers have two fundamental purposes, namely:

a) to provide a detailed example of a suggested solution to an examination question; and

b) to assist students with their research into the subject and to further their understanding and appreciation of the subject.

Introduction

This Revision WorkBook has been designed specifically for those studying company law to undergraduate level. Its coverage is not confined to any one syllabus, but embraces all the major company law topics to be found in university examinations.

Each chapter contains a brief introduction explaining the scope and overall content of the topic covered in that chapter. There follows, in each case, a list of key points which will assist the student in studying and memorising essential material with which the student should be familiar in order to fully understand the topic.

Additionally in each chapter there is a key cases and statutes section which lists the most relevant cases and statutory provisions applicable to the topic in question. These are intended as an aid to revision, providing the student with a concise list of materials from which to begin revision.

Each chapter usually ends with several typical examination questions, together with general comments, skeleton solutions and suggested solutions. Wherever possible, the questions are drawn from the University of London external company law papers, with recent questions being included where possible. However, it is inevitable that, in compiling a list of questions by topic order rather than chronologically, not only do the same questions crop up over and over again in different guises, but there are gaps where questions have never been set at all.

Undoubtedly, the main feature of this Revision WorkBook is the inclusion of as many past examination questions as possible. While the use of past questions as a revision aid is certainly not new, it is hoped that the combination of actual past questions from the University of London LLB external course and specially written questions, where there are gaps in examination coverage, will be of assistance to students in achieving a thorough and systematic revision of the subject.

Careful use of the Revision WorkBook should enhance the student's understanding of company law and, hopefully, enable you to deal with as wide a range of subject matter as anyone might find in a company law examination, while at the same time allowing you to practise examination techniques while working through the book.

Abbreviations

Throughout this Revision WorkBook the abbreviations CA and IA are used for Companies Act and Insolvency Act respectively. If examination candidates choose to use similar abbreviations when answering examination questions, the full name of the relevant Act should always be given alongside the abbreviated form where it first appears, as in the suggested solutions in this book.

Studying Company Law

Company law is a subject which is heavily regulated by statute – companies do not exist at common law. Students coming fresh to the subject may therefore form the impression that a knowledge of the statutes is the most important asset for a company lawyer. This is not entirely true. Although the statutes form the basis of the subject, there is also a vast amount of case law, some of which interprets the statutes, while other parts lay down principles which are not to be found in the statutes at all. The subject is one which may also overlap with other areas of law, in particular equity and trusts and contract. There are also occasional criminal liabilities, but it is safe to say that most undergraduate company law courses place relatively little emphasis on these with the possible exception of insider trading and the emerging law relating to corporate manslaughter.

Because of the amount of statutory regulation and case law in this subject, it is important for students to look for underlying principles in the subject. If these are grasped, it may well be possible to work out a sensible answer to a problem question even when much of the detailed law has been forgotten. Thus, it is important to know that company law normally operates on a principle of majority rule, that directors are in a fiduciary position in the company, and that the ultimate control rests in the general meeting.

Another important theme running through company law is that of maintaining a balance between the interests of shareholders, creditors and directors. Many apparently complex problems can be reduced to examples of this conflict.

In examinations essay questions tend to fall into two types. One type asks for an account of a particular area of the law. In attempting these questions it is important to identify carefully which area is being asked about and to stick to the point – company law topics are often interwoven, and it is easy to be lured into irrelevancy. It is also necessary to know the material thoroughly. These questions should be avoided by students who are relying on grasp of principle rather than detailed knowledge. The second type of essay question asks about issues of policy, often couched in terms which suggest that the law in a particular area is defective. Obviously, some knowledge of the law is required to answer these questions, but they are also suitable for those with a good grasp of principle.

Problem questions frequently cover a number of different areas. For this reason it is important to look closely at them and to ensure that all the areas are covered. In particular, remember to look at the situation from the point of view of all the parties. Remember that the remedies available to the company are not necessarily the same as those available to the shareholders, and that the directors are separate from the company. Some problems may ask about actions which appear to prejudice the creditors, even though the creditors are not mentioned in the problem: remember to consider their remedies as well.

At the time of writing, company law reform is on the cards. The DTI has submitted a detailed report to the Government.

Revision and Examination Technique

Revision Technique

Planning a revision timetable

In planning your revision timetable make sure you do not finish the syllabus too early. You should avoid leaving revision so late that you have to 'cram' – but constant revision of the same topic leads to stagnation.

Plan ahead, however, and try to make your plans increasingly detailed as you approach the examination date.

Allocate enough time for each topic to be studied. But note that it is better to devise a realistic timetable, to which you have a reasonable chance of keeping, rather than a wildly optimistic schedule which you will probably abandon at the first opportunity!

The syllabus and its topics

One of your first tasks when you began your course was to ensure that you thoroughly understood your syllabus. Check now to see if you can write down the topics it comprises from memory. You will see that the chapters of this WorkBook are each devoted to a syllabus topic. This will help you decide which are the key chapters relative to your revision programme, though you should allow some time for glancing through the other chapters.

The topic and its key points

Again working from memory, analyse what you consider to be the key points of any topic that you have selected for particular revision. Seeing what you can recall, unaided, will help you to understand and firmly memorise the concepts involved.

Using the WorkBook

Relevant questions are provided for each topic in this book. Naturally, as typical examples of examination questions, they do not normally relate to one topic only. But the questions in each chapter will relate to the subject matter of the chapter to a degree. You can choose your method of consulting the questions and solutions, but here are some suggestions (strategies 1–3). Each of them pre-supposes that you have read through the author's notes on key points and key cases and statutes, and any other preliminary matter, at the beginning of the chapter. Once again, you now need to practise working from memory, for that is the challenge you are preparing yourself for. As a rule of procedure constantly test yourself once revision starts, both orally and in writing.

Strategy 1

Strategy 1 is planned for the purpose of quick revision. First read your chosen question carefully and then jot down in abbreviated notes what you consider to be the main points at issue. Similarly, note the cases and statutes that occur to you as being relevant for citation purposes. Allow yourself sufficient time to cover what you feel to be relevant. Then study the author's skeleton solution and skim-read the suggested solution to see how they compare with your notes. When comparing consider carefully what the author has included (and concluded) and see whether that agrees with what you have written. Consider the points of variation also. Have you recognised the key issues? How relevant have you been? It is possible, of course, that you have referred to a recent case that is relevant, but which had not been reported when the WorkBook was prepared.

Strategy 2

Strategy 2 requires a nucleus of three hours in which to practise writing a set of examination answers in a limited time-span.

Select a number of questions (as many as are normally set in your subject in the examination you are studying for), each from a different chapter in the WorkBook, without consulting the solutions. Find a place to write where you will not be disturbed and try to arrange not to be interrupted for three hours. Write your solutions in the time allowed, noting any time needed to make up if you are interrupted.

After a rest, compare your answers with the suggested solutions in the WorkBook. There will be considerable variation in style, of course, but the bare facts should not be too dissimilar. Evaluate your answer critically. Be 'searching', but develop a positive approach to deciding how you would tackle each question on another occasion.

Strategy 3

You are unlikely to be able to do more than one three hour examination, but occasionally set yourself a single question. Vary the 'time allowed' by imagining it to be one of the questions that you must answer in three hours and allow yourself a limited preparation and writing time. Try one question that you feel to be difficult and an easier question on another occasion, for example.

Misuse of suggested solutions

Don't try to learn by rote. In particular, don't try to reproduce the suggested solutions by heart. Learn to express the basic concepts in your own words.

Keeping up-to-date

Keep up-to-date. While examiners do not require familiarity with changes in the law during the three months prior to the examination, it obviously creates a good impression if you can show you are acquainted with any recent changes. Make a habit of looking through one of the leading journals – *Modern Law Review*, *Law Quarterly Review* or the *New Law Journal*, for example – and cumulative indices to law reports, such as the *All England Law Reports* or *Weekly Law Reports*, or indeed the daily law reports in *The Times*. The *Law Society's Gazette* and the *Legal Executive Journal* are helpful sources, plus any specialist journal(s) for the subject you are studying.

Examination Skills

Examiners are human too!

The process of answering an examination question involves a communication between you and the person who set it. If you were speaking face to face with the person, you would choose your verbal points and arguments carefully in your reply. When writing, it is all too easy to forget the human being who is awaiting the reply and simply write out what one knows in the area of the subject! Bear in mind it is a person whose question you are responding to, throughout your essay. This will help you to avoid being irrelevant or long-winded.

The essay question

Candidates are sometimes tempted to choose to answer essay questions because they 'seem' easier. But the examiner is looking for thoughtful work and will not give good marks for superficial answers.

The essay-type of question may be either purely factual, in asking you to explain the meaning of a certain doctrine or principle, or it may ask you to discuss a certain proposition, usually derived from a quotation. In either case, the approach to the answer is the same. A clear programme must be devised to give the examiner the meaning or significance of the doctrine, principle or proposition and its origin in common law, equity or statute, and cases which illustrate its application to the branch of law concerned. Essay questions offer a good way to obtain marks if you have thought carefully about a topic, since it is up to you to impose the structure (unlike the problem questions where the problem imposes its own structure). You are then free to speculate and show imagination.

The problem question

The problem-type question requires a different approach. You may well be asked to advise a client or merely discuss the problems raised in the question. In either case, the most important factor is to take great care in reading the question. By its nature, the question will be longer than the essay-type question and you will have a number of facts to digest. Time spent in analysing the question may well save time later, when you are endeavouring to impress on the examiner the considerable extent of your basic legal knowledge. The quantity of knowledge is itself a trap and you must always keep within the boundaries of the question in hand. It is very tempting to show the examiner the extent of your knowledge of your subject, but if this is outside the question, it is time lost and no marks earned. It is inevitable that some areas which you have studied and revised will not be the subject of questions, but under no circumstances attempt to adapt a question to a stronger area of knowledge at the expense of relevance.

When you are satisfied that you have grasped the full significance of the problem-type question, set out the fundamental principles involved.

You will then go on to identify the fundamental problem (or problems) posed by the question. This should be followed by a consideration of the law which is relevant to the problem. The source of the law, together with the cases which will be of assistance in solving the problem, must then be considered in detail.

Very good problem questions are quite likely to have alternative answers, and in advising a party you should be aware that alternative arguments may be available. Each stage of your answer, in this case, will be based on the argument or arguments considered in the previous stage, forming a conditional sequence.

If, however, you only identify one fundamental problem, do not waste time worrying that you cannot think of an alternative – there may very well be only that one answer.

The examiner will then wish to see how you use your legal knowledge to formulate a case and how you apply that formula to the problem which is the subject of the question. It is this positive approach which can make answering a problem question a high mark earner for the student who has fully understood the question and clearly argued their case on the established law.

Examination checklist

a) Read the instructions at the head of the examination carefully. While last-minute changes are unlikely – such as the introduction of a compulsory question or an increase in the number of questions asked – it has been known to happen.

b) Read the questions carefully. Analyse problem questions – work out what the examiner wants.

c) Plan your answer before you start to write.

d) Check that you understand the rubric before you start to write. Do not 'discuss', for example, if you are specifically asked to 'compare and contrast'.

e) Answer the correct number of questions. If you fail to answer one out of four questions set you lose 25 per cent of your marks!

Style and structure

Try to be clear and concise. Fundamentally this amounts to using paragraphs to denote the sections of your essay, and writing simple, straightforward sentences as much as possible. The sentence you have just read has 22 words – when a sentence reaches 50 words it becomes difficult for a reader to follow.

Do not be inhibited by the word 'structure' (traditionally defined as giving an essay a beginning, a middle and an end). A good structure will be the natural consequence of setting out your arguments and the supporting evidence in a logical order. Set the scene briefly in your opening paragraph. Provide a clear conclusion in your final paragraph.

Table of Cases

Table of Statutes

Chapter 1

Corporate Personality

1.1   Introduction

1.2   Key points

1.3   Key cases and statutes

1.4   Questions and suggested solutions

1.1 Introduction

Corporate personality may be defined as the doctrine that a company is for legal purposes an independent person having an existence separate from that of the human beings who own, manage and serve it. For the most part the doctrine is well settled, though there are still some difficulties is working out certain of the implications of the doctrine. These difficulties are considered in the key points section below.

1.2 Key points

Concept of incorporation

A company is formed by the process of 'incorporation'. This is an administrative procedure, and its correct completion is both necessary and sufficient for the company to exist as an independent legal entity.

Legal capacity and personality

Once a company is duly incorporated it has both legal personality and legal capacity.

Legal personality means that the company exists as a legal person. It is distinct from its shareholders, directors and employees. As a separate person it has its own interests, which must be considered separately from those of the humans involved with it.

Legal capacity means that the company can own property and can make contracts in its own name and on its own behalf. In practice this will be done through the agency of human beings, but it is essential to understand that as a matter of law these acts will be the acts of the company.

Groups of companies

Particular difficulties arise where there are groups of companies. A company may own some or all of the shares in another company. Where one company has a majority of the shares in another company, the first is said to control the second, and the two companies form a group. In practice groups of many companies are found.

In principle each company in the group remains a separate legal entity, with its own property and its own rights and liabilities. This principle is sometimes used as a way of minimising or avoiding liabilities, and this may lead to an argument that some or all of the companies in a group should be regarded as a single entity. This is considered further under 'the veil of incorporation' below.

The veil of incorporation

When a company has been formed it is said to be protected by the 'veil of incorporation'. This means that it is not open to outsiders to argue that the company is really the same person as those controlling it (*Salomon* v *Salomon & Co* [1897] AC 22). The *Salomon* principle was further re-emphasised in *Polly Peck International plc (In Administration)* [1996] 2 All ER 433.

The corollary to this fundamental principle is that a company's directors and shareholders may contract with it (*Lee* v *Lee's Air Farming* [1961] AC 12), do not generally incur liability for its debts or defaults, and are not entitled to its property (*Macaura* v *Northern Assurance Co Ltd* [1925] AC 619). There are, however, exceptions to this principle.

Agency

A company may be found to be acting as the agent of its principal shareholders and/or directors, although there is no general presumption that this is so; for an explanation of the principles see *Smith, Stone & Knight Ltd* v *Birmingham Corporation* [1939] 4 All ER 116.

Trust

Where shares in a company are held on trust, the court may occasionally be prepared to look at the terms on which they are held (*Abbey Malvern Wells Ltd* v *MLGP* [1951] Ch 728), but it seems that this exception will apply only rarely.

Statute

Some statutory provisions, eg Insolvency Act 1986, ss212–215 and Companies Act 1985, ss24, 117(8) and 349(4), impose personal liability on directors or members in certain circumstances.

Interpretation

The court may look to the 'economic reality' to assist it in interpreting statutes, contracts and other documents (*DHN* v *Tower Hamlets London Borough Council* [1976] 3 All ER 462, where a group was treated as a single economic unit for the purposes of a statutory compensation payment).

Corporate façade

This is said to be the only true case of 'piercing' or 'lifting the veil' where a company has been used as a 'mere façade' to conceal the true facts. Examples include using a company as a vehicle to: avoid a conveyance (*Jones v Lipman* [1962] 1 WLR 832); evade a covenant in restraint of trade (*Gilford Motor Co v Horne* [1933] Ch 935); avoid payment of damages (*Creasey v Breachwood Motors Ltd* [1992] BCC 638); and gain an advantage improperly (*Re F G Films Ltd* [1953] 1 WLR 483).

While the Court of Appeal in *Adams v Cape Industries plc* [1991] 1 All ER 929 refused to accept that the court can lift the veil whenever it is 'necessary to achieve justice' (per Cumming-Bruce LJ in *Re A Company* [1985] BCLC 333), it nevertheless declined to give any guidance on how the court should decide when the company has been used as a 'mere façade'. However, it seems there is nothing wrong per se in a company arranging its affairs in reliance on the *Salomon* principle so as to minimise or avoid its liabilities.

1.3 Key cases and statutes

* *Abbey Malvern Wells Ltd v MLGP* [1951] Ch 728
  Where shares are held by a company on trust the court may look at the terms on which they are held

* *Adams v Cape Industries plc* [1991] 1 All ER 929
  Refusal by the courts to accept that the court can lift the corporate veil whenever it is necessary to achieve justice, but no further guidance given

* *Creasey v Breachwood Motors Ltd* [1992] BCC 638
  Company used to avoid payment of damages

* *DHN v Tower Hamlets London Borough Council* [1976] 3 All ER 462
  A group was treated as a single economic entity

* *F G Films Ltd, Re* [1953] 1 WLR 483
  Use of a company to gain an improper advantage

* *Gilford Motor Co v Horne* [1933] Ch 935
  Company used to avoid covenant in restraint of trade

* *H and Ors (Restraint Order: Realisable Property), Re* [1996] 2 All ER 391
  The Court of Appeal regarded property of certain companies as that of shareholders where there was evidence that the company structure had been used to avoid excise duty

* *International Credit and Investment Co (Overseas) Ltd v Adham* [1998] BCC 134
  Freezing orders made against persons associated with a company where a receiver was appointed over the company's property to prevent its disposal

- *Jones* v *Lipman* [1962] 1 WLR 832
  Company used as a facade to avoid a conveyance

- *Lee* v *Lee's Air Farming* [1961] AC 12
  A company may contract with its directors and shareholders even though in practice they are one and the same

- *Macaura* v *Northern Assurance Co Ltd* [1925] AC 619
  A company director is not entitled to the property of the company

- *Mephistopheles Debt Collection Services (A Firm)* v *Lotay* [1994] 1 WLR 1064
  Only a company enjoys separate legal personality

- *Polly Peck International plc (In Administration)* [1996] 2 All ER 433
  Salomon principle upheld

- *Salomon* v *Salomon & Co* [1897] AC 22
  Bedrock case concerning the separation of a company from the people that control it

- *Seaboard Offshore Ltd* v *Secretary of State for Transport* [1994] 2 All ER 99
  A company was not vicariously liable for the acts of all its employees

- *Smith, Stone & Knight Ltd* v *Birmingham Corporation* [1939] 4 All ER 116
  A company may be found to be acting as agent for its principal shareholders

- *Trustor AB* v *Smallbone* (2001) The Times 30 March
  Director of company transferred money from company's account directly to himself and used it

- Companies Act 1985

  - s24 – personal liability on reduction in members

  - s117(8) – plc requirements as to shareholding

  - s349(4) – personal liability where another is authorised to sign a document

- Insolvency Act 1986, ss212 to 215 – imposes personal liability on directors in misfeasance proceedings

1.4 Questions and suggested solutions

QUESTION ONE

'B C Hunt has written of "that brilliant intellectual achievement of the Roman lawyers, the juristic person, a subject of rights and liabilities as a natural person". Although so anticipated, to some extent, the achievement is no less remarkable in English law where a corporate legal entity has been evolved which has shown itself to be fully adequate to meet the vastly greater and more complex needs of modern times and, so far, capable of adaptation and development to maintain its usefulness.'

Discuss with reference to the development of the corporate entity doctrine in English company law.

University of London LLB Examination
(for External Students) Company Law June 1995 Q1

General Comment

The proposition requires an overview of the origin and rationale for the *Salomon* v *Salomon & Co* [1897] AC 22 principle and of the circumstances in which the courts will look behind the corporate veil.

Skeleton Solution

Outline of *Salomon* principle – brief rationale for the idea – examples of lifting the veil – group activities – deliberate abuse of corporate form to avoid obligations or restrictions – judicial analysis of facts on agency or instrument basis – statutory incursions into the principle – abuse of controlling positions within closely held companies.

Suggested Solution

The development of the concept of corporate legal entity owes much to *Salomon* v *Salomon & Co* [1897] AC 22, where the House of Lords established the principle that incorporation creates a legal entity completely separate and distinct from its members. There is no agency or fiduciary relationship created between company and member, and the fact of incorporation, without more, does not make the members liable for company debts beyond the limit of their share liability. This, and the development of limitation of liability by share or guarantee, has created a highly flexible method of conducting business of almost unlimited scope and scale. The system offers considerable protection to creditor, member, employee and director, while maintaining a form that is subject to the control of the law to a remarkable degree. The true worth of the system can be seen in cases where there is attempted abuse of limited liability or company law, or where injustice would follow too strict an application of the principle. The courts are quite willing to lift the 'veil of incorporation' in appropriate cases and certain situations illustrate this well.

Corporate groups and dominance by holding companies

The leading case is *Smith, Stone & Knight Ltd* v *Birmingham Corporation* [1939] 4 All ER 116, where the court reviewed the question of a holding company's entitlement to disturbance compensation for property occupied in the name of, and for the purposes of, a subsidiary. The judgments suggest tests to ascertain the reality of who traded there: was it a truly independent subsidiary or a mere corporate shadow of the holding company? The court looked behind the veil and saw clearly that the subsidiary had little existence beyond paper and that the holding company should succeed in obtaining compensation. A similar result was seen in *DHN* v *Tower Hamlets London*

Borough Council [1976] 3 All ER 462. Significant factors in such a consideration are the incidence of day-to-day control and management, or lack of it. The financial substructure of the subsidiary was looked at in *Re F G Films Ltd* [1953] 1 WLR 483 and *Littlewoods Mail Order Stores Ltd* v *Inland Revenue Commissioners* [1969] 1 WLR 1241. If, however, a holding company transfers property legally to its subsidiary to gain a perceived business advantage, it cannot expect the courts to lift the veil for the purpose of regaining an immunity for unlimited tortious liability which it lost in transferring the property: *William Cory & Sons Ltd* v *Dorman Long & Co Ltd* [1936] 2 All ER 386.

Abuse of corporate form to evade obligations or restrictions

In *Re Bugle Press Ltd* [1961] Ch 270, the court lifted the veil to disclose a company acquired and used for the sole purpose of taking advantage of statutory rights available to takeover bidders. The company was used by holders of 90 per cent of the shares in the target company who could not, without this device, bring themselves within s428 Companies Act (CA) 1985 as an 'offeror'. The court refused to sanction such tactics. A fairly common abuse is the transfer of property into, or out of, companies to prevent creditors, trustees in bankruptcy or other claimants succeeding to it or acquiring it. In this situation the court will look at the reality of the transaction, and disregard abuse and sham as in *Jones* v *Lipman* [1962] 1 WLR 832, (attempt to avoid specific performance of house transfer). In *Wallersteiner* v *Moir (No 1)* [1974] 3 All ER 217, a most serious abuse of the corporate form required the court to pierce the veil.

Judicial analysis of facts on agency or instrument basis

Despite the pronouncements to the contrary in *Salomon* v *Salomon & Co* [1897] AC 22, the courts will, where appropriate, give serious consideration to whether a company can be the agent or instrument of its members. Agency arguments particularly appeal to the courts in taxation cases, as in *Apthorpe* v *Peter Schoenhofen Brewing Co Ltd* (1899) 80 LT 395 and *Firestone Tyre and Rubber Co* v *Llewellin* [1957] 1 WLR 464, but arguments in the group cases seem also to rest upon agency. Nevertheless, the courts look for much more than mere shareholding to show agency, particularly between holding company and subsidiary. In *Kodak Ltd* v *Clark* [1902] 2 KB 450, a 98 per cent holding of the shares in an American subsidiary was not enough to make it an agency relationship. In *Lennard's Carrying Co* v *Asiatic Petroleum* [1915] AC 705, the point is made that if a company is truly the creature of its controller or owner, then it will be liable for his acts or omissions in using the medium of the company to achieve his ends.

Statutory intervention upon the doctrine

Statute has created significant inroads upon the corporate entity doctrine both in the area of pending or actual insolvency as well as in cases of fraudulent, negligent or abusive control and manipulation of companies. In cases of fraudulent or wrongful trading under ss213, 214 and 216 Insolvency Act (IA) 1986 (restrictions upon use of company names), personal liability for the debts of the company can be visited upon directors and shadow directors (s214 IA 1986) and those persons along with others (s216 IA 1986). In various other breaches of company legislation, personal liability for debt or loss can be imposed upon directors and controllers but these matters are not so much a lifting of the veil but rather a statutory provision of remedies to prevent the *Salomon* v *Salomon & Co* [1897] AC 22 principle being invoked as a defence.

Abuse of controlling positions within closely held companies

Cases such as *Scottish Co-operative Wholesale Society* v *Meyer* [1959] AC 324 and *Ebrahimi* v *Westbourne Galleries Ltd* [1973] AC 360 show the possibilities for the unconscionable and unfair prejudice to the legitimate expectations of members of closely held companies by the simple expedient of controlling members conducting the affairs of the company in an abusive way. On one view, such acts are the acts of the company itself, but the corporate entity is flexible enough to allow the courts to use equitable principles to prevent abuse without destroying the essential principle of majority control. This has also led to the statutory protections provided by ss459, 460 and 461 CA 1985 and the whole development of the law on minority protection illustrates the capacity of the corporate entity doctrine to be successfully adapted to the almost limitless range of company types and sizes whilst preserving the possibility for judicial intervention against abusive control.

In summary, it is submitted that the proposition of B C Hunt is eminently supportable.

QUESTION TWO

Ash Ltd and Smoke Ltd are both wholly owned subsidiaries of Fire Ltd. Fire Ltd has substantial assets and has a policy of issuing substantial annual dividends to all of its shareholders. Turf, Coal and Log are directors of all three companies.

Ash Ltd has been making losses on all commercial activities during the last three years. Fire Ltd has provided finance to cover these losses. In January of the current financial year the trading activities of Fire Ltd suffer a severe downturn. Fire Ltd will not have any surplus to meet the expected shortfall in the accounts of Ash Ltd. As a consequence, Turf, Coal and Log decide they will no longer allow Fire Ltd to meet any of the debts of Ash Ltd and will allow Ash Ltd to go into insolvent liquidation. Nevertheless they allow Ash Ltd to continue trading until the end of the financial year in April. In May, Ash Ltd went into insolvent liquidation. Grass, who is an unsecured creditor of Ash Ltd, has sustained substantial losses.

Smoke Ltd produces toxic chemicals for the nuclear power industry. During production toxic chemicals are released accidentally into the atmosphere. As a consequence several local residents, including John, are severely injured and there is substantial environmental damage. Substantial claims are made against Smoke Ltd but it transpires that Smoke Ltd has insufficient assets to meet these claims.

Advise Grass and John.

University of London LLB Examination
(for External Students) Company Law June 2000 Q7

General Comment

This question involves a consideration of when the courts will lift the corporate veil, for example when construing a contract, statute or document, or when a company is a mere façade concealing the true facts, or if the company is an agent of another.

Skeleton Solution

Wrongful trading, separate legal identity and lifting the veil – is a parent company liable for the debts of a subsidiary? – consider the single economic unit exception to the rule in *Salomon* v *Salomon* – s214 Insolvency Act 1986: have the directors incurred personal liability?

Suggested Solution

Section 214 Insolvency Act (IA) 1986 deals with the issues on wrongful trading and applies where a director knew or ought to have concluded that a company had no reasonable prospect of not going into insolvent liquidation and did not take every step that they should have taken to minimise potential loss to the company's creditors. Section 214 IA 1986 will apply where a company goes into liquidation at a time when it does not have sufficient assets to pay off its debts, and Ash Ltd clearly does not have the ability to pay off its debts. The standard for determining what the directors of Ash Ltd should or should not have known is that of the general knowledge, skill and experience which might reasonably be expected of any person in the directors' position and those directors in particular, and so it combines both a subjective and an objective standard. It also means that any personal qualifications and experience are to be taken into consideration, as well as the more general criteria in deciding whether or not a director has acted correctly: *Norman* v *Theodore Goddard* [1992] BCC 14.

It is a question of fact to determine the stage at which the directors concluded that insolvent liquidation was inevitable and it may have been before the decision was taken. But the problem here is that this requirement seems to test the actual performance of an individual by reference to matters of which he may have been ignorant. The words 'every step' also pose a problem, as they are vague and it is uncertain how broad the requirement actually is. There has apparently been a general drift towards insolvency which, according to the question, would have been evident from the accounts and in line with the decision in *Re Produce Marketing Consortium Ltd (No 2)* [1989] BCLC 520 where the directors were held liable to contribute to the assets of the company. And they were not able to defend themselves on the grounds that they had acted reasonably and ought fairly to be excused. The appropriate amount which the directors were to be ordered to contribute to the company's assets was the amount by which its assets could be seen to have been depleted by their conduct, so this section looks to compensate the company rather than punish the directors.

However, it is difficult to obtain a contribution for wrongful trading as shown in *Re Sherborne Associates Ltd* [1995] BCC 40. After deciding that a claim for wrongful trading survived the death of one of the directors, the court declined to make an order for contribution from the directors because at the time that the liquidator considered that the directors should have known that there was no reasonable prospect of the company avoiding insolvency, the court considered that the company could have made a turn round and that this was a reasonable belief for the directors to hold. The cases of *Re Farmizer (Products) Ltd* [1995] BCC 926 and *Re Oasis Merchandising Services Ltd* [1995] BCC 911 reinforce the idea that proceedings for wrongful trading are only likely to be brought in clear, straightforward cases.

Is the parent company liable for the debts of the subsidiary?

From the case of *Salomon* v *Salomon & Co* [1897] AC 22, which first held that the distinction between a company and its members is called the veil of incorporation, it is clear that each company is to be considered as a separate legal entity and this has been upheld in the case of *The Abazero* [1977] AC 774. However, in *DHN* v *Tower Hamlets London Borough Council* [1976] 3 All ER 462 the group of companies was treated as the economic entity and so all the subsidiaries were treated as one company, but the case of *Woolfson* v *Strathclyde Regional Council* 1978 SLT 159 distinguished the *DHN* case to hold that a company and its wholly owned subsidiary were separate entities. There is therefore uncertainty about this area of law.

However, *Re Southard & Co Ltd* [1979] 1 All ER 582 held that a parent company is not responsible for the debts of its subsidiary, and *Adams* v *Cape Industries plc* [1991] 1 All ER 929 has reduced the importance of the *DHN* case still further. It is not possible to propose a principle or a consistent policy which will be applied by the courts in lifting the veil of incorporation. Despite evidence of some relaxation in the strict approach to lifting the veil the case of *Adams* v *Cape Industries plc* marks a return to the rigid application of the *Salomon* principle. In the *Adams* case the court had to decide whether a parent company was present in the United States through one of its subsidiaries If it was, then the plaintiff could enforce an award of damages made against the subsidiary, a company registered in England. The arguments for this were that the companies in the group were a single economic entity, that the corporate structure was a mere façade concealing the true facts and that the subsidiary in the United States was the parent's agent. All these arguments failed. The modern trend of the courts is therefore to refuse to lift the veil between parent companies and their subsidiaries.

Conclusion

It is therefore most unlikely that Grass will be able to persuade the courts to lift the veil to enable Grass to seek compensation from Fire Ltd, even though he will probably be able to seek relief using s214 IA 1986. John will need to establish an exception to *Salomon* v *Salomon & Co* [1897] AC 22 to seek compensation from the parent company, but as we have seen the courts are now reluctant to do this. The only possibility that John might have would be to bring an action along the lines of *Lubbe* v *Cape plc* [1998] CLC 1559 where the argument ran that the holding company controlled its subsidiaries and through the careless disregard of its own directors for the foreseeable risks of injury the holding company was primarily negligent and therefore had some liability to the people who were injured.

QUESTION THREE

'English company law has become more and more out of touch with business and its needs ... and has lost sight of the commercial values and priorities which it ought to recognise and serve ... The challenge for us now is to find some way forward which ensures that the law does respond to business needs and moves in sympathy with commercial trends.'

Discuss. What should be the 'way forward' for company law?

University of London LLB Examination
(for External Students) Company Law June 1996 Q2

General Comment

This question offers a wide range of possible themes to the well-read student. The premise is clearly that English company law is too inflexible to meet 'business needs' and 'commercial trends'. An answer can be framed according to the candidates view of social legal and economic functions of company law, as it stands, and of the merits or disadvantages of deregulation. The suggested solution below is based upon the view that the corporate form has always been seen, and will continue to be seen, by the unscrupulous as a convenient vehicle for fraud, tax evasion and dishonesty of all types in the absence of close regulations of companies, directors and members. Answers favouring the views expressed in the quotation would be equally acceptable if supported by good argument.

Skeleton Solution

Origins of modern Companies Acts, legislation seen as the answer to abuse of the corporate form – use and abuse of corporate form as a legal entity – strict view of English law of directors as fiduciaries – consequences for commerce and business of further deregulation – attempts to ease the regulatory burden – conclusion, values and priorities can vary according to the standpoint of the observer.

Suggested Solution

Modern English company law is the result of a very long process in which the courts and Parliament have attempted to harness the beneficial, socially useful and responsible employment of the corporate form by entrepreneurial persons to the public good. The only reasons why the law should get involved in this area at all are to resolve disputes where there is uncertainty and to prevent abuses by unscrupulous and dishonest persons. Anyone reading through the evidence given to Mr Gladstone's Select Committee on Joint Stock Companies (1843), out of which the modern

Companies Acts were born, could not fail to understand that the companies of that relatively unregulated period were a byword for fraud and dishonesty. No doubt there were companies which exercised probity but these appear to have been few and far between. The possibility of any further useful development of the corporate form (other than as an engine of fraud) was, in the absence of strict regulation, nil. The urge to make a quick profit by the many was too strong for the honest few. This, of itself, shows that 'commercial values and priorities' can be looked at from very different perspectives.

One of the early problems for the law (and one upon which the quotation is premised) is that regulation stifles the spirit and frustrates the intentions of the entrepreneur. This question of regulation without stultification came squarely to the fore in the well known case of *Salomon* v *Salomon & Co* [1897] AC 22, where the question for the House of Lords boiled down to one of whether a man of business could, within the law, adopt the corporate form for his own already established business, see that business fail disastrously within a short time and still walk clear from the wreckage, relatively untouched, the loss having fallen on the corporate creditors. The answer was that he could, the creditors having dealt with the incorporated entity. The point being that the regulating and frustrating aspects of the law were more than outweighed by the privilege of the limitation of the corporation or members' liability. No doubt, if the 'way onward' for English company law involved some loss of protection from personal liability there would be even louder complaints that the law has 'lost sight of commercial values'. One cannot have one's cake and eat it as well.

The courts have long recognised the dangers of legislative stifling of the competitive and acquisitive urges that contribute so much to the success of all types of companies upon which the economic health of the nation depends. The maximum degree of flexibility is given to the courts by the simple stratagem of allowing discretionary principles of equity to have an important role in company matters. Such diverse matters as the treatment of directors as fiduciaries to their company as in *Industrial Development Consultants Ltd* v *Cooley* [1972] 2 All ER 162; the application of equitable principles to the control and ownership of closely-held companies as in *Ebrahimi* v *Westbourne Galleries Ltd* [1973] AC 360; the unfair prejudice remedy provided by s459 Companies Act (CA) 1985; the 'proper purposes' doctrine for the exercise of director powers as in *Parke* v *Daily News Ltd* [1962] Ch 927 or as in *Howard Smith Ltd* v *Ampol Petroleum Ltd* [1974] AC 821 and innumerable other situations illustrate that the courts are very aware that only the flexibility of equitable principles will cover the enormous variety of shapes, sizes and types into which registered companies fall. Short of having a very large number of different legislative and common law frameworks for the widely varying company types, involving enormous problems of demarcation, the present combination of common law, legislation and equity seems to be the best compromise between unlimited freedom to run a company by whoever controls it and complete regulation by the state.

The short term consequences for commercial and business interests of further deregulation may appear to be highly attractive. The opportunity to make a quick 'killing' and to get clear leaving a disastrous situation to someone else to clear up has very different consequences in the long term. In a very short time, indeed, highly deregulated companies would find that the supply of persons willing to deal with them and extend credit to them would rapidly shrink. Distrust and uncertainty would bring the trade of such organisations to a halt and capital availability, whether by share or under debenture, would dry up.

This is not to say that there have not been attempts to ease the burden of regulation. The Companies Act 1989 introduced the so-called elective regime for private companies which allows the company, on receipt of elections by all members entitled to vote at a general meeting, to agree to a written resolution and to act without a meeting being held at all: s381A(1) CA 1985 as inserted by s113(1) CA 1989. This resolution may be used to by-pass fundamental requirements of CA 1985 such as extending the statutory period for dealing with unissued shares or dispensing with annual accounts, direction and auditors reports etc being presented to the AGM, dispensing with the AGM and adjusting the requisite voting rights necessary for majority control. This regime may prove to be of very considerable importance in the development of the private company as distinct from public companies and could influence group development plans but it has considerable potential for abuse. Time alone will show whether this potential is realised.

In conclusion, it is submitted that the dangers and problems identified by Mr Gladstone's Select Committee in 1843 have not disappeared altogether. Even with close regulation, company fraud and director wrongdoing has been at very high levels in recent time. The dangers in further deregulating are obvious and the 'commercial values and priorities' which company law 'ought to recognise and serve' should be seen in their true perspective. It all depends upon who holds the value or the priority.

QUESTION FOUR

Health Industries plc is a large, well-established drug company which is the head of a large group of companies including Property Limited, a wholly-owned subsidiary which owns all the premises used by Health Industries in its business, and Testing Limited, another wholly-owned subsidiary which was set up specifically to carry out commercially risky ventures in the search for profitable new drugs. The Board of Directors of Health Industries consists of seven members, but the managing director, Larry Lincoln, is the dominant force. The board generally agrees with his proposals and he has become clearly associated in the mind of the public with Health Industries plc.

Last year the local authority governing the area where Health Industries carries on part of its business expropriated certain land under its statutory powers as part of a slum clearance programme. This included land owned by Property Limited. The compensation offered under the scheme established by the expropriating statute provided for compensation to be paid to 'the owner of the expropriated land according to the open market value of the land plus the assessed damages for any loss of profits suffered by the owner'. The compensation offered by the local authority to Property Limited has ignored the loss, amounting the £150,000, suffered by Health Industries plc in having to relocate its operations elsewhere.

More recently, Testing Limited undertook experiments to try to develop a drug to cure certain types of cancer. In a high profile advertising campaign, Larry Lincoln made a personal appeal on behalf of Testing Limited for volunteers for this experiment. The advertising campaign ran for several days on television and in national newspapers, and 100 volunteers were selected. The experiment went disastrously wrong; several volunteers died, others were permanently maimed. The experiment was not properly researched and there is clear evidence of negligence. Testing Limited has assets of £2,000 to £3,000 and now faces claims of several millions. Test cases have been brought against both Testing Limited and Health Industries plc.

Advise Health Industries plc.

University of London LLB Examination
(for External Students) Company Law June 1992 Q7

General Comment

This question concerns separate corporate legal personality and its exceptions and ramifications. Any serious student of company law must have considered the topic, and ought not to have had difficulty in obtaining at least a fairly good mark.

Skeleton Solution

Separate personality of a company – exceptions – illustrative cases.

Suggested Solution

An incorporated company is in law an entirely distinct and separate legal person from its members. In *Salomon v Salomon & Co* [1897] AC 22 Mr Salomon, who had previously carried on a boot and shoe business as an individual, caused a company to be incorporated and became the holder of almost all of its shares. He then sold and transferred his business to the company and took a secured debenture on its assets for the unpaid balance of the purchase price. When the company became insolvent, the House of Lords held that Mr Salomon, as a secured creditor, had a prior claim to the assets to the claims of the company's unsecured creditors; as distinct legal persons Mr Salomon and the company could trade with each other notwithstanding Mr Salomon's control of the company.

Lee v *Lee's Air Farming* [1961] AC 12, or analogous cases, could also be cited and discussed with advantage.

The *Salomon* v *Salomon & Co* [1897] AC 22 principle will equally well apply to Health Industries plc and its two wholly-owned subsidiaries; each company is a distinct legal person.

Nevertheless, there are circumstances in which the courts will not apply the doctrine of corporate personality distinct from that of membership. An illustrative case is *Gilford Motor Co v Horne* [1933] Ch 935 where the court refused to allow an individual who was bound by a valid restrictive covenant to evade performance by forming a company, with himself as its only substantial shareholder, which would proceed to break the covenant. How wide are the circumstances, apart from fraud, in which the courts will disapply the *Salomon* principle is unclear.

As regards the expropriation of land owned by Property Ltd, it is clear that Property Ltd, which is not a trader, has not lost any profits thereby. But if Health Industries plc and Property Ltd were to be regarded in this context as a single entity, a loss of profit would be incurred. There are two contrasting cases on this point and in the context of similar facts to these of our problem. In *DHN v Tower Hamlets London Borough Council* [1976] 3 All ER 462 the Court of Appeal allowed the holding company to claim compensation for disturbance to the business which it carried out on land compulsorily to be acquired from its wholly-owned subsidiary. But in *Woolfson v Strathclyde Regional Council* 1978 SLT 159 the court declined to allow a claim where the circumstances were in many respects similar, save that there the company which ran the business did not control the owners of the land. *Woolfson*'s case casts some doubt upon the *Tower Hamlets* decision; nevertheless it is submitted that, unless and until it is overruled, the *Tower Hamlets* ruling governs this part of the problem. The Court of Appeal in *Adams v Cape Industries plc* [1991] 1 All ER 929 accepted that in cases turning on the construction of a statute, contract or other document the court may look at the economic reality and treat a group of companies as a single economic unit, treating *Tower Hamlets* as such a case. Alternatively it may be possible to show that the subsidiary was acting as the agent of the parent company, as was found to be the case in *Smith, Stone & Knight Ltd v Birmingham Corporation* [1939] 4 All ER 116. (This, if established, would be another ground for claiming loss of profit from the land acquisition.) The relevant factors listed in *Smith*'s case cannot be easily applied to our problem, since in *Smith*'s case each company was carrying on a business and naturally the judgment was directed to that situation.

Finally, it may be mentioned that a director is not, as such, liable for torts committed by the company of which he is a director; he would be liable if he authorised the tort or personally took part in controlling it. It does not appear that Larry Lincoln has done either of these things.

Chapter 2

The Memorandum of Association and Legal Capacity

2.1   Introduction

2.2   Key points

2.3   Key cases and statutes

2.4   Questions and suggested solutions

2.1 Introduction

The memorandum and articles of association together are the constitution of the company, the former specifying the form and legal capacity this artificial legal person is to have, and the latter regulating its internal dealings. Both are registered at Companies House. Alterations to the memorandum, legally the most important of the two documents, must follow specified procedures depending on the clause to be altered.

For many years, the ultra vires rule (explained below), centering on the objects clause in the memorandum of association, often thwarted attempts by third parties to sue the company in contract and generated an enormous body of case law containing many fine distinctions. The rule, although it still exists, has been deprived of its teeth by the Companies Act (CA) 1989.

2.2 Key points

The objects clause

The objects clause in the memorandum is probably its most important clause. Under s5 CA 1985, it could only be altered for specified purposes and only by following the correct procedure, which includes a special resolution and a right for a dissenting minority to apply to the court for cancellation. The objects clause in the memorandum gives a company its legal powers. It states what businesses the company is formed to carry on and what powers it may exercise in the course of carrying on those businesses.

Ultra vires

The ultra vires rule states that a body must not act outside the powers (sometimes also referred to as capacity or authority) bestowed on it. Applied to companies it has meant that a company cannot carry on any business not specified in its objects clause (*Ashbury Railway Carriage and Iron Co Ltd* v *Riche* (1875) LR 7 HL 653), cannot exercise any power not mentioned, unless the court is prepared to imply it, nor exercise a power it possesses in pursuit of any unspecified object. Gratuitous payment by companies, such as pensions and payments to employees on the transfer of a business, have often been disallowed where there was no power to make them, on the ground that such payments could not be for the benefit of the company (see, eg, *Parke* v *Daily News Ltd* [1962] Ch 927). The immediate practical result was increasingly long objects clauses as companies strove to include any business they might wish to carry on, or power they might wish to exercise, together with a catch-all clause permitting the company to carry on any business which the directors thought fit (known as *Bell Houses* clause after *Bell Houses Ltd* v *City Wall Properties Ltd* [1966] 2 QB 656, the case in which it was first sanctioned).

Nevertheless, companies were still caught by the rule and, when it applied, any contract made in the course of carrying on the unauthorised business or exercising the unauthorised power was void, ie neither the company nor the other party to the transaction could enforce it.

The apparent harshness of this rule to third parties was justified by the rule that since the memorandum is a public document everyone is deemed to have knowledge of its contents (constructive notice). However, the courts recognised that the rule could be unfair, and a considerable body of case law was generated.

Directors' powers

Closely connected with the problem of ultra vires is that of directors' authority. The directors are agents of the company and clearly the company as principal cannot give directors powers which it does not itself have. Thus, directors who act ultra vires the company are clearly exceeding their powers (or authority) and are personally liable.

However, directors, like other agents, can exceed or breach their authority in other ways. They can only exercise powers delegated to them. This need not be a problem because usually all the powers of managing the company are bestowed on the directors by the articles of association. However, these powers are given to the board collectively, and a director who acts independently of the board exceeds his authority. Second, the company may have reserved certain powers to itself, or laid down a specific procedure to be followed before certain acts can be done or contracts made. If this is ignored, again the directors exceed their authority. Third, a director may not have been validly appointed.

The problem for the other party to transactions where the active directors lack express authority is whether the company is bound by the transaction. A director, like other agents, may have implied (usual) or ostensible authority, which may make the transaction enforceable against the company (see, eg, *Freeman & Lockyer* v *Buckhurst*

Park Properties (Mangal) Ltd [1964] 2 QB 480). Moreover, the rule in *Royal British Bank* v *Turquand* (1856) 6 E & B 327 states that a third party is not concerned to see that internal procedures have been followed, where he is not an 'insider' and could not have known whether they had been followed or not. Thus, certain transactions were enforceable even where the directors had exceeded their authority. Nevertheless, third parties could still be caught by the complex rules and could only hope that the company would ratify the transaction or rely on their remedies against the directors personally.

A clumsy attempt was made to deal with the problem in the notorious s9(1) European Communities Act 1972. The section was fraught with interpretative difficulties (for a discussion see *International Sales & Agencies Ltd* v *Marcus* [1982] 3 All ER 551), but the section was nevertheless carried through into the 1985 legislation and became s35 CA 1985.

The position of the members

Ultra vires is an exception to the rule in *Foss* v *Harbottle* (1843) 2 Hare 461 (see Chapter 11: *Minorities*), thus members can sue individually to restrain an ultra vires transaction, to rescind or to sue the directors for misfeasance. An ultra vires transaction cannot be ratified.

Where directors have exceeded their authority, the company may sue them for misfeasance but, if the directors have ostensible or implied authority, the company will be bound by the transaction. The members may be able to cure a defect in a transaction which is not ultra vires by ratification or by following the necessary procedure.

The Prentice Report

The Prentice Report ('Reform of the Ultra Vires Rule', DTI, 1987) recommended that companies should have the capacity to do any act whatsoever and need no longer have an objects clause, but unfortunately this was at variance with European Community law. Many of the recommendations in the Report were carried through into new legislation in 1989, but the Government at the time did not go so far as abolishing objects clauses, nor even the ultra vires rule.

The 1989 Act and the present law

The CA 1989 dealt with both the problems of third parties to ultra vires transactions and transactions involving lack of authority of directors. It did so by retrospectively inserting provisions into the CA 1985. The principal points to note are listed below.

a) Section 3A says a company may state that its object is to carry on business as a 'general commercial company'. The effect is that its object is to carry on any trade or business whatsoever and to have the power to do all such things as are incidental or conducive to carrying on any trade or business. This is an attempt to make long objects clauses redundant in many cases.

b) Under s35(1) CA 1985 (a new s35 is substituted in the Act by s108 CA 1989), the validity of any act done by a company shall not be called into question on the ground of lack of capacity by reason of anything in the company's memorandum. This effectively (if not actually) abolishes the ultra vires rule and now neither the company itself nor a third party can use ultra vires to challenge the validity of a transaction.

c) Subsection 35(2) preserves the members' right to restrain an action which (but for s35(1)) would be a breach of the ultra vires rule, unless the action is fulfilling a pre-existing legal obligation of the company.

d) Under subs(3), any act of the directors (even an ultra vires one) can be ratified by special resolution but, unless a separate special resolution is passed absolving them, the directors remain personally liable.

e) The new s35A substitutes the following for the old s35 formula:

> '(1) In favour of a person dealing with the company in good faith, the power of the board of directors to bind the company, or authorise others to do so, shall be deemed to be free of any limitation under the company's constitution.'

While this formula is not entirely problem-free, it includes a guide to interpretation (in subs(2)) and should prove a better attempt to legitimate, so far as third parties are concerned, unauthorised contracts made by directors.

f) Section 35B states that a party to a transaction is not bound to enquire whether that transaction is permitted by the company's memorandum or as to any limitation on the powers of the board to bind the company where the transaction falls within s35A. Even where s35A does not provide protection, s711A(1) effectively abolishes the doctrine of constructive notice as it relates to documents available for inspection at Companies House, but third parties must make such enquiries as ought reasonably to be made.

g) The distinction between 'outsiders' and 'insiders' in the rule in *Turquand*'s case (*Royal British Bank* v *Turquand* (1856) 6 E & B 327, as modified in *Morris* v *Kanssen* [1946] AC 459) is expressly retained. Should the other party to the transaction be a director, a 'connected person' or a company associated with a director, that party will not receive the protection of s35A and may have to account to the company or indemnify it if it sustains a loss. Nevertheless, the transaction may be ratified by special resolution (if it exceeds the company's own capacity) or ordinary resolution.

h) Companies are now specifically empowered to make provision for employees or former employees of the company or its subsidiaries, in connection with cessation of business or the transfer of its undertaking, even though such provision may not be in the best interests of the company.

2.3 Key cases and statutes

- *Ashbury Railway Carriage and Iron Co Ltd* v *Riche* (1875) LR 7 HL 653
  A company cannot carry on any business not specified in its objects clause

- *Bell Houses Ltd* v *City Wall Properties Ltd* [1966] 2 QB 656
  Development of catch-all clause in objects clause

- *Burge* v *Haycock* [2002] RPC 28
  In passing-off action 'trade' is given a wide interpretation to include professional and artistic work and the activities of a pressure group such as the Countryside Alliance

- *Department of Trade and Industry* v *Cedenio* (2001) The Times 22 March
  Where a company uses a business name other than its own, all that is required is a name and address – there is no requirement that the name is that of the proprietor, or the address is the address for service

- *Foss* v *Harbottle* (1843) 2 Hare 461
  Gives ultra vires as an exception to the rule in this case

- *Freeman & Lockyer* v *Buckhurst Park Properties (Mangal) Ltd* [1964] 2 QB 480
  A director may have implied or ostensible authority which may make a transaction enforceable against a company

- *International Sales & Agencies Ltd* v *Marcus* [1982] 3 All ER 551
  Contains discussion of difficulties encountered by s9(1) European Communities Act 1972

- *Morris* v *Kanssen* [1946] AC 459
  Modifies the rule in *Turquand*'s case

- *Royal British Bank* v *Turquand* (1856) 6 E & B 327
  The indoor management rule

- *Williams* v *Natural Life Health Foods Ltd* [1997] 1 BCLC 131
  Managing director of company held personally liable for negligent misstatements made during negotiations

- Companies Act 1985

  - s3A – company may have general objects clause

  - s35(1) – effectively abolishes ultra vires for external contracts

  - s35(2) – effectively retains the rule for members so that they still have a right of action

  - s711A(1) – effectively abolishes constructive notice, but has not yet been brought into force

- Companies Act 1989, ss108 and 109 – now subsumed into Companies Act 1985

2.4 Questions and suggested solutions

QUESTION ONE

Utopia Ltd has articles in the form of Table A and the objects clause in the memorandum is silent as to the making of gifts. In 1995 the board of directors appointed MD to be the managing director under a service contract lasting ten years. The board of directors has given MD full powers to act for the company in all transactions involving up to £100,000. Matters involving larger sums are to be referred to the board of directors. The business of Utopia Ltd is the manufacture of drugs. MD appoints a team to research into new drugs and as a result has discovered a new drug called Miagra, which will alleviate all known headaches. MD is grateful to the National University for their help in this project and has donated £80,000 to the department of pharmaceuticals at the National University. MD has also donated £10,000 to the National Opera and £10,000 to the New Labour Alliance political party. The board has discovered that the development of this new drug will necessitate the acquisition of a new factory for £500,000 and will require substantial investment in new machinery. The board has discovered what MD has done, and wishes to order him to halt negotiations for the purchase of a factory as he has no authority to proceed with the purchase. They also want MD to cancel the various donations. Failing this they wish to dismiss MD from his post.

Advise the board of directors accordingly.

University of London LLB Examination
(for External Students) Company Law June 1999 Q5

General Comment

The issues of ultra vires and breach of directors duties are very closely intertwined and the internal effects of the ultra vires rule are difficult to distinguish from breach of duty. The objects of a company must be stated in the memorandum. The primary purpose of this rule is to protect investors, so a company should not carry out acts or enter into transactions which are beyond the company's capacity. This problem covers a variety of situations, but deals with issues around the edge of the main topics introduced. Students should therefore be very careful to address the points actually asked and not to write a general answer describing the areas covered.

Skeleton Solution

The donations made by MD are subject to the ultra vires rule and so the company's objects clause needs to be considered – *Hutton* v *West Cork Railway Co* and *Evans* v *Brunner Mond* – the donations need to be considered separately – the transaction of £500,000 exceeds the delegated authority given to MD – if the transactions are ultra vires what is the effect on the third parties involved? – probably be protected by s35(1) Companies Act 1985 – members of the company can bring an action to restrain or ratify ultra vires acts – the board of directors should look at MD's service contract (exceeds the normal permitted length of five years) – the members in a general meeting may also be able to dismiss MD under the provisions of s303 Companies Act 1985.

Suggested Solution

The terms of MD's service contract need to be examined as the length is stated to be for ten years. Article 84 Table A vests in the directors as a group the authority to enter into a service contract with another director, which is more liberal that the statutory requirements covering service contracts. However, the service contract will not be binding unless it has been approved by the whole board: *UK Safety Group Ltd* v *Heane* [1998] 2 BCLC 208. Because the contract has been granted for ten years it falls within the ambit of s319 Companies Act (CA) 1985 which states that if a director has a contract which exceeds five years and that contract contains a term which restricts the right of the company to terminate the contract, then the contract must be approved by the general meeting before it is entered into. Before the resolution is passed a written memorandum setting out the proposed agreement must be available for inspection by the members for at least 15 days before the meeting and at the meeting itself. However, as the purpose of this section is to protect the shareholders, the specific requirements of s319 can be waived if there is a unanimous informal approval of the shareholders.

In the event that this contract contains the restrictions and has not been approved it will be void to the extent it contravenes the section, that is to say the additional five years will be discounted and it will be deemed to contain a term entitling the company to determine by reasonable notice, so it may be possible for MD to be dismissed without being able to bring an action for breach of contract. The Combined Code of the Committee on Corporate Governance, the code of best practice, requires contract and notice periods of one year only so that directors cannot get excessive compensation in the event of their contract being terminated. Although the code applies to public listed companies, it is used to guide the behaviour of private companies too. The Law Commission has now recommended that the time limit in s319 should be reduced to three years.

Even if MD's contract is valid, it may still be possible to use s303 CA 1985 to dismiss him. In order to do this the board will need to secure an ordinary resolution in a general meeting. Again, we are not told if the directors themselves are shareholders. If the directors hold the majority of shares between them there will be no difficulty in securing the resolution. If the shareholders are other people, then the directors will need to canvass their opinions. The potential difficulties attached to this method of dismissal are that it could be expensive if MD has a clause in the contract relating to severance pay, and there may also be a breach of contract entitling MD to damages. Secondly, MD may have a *Bushell* v *Faith* [1970] AC 1099 type arrangement in his contract giving him weighted voting rights in times of adversity. These clauses are quite common in small private companies, but this will only be an issue if MD is a shareholder.

Turning to the issue of the three donations, the question is whether they are ultra vires under s35 CA 1985. To determine this one would need to see the objects clause of the company. If there are no express powers given in the memorandum the extent of the company's implied powers to make gifts must be determined. The case law suggests that whatever can fairly be regarded as incidental to, or consequential on, the stated objects could be implied: *Attorney-General* v *Great Eastern Railway* (1875) LR 7 HL 653; *Hutton* v *West Cork Railway Co* (1883) 23 Ch D 654. However, the case of *Evans* v *Brunner Mond* [1921] 1 Ch 359 held that even if the majority of the shareholders think a proposed act is beneficial to the company a dissenting member may still challenge that act. However, the court accepted the validity of a provision at the end of the company's objects clause which gave the company or its directors power to do all such other things as are incidental or conducive to the attainment of the company's objects. If any of the donations are found to be ultra vires it would seem that s35 CA 1985 will probably protect innocent third parties. The company will be bound unless MD has exceeded any limitations put onto his authority by the board. If he has then he will become personally liable to restore the funds to the company, which may or may not be a practical solution. Section 35B CA 1985 provides that third parties to a transaction do not have to make enquiries about any limitations that have been put on a director's powers. If the donations are ultra vires the objects clause, the shareholders may ratify the act or sue for damages.

With regard to the political donation it should be disclosed in the directors' report as it exceeds £200, but if it is not this will not invalidate the donation. Practically speaking the change to the ultra vires rule means that there is no longer statutory control over the making of donations to political parties. However, directors remain subject to fiduciary duties and they must make decisions about the use of company money in accordance with their duties to act in the best interests of the company.

However, in addition to the ultra vires rule, the board of directors has given MD authority to deal with transactions up to £100,000 and said that matters involving larger sums are to be referred to the board. Although the donations fall short of this limit, the acquisition of the new factory for £500,000 is above the limit and so MD is exceeding his authority in this transaction. Under the terms of art 72 Table A the board of directors may delegate powers to MD and those powers may be subject to any limitations or conditions that the board wishes to impose. The board can revoke this delegation at any time.

Although outsiders dealing with authorised agents of the company will generally be protected by the rule in *Turquand*'s case (*Royal British Bank* v *Turquand* (1855) 5 E & B 248), provided they are not aware of any irregularity in the proceedings, this rule may not help when considering the powers of individual officers. There are two types of authority, actual and ostensible. MD will exceed his actual authority in negotiating for the factory at £500,000. So MD will have no actual authority to enter into this transaction, but he may have ostensible authority as this relates to how outsiders see MD's position. This means that an outsider dealing with MD who is not aware of the restriction may be able to hold the company to the transaction.

Conclusion

The board should instantly revoke the powers given to MD to negotiate the purchase of the machinery. They should then call a general meeting to consider the donations, if they are found to be ultra vires the objects clause, and decide whether or not to ratify them. In addition, if MD's service contract is found to be acceptable under the terms of s319 CA 1985, they should call for MD's dismissal under s303 CA 1985, bearing in mind that they require an ordinary resolution to be passed to secure this and that they must give special notice for the resolution, ie 28 days.

QUESTION TWO

The objects clause of the memorandum of association of Southerly Breezes Ltd contains only the following.

The objects of the company are to manufacture and sell sailing yachts.

The company shall have power to do any act which is incidental or conducive to the attainment of the above objects.

The company is currently successfully engaged in its business of making and selling sailing yachts. Emily and Roland are the directors of the company but own no shares in it. In 1991 they were approached by Gina, a close friend of Roland, who was seeking a guarantee of a loan of £100,000 which she was negotiating with Spartan Bank plc. The directors said 'a friend in need is a friend indeed' and, having sent a copy of the memorandum of the company to the bank, caused the company to give a guarantee to the bank in respect of the £100,000.

In March 1993 Gina was made bankrupt and the bank commenced an action against the company on the guarantee. In May 1993 a specially convened meeting of the shareholders of the company passed the following resolutions by 51 per cent majority vote.

a) Ratifying the directors' actions in giving the guarantee and authorising payment under it.

b) Authorising a donation of £25,000 to the general funds of the Green Party.

Harvey, who is holder of 49 per cent of the shares, voted against the resolutions at the meeting. Advise him as to whether there are any legal grounds for getting the resolutions set aside.

University of London LLB Examination
(for External Students) Company Law June 1993 Q6

General Comment

A question requiring the candidate to illustrate a clear understanding of ultra vires, directors' authority, and the effect on the rules of Companies Act (CA) 1989. Candidates are asked to advise a minority shareholder rather than the third party to the transactions, which is more usual.

Skeleton Solution

Objects clause – corporate gifts – capacity – express and implied powers – ultra vires – breach of authority – ss35 and 35A CA 1985 – ratification.

Suggested Solution

This question focuses on express and implied powers, the problems of a company's capacity and breach of directors' authority from a member's point of view. Both transactions are effectively gifts.

The capacity of a company to perform acts and enter into contracts is prescribed by the objects clause in its memorandum of association. An objects clause typically contains objects, which are the businesses a company is empowered to carry on and powers, which are the acts a company is permitted to do in pursuit of its objects. A company acts outside its powers (ultra vires) if it carries on any business or exercises any power not authorised by its objects clause (*Ashbury Railway Carriage and Iron Co Ltd* v *Riche* (1875) LR 7 HL 653), or even if it exercises a power contained in its objects clause if it does so for an unauthorised object (*Introductions Ltd* v *National Provincial Bank* [1970] Ch 199).

At common law, various consequences result from a company acting ultra vires. First, any contract made in the course of acting ultra vires is void and unenforceable by either the company or the other party (unless the latter can show he is not affected by constructive notice of the company acting ultra vires). Second, directors being agents of the company, can only exercise powers delegated to them. The company cannot, however, delegate powers it does not itself have, and thus by acting ultra vires the company, the directors exceed their own authority. As a result, they are personally liable to third parties, to the company and to members. Third, as the company does not have the powers itself, the general meeting cannot (at common law) ratify the directors' abuse of authority.

However, even where the company does have the capacity to do a particular act by virtue of its objects clause, the act may still be a breach by the directors of their authority for it may not have been done in the proper way, or it may have been done for improper purposes, for example. Agency rules apply at common law to cover this type of situation. If the director or directors who make the contract appear to the other party to have the authority to do so (ostensible authority) then the company will be bound by the contract (*Freeman & Lockyer* v *Buckhurst Park Properties (Mangal) Ltd* [1964] 2 QB 480). As between the company and the directors, however, the active directors in the transaction are personally liable to the company for any loss which it may suffer, although the company may ratify an abuse of authority (if it is not also ultra vires) by ordinary resolution, binding itself under the contract.

As will be explained below, the common law consequences of both ultra vires acts and acts which exceed the directors' authority have been affected by the Companies Act (CA) 1989.

The two transactions here must be treated separately. Resolution (a) is concerned with ratification of an act already performed by the directors, and resolution (b) with an act to be performed by the company itself.

As regards the guarantee, Southerly Breezes Ltd has only one object in the first paragraph of its objects clause. It also has one very wide power in the second paragraph which is unlikely to be construed as a substantive object and must therefore be an ancillary power (*Re Horsley & Weight Ltd* [1982] Ch 442). Therefore, while the second paragraph could comprise the guaranteeing of loans, to be intra vires they should be connected with the business of manufacturing and selling sailing yachts.

Some case might be made out that the loan was in connection with the business of the company but, on the facts given, it seems most likely that it was not and the exercise of the power to guarantee the loan would therefore have been ultra vires and the guarantee void.

However, s108 CA 1989 inserted some new provisions (s35 and s35A) into the CA 1985 aimed at validating ultra vires transactions and others that exceed or breach directors' authority. Section 35(1) provides that the validity of any act done by a company shall not be called into question on the ground of lack of capacity by reason of anything in the company's memorandum. In this case this means that the company cannot use the ultra vires rule to avoid payment under the guarantee. This is relevant since, if the guarantee was validly given, it matters little as between the members and the bank whether it was retrospectively ratified.

Nevertheless, it could still be argued that the directors have exceeded their authority, not only by acting ultra vires but by using their power to give guarantees for an improper purpose. This would not be enough to invalidate the guarantee if they had ostensible authority. However, a claim that they had ostensible authority might be countered by saying that the bank had a copy of the memorandum of the company and knew the contents of its objects clause. Depending on what the loan was for, it could be argued that the bank ought to have known that the directors did not have authority to guarantee it, or at least should have been 'on enquiry'.

The CA 1989 again comes to the bank's aid because s35A CA 1985 (also inserted by s108 CA 1989) states that:

> '(1) In favour of a person dealing with a company in good faith, the power of the board of directors to bind the company, or authorise others to do so, shall be deemed to be free of any limitation under the company's constitution.'

In addition, s35B states that a party to a transaction is not bound to enquire whether that transaction is permitted by the company's memorandum. Good faith is presumed and s35A(2) states that a party shall not be regarded as acting in bad faith by reason only of knowing that an act is beyond the powers of the directors under the company's constitution.

The result is that the company probably has no option but to honour the guarantee in any case, causing it a loss of £100,000. While members have their right preserved under s32 CA 1985 to obtain an injunction to restrain the commission of an ultra vires act, such as payment under the guarantee, this right is not available if the company is fulfilling a pre-existing legal obligation. If the guarantee is validated by s35(1) and s35A as appears to be the case, the company cannot challenge the payment and must suffer a loss. The question is whether that loss could or should be recovered from the directors.

The sole purpose of resolution (a) seems to be to absolve the directors from liability. While s35(3) permits the company to ratify even an ultra vires act, it must do so by passing a special resolution (although an ordinary resolution would suffice were it not ultra vires). Furthermore, such ratification does not relieve the directors of personal liability and a separate special resolution must be passed in order to do so. In this case, the meeting has merely passed an ordinary resolution. As Harvey holds 49 per cent of the shares, the necessary special resolution could not be passed without his support. Thus, the resolution is invalid and the directors remain personally liable. While the action would usually need to be brought by the company by virtue of the rule in *Foss* v *Harbottle* (1843) 2 Hare 461, and the majority appear to support what the directors have done, Harvey has two points in his favour. First, the passing of a resolution by the incorrect majority is an exception to the rule (*Edwards* v *Halliwell* [1950] 2 All ER 1064), and an individual member can bring an action to have the offending resolution declared invalid. Second, ultra vires is also an exception.

Turning to resolution (b), there is no express power to make this payment. When the court can imply a power to make gratuitous payments has been the subject of much judicial and academic debate. In *Hutton* v *West Cork Railway Co* (1883) 23 Ch D 654 Bowen LJ said that there should be 'no cakes and ale except such as are required for the benefit of the company', and political donations might in some circumstances be regarded as being generally for the company's benefit. In *Re Lee, Behrens & Co Ltd* [1932] 2 Ch 46, Eve J laid down a three-stage test in order to determine the validity of corporate gifts. Besides being for the benefit of the company and bona fide they should also be reasonably incidental to the carrying on of the company's business, but in *Rolled Steel Products (Holdings) Ltd* v *British Steel Corporation* [1986] Ch 246 Slade J in his turn called the *Behrens* test 'misleading'. If on a true construction of the company's memorandum the act was capable of being performed as reasonably incidental to the attainment of its objects, it would not be ultra vires simply because the directors performed it for purposes other than those specified in the memorandum. Whether or not it is for the company's benefit may therefore be irrelevant.

Thus, if it is not capable of being reasonably incidental to the company's objects (and it is hard to see how it can be), the donation to the the Green Party is likely to be ultra vires. If the donation has not already been made then it may be open to Harvey to apply for an injunction against the directors to restrain payment under s35A(4) CA

1985. He may also have the resolution declared invalid, since the general meeting has no power to authorise an ultra vires payment.

If the £25,000 has already been paid, although s35(1) would seem to preclude recovery from the recipients, Harvey may seek to bring a derivative action against Emily and Roland to recover the sum. Harvey should also be advised that any derivative action may now be brought under s459 CA 1985, which enables the court to authorise any individual to bring proceedings on behalf of the company: s461(2)(c).

Chapter 3

The Articles of Association

3.1   Introduction

3.2   Key points

3.3   Key cases and statute

3.4   Questions and suggested solutions

3.1 Introduction

This chapter deals with the problems arising from the provisions contained in a company's articles of association, and in particular from the concept that these articles form a contract involving the members and the company.

3.2 Key points

Companies Act 1985: s14

This section provides that the memorandum and articles of association are a contract binding as if they had been signed and sealed by every member of the company. In *Wood v Odessa Waterworks Co* (1889) 42 Ch D 636 it was held that this provision must be read as if it also deemed the company to have signed and sealed the articles. The contract is multi-partite, involving the members inter se and each member individually with the company.

The s14 contract may be enforced by any member of the company, but there is some uncertainty as to the rights which may be enforced by means of s14. One view is that s14 may only be used in connection with what are sometimes termed 'membership rights', ie those rights whose violation will affect the member in his capacity as a member. However, it is suggested that the better view is that the rights of the member include the right to have the company's affairs managed in accordance with any provisions in the articles, irrespective of theoretical debates about the nature of membership rights.

The narrower view of the s14 contract rests on the decision of Astbury J in *Hickman v Kent or Romney Marsh Sheepbreeders' Association* [1915] 1 Ch 881, whilst the broader view appears in *Quinn & Axtens v Salmon* [1909] AC 442. Later cases provide support for both interpretations and, while judges generally express the narrower proposition, there is much academic support for the wider view.

Suing on the basis of 'membership rights' under the s14 contract is one way of circumventing the rule in *Foss* v *Harbottle* (1843) 2 Hare 461 (see Chapter 11: *Minorities*), and the debate therefore has more than mere academic significance. The court has generally refused to enforce 'non-membership rights' contained in the articles, however. In *Eley* v *Positive Government Security Life Assurance Co* (1876) 1 Ex D 88 it was held that the s14 contract could not be used to enforce the right, contained in the articles, to be the company solicitor. This refusal to allow 'outsiders' to sue on the contract extends equally to directors (see, eg, *Beattie* v *Beattie* [1938] P 99), but articles have been allowed to evidence the terms of an agreement between the company and its directors (*Re New British Iron Co, ex parte Beckwith* [1898] 1 Ch 324). This problem in relation to directors has declined in importance, since virtually all directors now have service contracts. However, the articles may be held to supplement a service contract as in *Re Richmond Gate Property Co Ltd* [1965] 1 WLR 335. One should also bear in mind that removing a director from office even in accordance with the articles may be a breach of his service contract, entitling him to claim damages (*Southern Foundries Ltd* v *Shirlaw* [1940] AC 701).

Case law suggests that there are certain respects in which the s14 contract differs from an ordinary contract. Thus, it is not subject to rectification, even where it appears that the normal requirements for this remedy are fulfilled: *Scott* v *Frank Scott (London) Ltd* [1940] Ch 794. Nor can damages be awarded against the company for a breach of the contract, since this would be a misuse of the company's funds: *Houldsworth* v *City of Glasgow Bank* (1880) 5 App Cas 317.

Altering the articles

Section 9 Companies Act (CA) 1985 permits the alteration of the articles by special resolution. Difficulties sometimes arise where it is alleged that the majority has made an alteration for the purpose of treating the minority unfairly. *Allen* v *Gold Reefs of West Africa* [1900] 1 Ch 656 establishes that the power to alter the articles must be exercised bona fide in the best interests of the company.

The modern tendency is not to have in articles of association the type of provision which was subject to a challenged alteration in many of the older cases. Instead, such provisions, concerning expulsion of directors, voting rights, etc, are more usually found in directors' service contracts or shareholders' agreements. Cases of challenged alterations to articles are therefore now infrequent. Moreover, the court has generally upheld alterations where the plaintiff cannot show bad faith was involved, which has often discouraged litigants. Variation of class rights (ie membership rights attaching to a particular class of shares), involving an alteration to articles, might give scope for a legal challenge under this heading. (As to class rights, see further Chapter 6: *Shares*.) Action under s459 CA 1985 (conduct unfairly prejudicial to members) would now, however, seem to be the best method of challenging most alterations.

Any provision in the articles purporting to make them unalterable is void. However, there is no objection to weighted voting rights (*Bushell* v *Faith* [1970] AC 1099). By the same token, it seems, shareholders may enter enforceable agreements as to how they will vote in the event of a resolution to alter the articles but, if the company is made a party to such a shareholders' agreement so as to fetter its statutory right to alter the articles, the agreement will be void, at least as concerns the company, according to the House of Lords' judgment in *Russell v Northern Bank Development Corporation Ltd* [1992] 1 WLR 588.

3.3 Key cases and statute

- *Allen v Gold Reefs of West Africa* [1900] 1 Ch 656
  Power to alter articles must be exercised bona fide in the best interests of the company

- *Beattie v Beattie* [1938] P 99
  Extends the refusal in *Eley v Positive Assurance Co Ltd* to directors

- *Bushell v Faith* [1970] AC 1099
  Can have weighted voting rights

- *Eley v Positive Government Security Life Assurance Co* (1876) 1 Ex D 88
  Refusal to allow outsiders to sue on the s14 contract

- *Hickman v Kent or Romney Marsh Sheepbreeders' Association* [1915] 1 Ch 881
  Supports narrow view of s14 contract

- *Houldsworth v City of Glasgow Bank* (1880) 5 App Cas 317
  Damages cannot be awarded against a company for breach of s14 contract

- *Quinn & Axtens v Salmon* [1909] AC 442
  Supports wider view of s14 contract

- *Rayfield v Hands* [1960] Ch 1
  Articles requiring directors to hold at least one share and to buy shares of any member who wished to sell – enforceable under s14 as between members (in practice, this issue is usually avoided by providing in the articles that the company, whose position under s14 is clear, shall be the intermediary between members in share transactions)

- *Richmond Gate Property Co Ltd, Re* [1965] 1 WLR 335
  Articles were held to supplement a director's service contract

- *Scott v Frank Scott (London) Ltd* [1940] Ch 794
  Section 14 contract is not subject to rectification

- *Wood v Odessa Waterworks Co* (1889) 42 Ch D 636
  Company must be deemed to have signed and sealed its articles

- Companies Act 1985

  - s9 – permits the alteration of the articles by special resolution

- s14 – the memorandum and articles of association are a binding contract
- s459 – allows an action for conduct which is unfairly prejudicial to the members

3.4 Questions and suggested solutions

QUESTION ONE

Computer Mouse Ltd was formed in 1997 with an issue share capital of 3,000 £1 shares and carries on a small business manufacturing computer mouse pads. The shares are held equally by the three directors, Ann, Ben and Cal. The memorandum of association provides, inter alia, that the shares shall have one vote each.

By January 1998 the company was in need of further funds and Ann, Ben and Cal entered into an agreement contained in a document which was signed by each of them. The agreement provided as follows.

a) Ann, Ben and Cal will each make an interest free loan to the company of £25,000 repayable in instalments of £5,000 over five years commencing January 1999.

b) The company being desirous of issuing 3,000 shares at a price of £2, it is hereby agreed that Ann, Ben and Cal shall each take up 1,000 shares.

c) On a resolution to remove a director under s303 of the Companies Act 1985, the votes attached to the shares held by the director who is the subject of the resolution shall treble.

d) The company is deemed to be party to this agreement

e) This agreement is intended to bind any persons into whose hands shares of the company may come. Accordingly the existing shareholders undertake that any contract for the sale of their shares shall contain an undertaking by the transferee that he shall enter into this agreement and be bound by all the clauses of this agreement, including this one.

Ann has not yet complied with clause (a) and (b) of the agreement above and regrets signing the agreement. She seeks your advice as to whether any of the agreement is enforceable.

Ann also wishes to know whether, and if so how, Ben and Cal could alter the memorandum to vary the rights attached to their ordinary shares so as to give themselves, but not Ann, two votes per share.

Advise Ann.

University of London LLB Examination
(for External Students) Company Law June 1999 Q6

General Comment

This question tackles the issue of the shareholders' agreement and how that relates to the articles of association of a company. Whilst the power of management is generally distributed by the company's articles, its actual exercise may be restricted by the shareholders' agreement. It requires a general understanding of the law of contract.

Skeleton Solution

Shareholder agreements and their validity; the issues contained in the shareholders' agreement; alteration of the memorandum of association, variation of class rights – *Russell v Northern Bank Development Corporation Ltd* (validity of shareholder agreements; how they relate to the articles of association – shareholder agreements can be valid as personal agreements between the parties, but that agreement is subject to the general principle of company law that a company cannot contract out of its statutory powers under s9 Companies Act 1985 – ss2(7) and 17 Companies Act 1985 (limit the alteration of the memorandum) and s125(5) Companies Act 1985 (if class rights have been affected).

Suggested Solution

A company cannot deprive itself of the power to alter its articles by special resolution by a statement to that effect in its articles, but it may be able to achieve the same effect by entering into a contract outside the articles. The conflicting case law that has surrounded this area has been the subject of a definitive ruling by the House of Lords in 1992.

In the case of *Russell v Northern Bank Development Corporation Ltd* [1992] 1 WLR 588 a company contracted not to alter the nominal capital clause in its memorandum and the House of Lords held that any provision in a company's memorandum or articles which purports to limit the exercise of the statutory power to alter the memorandum or articles can have no effect. Their Lordships considered that such a contract was as obnoxious as any provision to that effect in the articles themselves, and that it would be equally as invalid and unenforceable even by way of damages. However, it was recognised that existing members of a company could make an enforceable contract between them regarding the way in which they would exercise their votes, even though this would have the same effect. So a company may not contract to alter its articles , but its shareholders may agree amongst themselves that they will not vote in favour of a proposal to alter the articles and this agreement may be enforced by an injunction. Such contracts are called shareholders' agreements and are valid contracts.

Turning to the individual clauses, the two clauses which require detailed analysis are clause (c) and clause (e).

Clause (c) contains what is known as a *Bushell v Faith* [1970] AC 1099 clause. In this case the company's articles gave shareholders weighted voting rights in certain circumstances and the practical outcome of this clause was that resolutions on certain issues could be prevented from being passed. The Court of Appeal considered the effect that such a clause would have to prevent a company from altering its articles. It was argued that such a clause could not be permitted to stand because it would have the effect of being contrary to s9 Companies Act (CA) 1985 and deprive the company of the right to alter its articles. However, Russell LJ held that a provision relating to voting rights which had the effect of making a special resolution incapable of being passed is not the same thing as binding a company not to alter its articles. The shareholders who benefit from the weighted voting rights have to decide to vote in a particular way and there is a distinction between voting rights attached to shares and the scope of s303 CA 1985. So although this provision has the effect of negating s9 CA 1985, it follows from *Bushell v Faith* [1970] AC 1099 that the result of the action is not what is to be regarded. Lord Upjohn commented that Parliament has never sought to fetter the right of a company to issue a share with whatever rights or restrictions they may desire. The section requires the passing of an ordinary resolution, it does not require that the vote should be taken on a poll, so the introduction of weighted voting rights does not make a mockery of s303.

Clause (e) will not be valid as a shareholders' agreement can only bind the parties to it. A shareholders' agreement is a purely contractual document and operates as any other contract. The articles and memorandum of a company are different, because although they are based in contract they also have the ability to bind successors in title along the lines of a restrictive covenant in a lease.

With regard to the question of altering the class rights attaching to the shares, generally the power to alter the memorandum is found in s17 CA 1985. However, s17 cannot be used to vary the special rights attached to a class of shares unless either the memorandum or the articles provide for the variation of those rights, in which case the procedure set out in the memorandum or articles must be adhered to. If there is no such provision, and the question does not give this information, then such an alteration can only be made if all the members agree to it: s125(5) CA 1985. The only other way that such an alteration could be made would be by way of a court-sanctioned arrangement under s425 CA 1985.

Minority protection for Ann

The question of whether a shareholders' agreement can oust the operation of s459 CA 1985 was considered in *North Holdings Ltd v Southern Tropics Ltd* [1999] BCC 746 and the Court of Appeal held that the existence of a shareholders' agreement did not defeat s459, so Ann will still be entitled to consider bringing an action for unfair prejudice despite the existence of the *Bushell v Faith* [1970] AC 1099 clause in the agreement.

The advice to Ann is that the agreement is valid as between the members that have entered into it. However, it cannot bind successor shareholders. If the memorandum or articles provide that matters relating to class rights can be altered then Ben and Cal would need a special resolution to achieve this. If there is no such clause, then the alteration could only be achieved through unanimity of the shareholders.

QUESTION TWO

Ox Ltd was formed in 1986 and carries on a business manufacturing nuts and bolts. The memorandum of association provides, inter alia, that the share capital of the company is divided into 50,000 £1 ordinary shares and 10,000 £1 preference shares. Further, the preference shares are there expressed to carry rights to a 16 per cent preference dividend. All the share capital has been issued.

In 1989, after lengthy negotiations, Ox Ltd purchased a factory from Pin Ltd, a company which has owned 5,000 of the ordinary shares in Ox Ltd since its formation in 1986. As part of the consideration for the purchase, it was agreed that the articles of association of Ox Ltd would be altered so as to give Pin Ltd special pre-emption rights in the event of other members of Ox Ltd wishing to sell their shares. The alteration of articles was carried out by Ox Ltd early in 1990.

The board of directors of Ox Ltd now wish to remove from the articles the rights of Pin Ltd in respect of pre-emption, although they are aware that Pin Ltd would oppose this. They also wish to reduce the preference dividend from 16 per cent to 10 per cent. They have heard that 85 per cent of the preference shareholders would be prepared to accede to this reduction since they have all become aware that the company is in financial difficulties and wish to help it. The remaining 15 per cent of the preference shareholders would be opposed to this reduction.

Advise the directors.

University of London LLB Examination
(for External Students) Company Law June 1993 Q7

General Comment

A question requiring the candidate to look very carefully at the problem. Once the 'perception threshold' of the question is broken the solution is not too difficult. A question likely to be avoided by many candidates and therefore an opportunity for the individual to distinguish him/herself. Variation of class rights is covered in Chapter 6: *Shares*.

Skeleton Solution

Articles of association: restrictions on alteration; bona fide for the benefit of the company; subjective or objective test – ascertainment of class rights: variation of class rights; what alterations constitute a variation? – rights of dissenting minority.

Suggested Solution

The directors of Ox Ltd ('the company') wish to alter its articles in order to achieve two things: firstly they wish to divest Pin Ltd of the pre-emption rights acquired on its sale of the factory to the company; secondly they wish to reduce the dividend attaching to the preference shares from 16 per cent to 10 per cent. We are told that both Pin Ltd and 15 per cent of the preference shareholders are unlikely to acquiesce to the alterations. There is therefore a possibility that the alterations might be challenged by either of the above groups on the basis that they constitute a variation of a class right necessitating approval by that class alone, and/or that the alterations are not in any event 'bona fide for the benefit of the company'.

Dealing firstly with the alteration removing Pin Ltd's rights of pre-emption, by virtue of s9 Companies Act (CA) 1985 any alteration to the articles requires a special resolution. As owner of 20 per cent of the ordinary shares in Ox Ltd, Pin Ltd is prima facie unable to defeat the resolution for alteration. Pin Ltd may however contend that the pre-emption rights currently enjoyed by it are 'class rights' attached to the shares currently held and therefore that any variation will require observance of the procedure for variation laid down in the articles or, alternatively, observance of s125 CA 1985. Are the rights enjoyed by Pin Ltd class rights?

Class rights are more often easier to recognise than to define. Frequently (although not invariably) the rights are expressly defined in the articles. Farrar (*Farrar's Company Law*, 3rd ed, p222) states that 'dissimilar interests alone, not arising from legal rights under the corporate constitution, cannot generally be regarded as sufficient ground for the separation of classes'. There was until relatively recently little authority as to what constitutes a class. A thorough review however was undertaken by Scott J in *Cumbrian Newspapers Group Ltd* v *Cumberland and Westmorland Herald Newspaper and Printing Co Ltd* [1986] 2 All ER 816 who adopted a tri-partite classification. Of particular significance to Pin Ltd in the present case is the third category of rights upheld by Scott J in this case. These were rights which although not attached to any particular class of shares were conferred on the beneficiary qua member. In that case the rights were enjoyed on condition that the plaintiff held at least 10.67 per cent of the issued ordinary share capital of the company. Applying this to the facts of the problem it can be seen that the pre-emption rights acquired by Pin Ltd were not referable to (and were unconnected with) its pre-existing membership of the company. They are not therefore rights enjoyed qua member and for that reason neither are they class rights. This alteration at least cannot therefore be a variation of a class right. Thus the only remaining option available to Pin Ltd is to contend that the alteration is not bona fide for the benefit of the company.

The duty of shareholders to vote bona fide in the interests of the company has received a chequered treatment in the authorities over the years. The duty was firmly established by the Court of Appeal in *Allen* v *Gold Reefs of West Africa* [1900] 1 Ch 656. The principal difficulty lies in knowing whether the test is to be applied according to the subjective view of the members or an objective view.

In *Shuttleworth* v *Cox Bros & Co (Maidenhead) Ltd* [1927] 2 KB 9, the Court of Appeal preferred not to interfere where there were grounds on which a reasonable shareholder would come to the same conclusion. This is at odds with the ratio of the Court of Appeal in *Greenhalgh* v *Arderne Cinemas Ltd* [1951] Ch 286 in which Lord Evershed MR adopted the test of the hypothetical shareholder, ie to ask whether what was proposed was for that person's benefit. The test proposed in *Greenhalgh* is of little value where there is a conflict as in the instant case between two groups. Lord Evershed MR did however indicate that discriminatory conduct might be a ground for intervention. In the instant case it is not known exactly why Ox Ltd wishes to remove the pre-emption rights or exactly how it is intended to be beneficial to the company. Pin Ltd would therefore appear to be in a position to commence proceedings under s459 CA 1985 in order to seek redress.

The reduction of the preference dividend from 16 per cent to 10 per cent is undoubtedly a variation of the rights attaching to those shares: *House of Fraser plc* v *AGCE Investments Ltd* [1987] AC 387; ie variation presupposes existence of the right, variation of the right, and the continued existence of the right. The resolution effecting the variation must therefore comply with any procedure laid down in the articles dealing with variation (if there is one): s125(4) CA 1985. If the articles do not provide any procedure for variation s125(2) provides a statutory procedure: this requires either a special majority of the holders of the class to consent in writing or an extraordinary resolution passed at a separate class meeting. The 15 per cent preference holders who object may apply to the court to have variation cancelled within 21 days of the consent/resolution being given/passed: s127(1) and (2). Where this mechanism is invoked the variation is of no effect unless approved by the court.

QUESTION THREE

Lorry Ltd is operating a road haulage business. It has an issued share capital of 900 £1 shares. Alan, Barry and Colin own 300 shares each. The articles of association of the company provide that, 'Alan, Barry and Colin are to be the directors of the company and each is to receive a salary of £25,000 per annum'.

The company was formed in 1987 and was immediately successful. Every year Alan, Barry and Colin have each drawn £25,000. No dividends have been paid on their shares but the huge profits of the company have been ploughed back into the business, so that now each £1 share is represented by assets worth about £1,000, and thus the total asset value of the company is about £900,000.

In 1990 Colin quarrelled with Alan and Barry over matters of business policy. After that, they made it difficult for Colin to have any real share in the management of the business because, although they still had regular weekly directors' meetings at which they were all present, Alan and Barry discussed and made all the business decisions in advance and invariably outvoted Colin at the board meetings. At first Colin complained bitterly about this, but after some months he lost all interest in the business and has not now attended a board meeting for nearly two years.

In recent months Colin has suspected that Alan and Barry have been diverting the company's haulage contracts to a newly formed company registered with the name Lorry (London) Ltd of which Alan and Barry are the sole shareholders and directors. Last week Colin confronted Alan and Barry with this and there was a violent quarrel.

They have just written to him informing him that he is 'sacked as director and will receive no more salary from the company'.

Advise Colin.

University of London LLB Examination
(for External Students) Company Law June 1993 Q4

General Comment

An eye for the salient facts and an appreciation of the limits of the remedies available are required.

Skeleton Solution

The s14 contract: 'outsider rights'; contracts extrinsic but identical to the articles – shareholder remedies: s459 CA 1985; s122 IA 1986 and limitations thereon; interrelation between derivative action and s459.

Suggested Solution

Colin has a plethora of remedies available to him. There are three main issues: (a) does Colin have a contractual remedy against Lorry Ltd on the basis of a contract contained in the articles; (b) is exclusion from the board actionable qua member; and (c) can Colin pursue any remedy against Alan and Barry on behalf of Lorry Ltd?

a) Section 14 Companies Act (CA) 1985 gives contractual effect to the memorandum and articles between the members inter se, and between the members and the company. The effect is that every member has a contractual right to enforce observance of the articles: *Wood* v *Odessa Waterworks Co* (1889) 42 Ch D 636. There are however important restrictions on the type of right which may be enforced. Most significantly the rights enforceable are only those which affect the member in his capacity as member: *Eley* v *Positive Government Security Life Assurance Co* (1876) 1 Ex D 88. In the instant case the relevant article provides that Colin is to be director. The right is therefore not conferred qua shareholder and prima facie Colin has no action on the basis of the contract contained in the articles.

   There are however two further possibilities. The first is that Colin may be able to bring an action qua member to have the articles enforced (the fact that this will result in his being reinstated as a director being incidental to the action). There is no direct authority in Colin's favour in point although the House of Lords in *Quinn & Axtens* v *Salmon* [1909] AC 442 upheld the plaintiff's injunction qua member although it affected him principally qua director. The second possibility is that the court would be prepared to imply a contract extrinsic but identical to the articles, alterable unilaterally by the company: *Re New British Iron Co, ex parte Beckwith* [1898] 1 Ch 324. On this basis Colin would at least be able to recover any arrears of salary.

b) As a shareholder Colin has potentially at his disposal two important remedies. He may petition the court for a just and equitable winding-up of Lorry Ltd pursuant to s122(1)(g) Insolvency Act (IA) 1986. Alternatively he may bring proceedings under s459 CA 1985 for unfairly prejudicial conduct. Frequently the same set of facts will give rise to the availability of either remedy. Exclusion from participation in management was recognised as a ground for just and equitable winding-up (at least in relation to quasi-partnership companies) by the House of Lords in *Ebrahimi* v *Westbourne Galleries Ltd* [1973] AC 360. As a condition precedent to granting relief the court will require to be satisfied as to the existence of one or more of the following criteria: (i) the company should have been formed on the basis of a personal relationship involving mutual trust and confidence; (ii) there should be some agreement that all or some of the shareholders participate in the management of the business; and (iii) there should be pre-emption rights over the shares. The crux of the matter is that the court will not intervene unless the agreement embodied in the articles does not properly define the parties' rights and expectations.

Colin is attempting to invoke an equitable jurisdiction and so the court will be interested in whether or not he has 'clean hands' and has delayed in seeking this remedy. Colin should also bear in mind that to have the company wound up will be to 'kill the goose that lays the golden eggs'. In view of the fact that the value of the company has increased from £900 in 1987 to £900,000 at the present day, Colin would be advised to view this remedy as a last resort.

By virtue of s461 the court has an almost unlimited discretion as to the appropriate order upon the hearing of a petition under s459 alleging unfairly prejudicial conduct. Commonly the order will be that petitioners' shares be purchased by the respondent. The range of remedies available should alone make this a more attractive choice of remedy to Colin. The paramount question is whether there has been any unfair prejudice.

In common with the remedy of the just and equitable winding-up, exclusion from management can form the basis of an unfair prejudice application: *Re London School of Electronics Ltd* [1986] Ch 211. As before the court will require to be satisfied that the removal from the board is both unfair and prejudicial. Mere removal alone will not suffice and so much depends on the basis upon which Colin became a member of Lorry Ltd. There is no requirement that Colin come to the court with clean hands although his non attendance at board meetings may influence the court as to the relief which it is prepared to grant. There is, however, one further element which may make a petition under s459 the most appropriate remedy.

c) Can Colin pursue any remedy against Alan and Barry for allegedly diverting contracts to the newly formed Lorry (London) Ltd? According to the rule in *Foss* v *Harbottle* (1843) 3 Hare 461 the proper plaintiff in an action in this respect would be Lorry Ltd. As malefactors and majority shareholders Barry and Alan are unlikely to procure Lorry Ltd to bring proceedings against themselves. Prima facie therefore there is a fraud on the minority of exactly the type contemplated in *Cook* v *Deeks* [1916] 1 AC 554 which Colin may attempt to redress on behalf of Lorry Ltd in a separate derivative action. It should be noted, however, that under s459 CA 1985 (as amended by CA 1989) conduct which is prejudicial to the interests of the 'members generally' will be actionable. Prior to this amendment conduct which affected all members equally (and therefore in reality the company itself) was not actionable. In the present case Alan and Barry's actions will ultimately diminish the value of theirs and Colin's holdings in Lorry Ltd. It is therefore open to Colin to remedy this loss to Lorry Ltd under s459. It should be noted that by virtue of s461(2)(c) the court may authorise civil proceedings to be brought in the name and on behalf of the company. This would thereby enable Colin to redress wrongs done to both himself and Lorry Ltd in a single petition under s459 by sidestepping the confusing rules governing common law derivative actions.

Chapter 4

Promoters and
Pre-incorporation Contracts

4.1   Introduction

4.2   Key points

4.3   Key cases and statutes

4.4   Questions and suggested solutions

4.1 Introduction

The title of this chapter really encompasses two separate areas of law. The first concerns the liability of promoters for statements contained in a company prospectus issued prior to a flotation, whilst the second concerns the extent to which the company can be made liable, after incorporation, for contracts entered into, purportedly on its behalf, prior to incorporation. The two areas are covered in the same chapter because they both relate to the very early stages of a company's existence and consequently often occur together in a problem question.

4.2 Key points

Flotation

Only a public company may offer its shares to the public. Securities of a public company (principally shares and debentures) may be listed on the Stock Exchange or be unlisted.

Section 142 Financial Services Act 1986 provides that such securities may only be admitted to the Official List of the Stock Exchange if they comply with Pt IV of the Act. The principal requirement (s144) is that the Stock Exchange Listing Rules (contained in what is known as the Yellow Book) be complied with. The Yellow Book is subject to revision from time to time, the latest being in January 1999.

The Listing Rules comprehensively set down conditions for admission, admission procedures, time limits and contents of the listing particulars and other offer documents issued by the company. Other offer documents include mini or abridged prospectuses. Prior Stock Exchange approval is required for publication of all such documents, and the Stock Exchange also has power to control advertisements for share offers.

Offers of unlisted securities are now controlled by the Public Offer of Securities Regulations 1995 which contains a similar regime to that envisaged in Pt V Financial Services Act 1986 (never implemented). The regulations which came into force in June 1995 replace Pt III Companies Act (CA) 1985. The new regime is not dissimilar to that for listed securities. Where securities are offered which are not admitted to official listing the person responsible for making the offer or invitation to make an offer must first register a prospectus with the Registrar of Companies and then make it available free to the public. Regulation 8 requires the prospectus to comply with the form and contents set out in the First Schedule, and regulation 9 imposes a general duty of disclosure. Advertisements (given a wide definition) cannot be issued unless they state that a prospectus will be published and give the address where it can be obtained.

Unlisted securities may nevertheless be traded. The Alternative Investment Market (AIM) has replaced the Unlisted Securities Market (USM) as the principal secondary market for securities of smaller and growing companies. These companies might not be able to satisfy the requirements for a full Stock Exchange listing, but still wish to raise capital by public issue, and sometimes a quotation on the secondary market may be a step towards full listing at a later stage. Entrance to the secondary markets is also controlled by Stock Exchange rules, although the requirements are less stringent than for a full listing. The investor in AIM quoted companies accepts a higher level of risk but still has some protection.

Whether securities are listed or unlisted, liability may be incurred by the company, its directors, and other persons responsible for the content of offer documents if they fail to comply with the procedural requirements, or if there are significant omissions from particulars, or if the documents contain false or misleading particulars. Liability can be statutory – principally s150 Financial Services Act 1986 (listed securities) and the Public Offer of Securities Regulations 1995, regulation 15 (unlisted), which provide for similar liabilities and exemptions – or at common law for deceit or misrepresentation. There may be civil as well as criminal liability for offenders, affording injured investors rights to compensation or rescission. Students should be familiar with all potential offences and remedies and with the defences, particularly the statutory defences, available.

Promoters

There is no statutory defintion of the term 'promoter', but it is generally understood to mean those who take on the task of forming the company and getting it under way in its business. The best description of a promoter is to be found in the case of *Whaley Bridge Calico Printing Co* v *Green and Smith* (1879) 5 QBD 109.

Promoters owe fiduciary duties to the company, although they cannot be treated as its agents during the period of promotion, for the company does not exist at that time. In particular they must not make a secret profit out of the process of formation: *Omnium Electric Palaces Ltd* v *Baines* [1914] 1 Ch 332. This is of particular importance if the promoters are intending to sell their own property to the company. Full disclosure of the circumstances must be made, either to the shareholders or to an independent board of directors. In many cases there will be no independent board, since it is likely that the promoters themselves will become the directors.

Promoters have a duty to account to the company for the profits of any property which they have bought for the purpose of selling it to the company. In equity the property belongs to the company, which is therefore entitled to insist on taking it over at cost price. Promoters also have a duty not to exercise undue influence over the decisions of the company.

Where promoters are in breach of their duties the company will be able to sue for any damages incurred, or claim an account of any profits made. If a contract has been improperly procured, then it is likely that the company will be able to rescind it.

In this area many of the remedies depend upon general contractual and tortious principles (including the tort of deceit). In any case it is necessary to consider the application of these principles.

Pre-incorporation contracts

When a company is in the process of formation it is common for contracts to be entered into on its behalf. This is a logical impossibility, since by definition the company does not exist at that point. After incorporation it may become necessary to consider who, if anyone, is liable on the contract.

Section 36C CA 1985 provides that a person who enters into a contract as purported agent for an unformed company is deemed to have made the contract in a personal capacity and is personally liable on it. This rule is subject to contrary agreement between the parties to the contract, but it is important to understand that the contrary agreement cannot serve to make the company liable on the contract.

The only way in which the company can become liable is if, after incorporation, it enters into a contract with the original creditor in the same terms as that of the orginal contract between the promoter and the creditor. It is not possible simply to ratify the original contract, since the principles of agency do not permit ratification of a contract made when the purported principal did not exist.

4.3 Key cases and statutes

- *BDG Roof Bond Ltd (In Liquidation)* v *Douglas* [2000] 1 BCLC 401
  Compliance with procedural requirements – off-market purchase of a company's own shares – members can waive requirements because they are the only persons it is intended to protect

- *Cotronic (UK) Ltd v Dezonie* [1991] BCC 200
  Contract void where a company does not exist and the formation of a new company is not in contemplation – defendant therefore excused from personal liability under s35C(1) CA 1985

- *Omnium Electric Palaces Ltd v Baines* [1914] 1 Ch 332
  Promoters must not make a secret profit out of the company formation

- *Oshkosh B'Gosh Inc v Dan Marbel Inc and Craze* (1988) 4 BCC 795
  Section 36C(1) CA 1985 does not apply to make a director personally liable where the company is waiting for a new certificate of incorporation to reflect a change of name

- *Phonogram v Lane* [1982] QB 938
  Section 36C(1) CA 1985 makes it clear that the words 'subject to any agreement to the contrary' require an express agreement and cannot be inferred by a promoter signing as agent for the company

- *Whaley Bridge Calico Printing Co v Green and Smith* (1879) 5 QBD 109
  Contains a good description of a promoter

- Companies Act 1985, s36C – promoters make contracts for unformed companies on a personal basis

- Financial Services Act 1986

  - s142 – plc securities may only be admitted to the Official List of the Stock Exchange if they comply with Pt IV of this Act

  - s144 – need to comply with Stock Exchange Listing Rules

  - s150 – liability for documents

- Public Offer of Securities Regulations 1995 replaces Pt III CA 1985 and Pt V Financial Services Act 1986 (unimplemented), significantly amending the rules relating to contents of prospectuses and liability for misstatement in relation to offers of unlisted securities

4.4 Questions and suggested solutions

QUESTION ONE

Dee and Ellie were directors of Choc-a-holic Ltd, a successful confectionery company which supplies 'environmentally-friendly' chocolates to high class retailers. Wishing to raise additional finance for further expansion, they sought advice from Lorings, a notable merchant bank. Subsequently Choc-a-holic Ltd issued £1 million ordinary shares and converted to a public company with the new name of Choc plc. The shares were offered for sale to the public and Choc plc obtained a listing on the Stock Exchange.

The listing particulars, which were issued on 3 January 1995, explained that the company only used organically produced ingredients that were environmentally friendly and that the company's expansion plans intended to build on this and a further 30 outlets had been obtained for the increased sale of the confectionery. The profits forecast stated that the company's profits were likely to increase by 50 per cent as a result of these expansion plans.

An EEC report was 'leaked' to the directors of the company which stated that Choc plc confectionery products did not comply with the new EEC approved definition of 'environmentally friendly' and that 99 per cent of the ingredients were from sources that did not comply with a new EEC Regulation's definition of 'organic.'

The directors chose to ignore the leaked report. The sale of the shares was a success. After trading in the shares commenced the EEC report was published. As a result the price of the company's shares has fallen by 90 per cent. All retail outlets are now refusing to stock the company's products. The Stock Exchange has suspended dealings and the company is expected to go into insolvent liquidation.

Advise Caramel who agreed to take 100 Choc plc shares on flotation, and Hazel who bought 100 shares on the market after trading in the shares commenced.

University of London LLB Examination
(for External Students) Company Law June 1995 Q5

General Comment

This question concerns liability for information about a company which ought properly to be provided by listing particulars and a knowledge of the statutory and common law remedies available. It is very important to deal in some detail with those remedies which operate against persons other than the company where insolvent liquidation appears likely.

Skeleton Solution

Outline provisions in Financial Services Act 1986 about general requirement of disclosure – class of claimants – statutory defences; s151 – insolvent liquidation and recovery from directors personally – compensation and measure of damages – alternative common law remedies.

Suggested Solution

Caramel and Hazel have each acquired 100 Choc plc shares and seem to have sustained a heavy loss as a result. The listing particulars emphasised the importance of 'organic' and 'environmentally friendly' factors, but Dee and Ellie find out, apparently before the sale of shares began, about their non-compliance. There are statutory remedies for persons suffering losses by reason of defects in listing particulars and these must be considered first.

Section 150 Financial Services Act (FSA) 1986 is relevant here and subs(1) and (3) impose liability to pay compensation to persons acquiring securities and suffering loss as a result of misleading statements or omissions in the particulars (subs1), or in supplementary listing particulars (subs3). Section 146 FSA 1986 imposes a general duty of disclosure in listing particulars, and this extends to such information as would normally be found to enable investors to assess 'the prospects of the issuer of the securities' (s146(1)(a) and Chapter 6, Pt 6 Stock Exchange Listing Rules), ie Choc plc. This information was absolutely crucial to an assessment of Choc plc's prospects. Provided there was sufficient time between the directors becoming aware of the problem and the onset of share dealing, there was a clear duty to issue supplementary particulars based on 'significant new matters' which would have needed to go into the listing particulars had they been known about earlier (s147(1)(a)).

Caramel purchased under the original flotation and Hazel bought on the open market after trading commenced, but we do not know whether this was before or after publication of the report. Caramel seems to be well within the class of persons contemplated by s150(1), as her loss was directly caused by the omission of supplementary particulars. Hazel's position is not so clear, because if she had purchased subsequent to the publication of the EEC report, the price may have begun to reflect the true situation. Certainly, this would be the case within a few days at most, but this a matter of evidence. There seems to be nothing in the legislation to prevent an open market purchaser being an 'acquirer' within the Act.

The next point is whether there are relevant defences against either of the investors. This seems to turn upon the chronological order of events and the defences are set out in s151 FSA 1986.

Section 151(1)(a) gives a defence if the particulars, when submitted, were believed to be true and that acquisition took place before it was reasonably practicable to correct matters. This might be available if the leak was close in time to the onset of dealing. There seems to be no reason to doubt the directors' belief in the truth of the particulars although, if they had no reasonable foundation for their belief through lack of inquiry, ie 'Nelsonian' (ie deliberate) blindness, s146(3) would preclude reliance upon this defence.

Section 151(2) might defend had the directors relied upon a statement by an expert on the points later defined by the EEC, although this sounds unlikely.

Section 151(5) might defend against Hazel but not Caramel. This is that the open market purchase was made in the light of knowledge of the 'change or new matter'. This, again, is a matter of evidence.

Section 151(6) would defend if the directors 'reasonably believed' that supplementary particulars were not called for. Much will depend upon just what was leaked and how authentic the information seemed. If the directors had the full substance of the report they will have no defence, but a mere 'whisper' might allow this defence to work.

It sounds as if insolvent liquidation is close, so an important question is: who may be liable to the investors? Section 150(1) imposes liability upon 'the persons responsible for' the particulars. This includes the 'issuer' (s152(1)(a)), and directors at the time the particulars were submitted (s152(1)(b)). This seems to catch the directors but, by the wording of s147(1) and (3) and s150(3), it is clear that for failure to issue supplementary particulars only the issuer is caught, not the persons responsible for the original particulars. All is not lost, however, because s147(3) imposes a duty upon the persons responsible for the original particulars to notify the issuer, ie Choc plc, of any 'new matter' requiring supplementary particulars. This will catch the directors quite neatly.

If Caramel and Hazel can get this far and the directors cannot find a defence, the question becomes one of what remedy is provided. The Act does not give much guidance, and merely refers to 'compensation' for loss, so damages are contemplated but nothing is said of the measure. The Companies Acts' measure of damages for untrue statements in prospectuses is usually the difference between the higher of (a) the market value at purchase (if any) and (b) the price actually paid (the flotation price in Caramel's case or the market price for Hazel), and the true value of the securities at that time when the untrue element in the prospectus is disregarded. This appears to be the approach under the FSA 1986 and the case of *Smith New Court Securities* v *Scrimgeour Vickers (Asset Management) Ltd* [1994] 2 BCLC 212 was decided on that basis.

Outside the FSA 1986 provisions, most avenues for Caramel and Hazel are based upon misrepresentation and would need, of necessity, to be pursued against the company. This seems of little use in the circumstances, although rescission would possibly be worth pursuing if circumstances changed. There could be some difficulty with this as Choc plc may not have been in being at the time of the particulars, so that the directors could not possibly have been its agents and therefore rescission would not be available (*Lynde* v *Anglo-Italian Hemp Spinning Co Ltd* [1896] 1 Ch 178). It would certainly be too late once the company was in liquidation (*Oakes* v *Turquand and Harding* (1867) LR 2 HL 325). There might be a reasonable possibility of pursuing the directors personally under *Hedley Byrne* principles (*Hedley Byrne & Co* v *Heller and Partners* [1964] AC 465) for negligent misstatement, and the House of Lords' decisions on reliance cases indicate a favourable reception. However, the existence of statutory duties and remedies such as those in the FSA 1986 probably stands in the way of a common law action purely for damages.

The point about the various remedies is that they are not mutually exclusive but are, in fact, cumulative, so that any or all of them are available and this is not affected by rescission (*Archer* v *Brown* [1985] QB 401). It is clear that double recovery would not be possible.

QUESTION TWO

In the summer of 1993, Ann Appleby and Betty Berry decided to form a company to manufacture wine but in view of their imminent holidays, agreed to do nothing about it until the Autumn. In August 1993, without telling Betty (who was still on holiday), Ann purchased a plot of land, 'Grapeacre', located in southern England. The purchase was made at a properly conducted auction for a price of £200,000 (about half its true market value at that time) and was transferred into the sole name of Ann.

In November 1993 Ann explained to Dave Daft that she was forming a wine manufacturing company to be called 'Wino Ltd'. She arranged that he would supply a hydraulic grape press to be delivered to the factory on Grapeacre in February 1994 in return for a price of £50,000 payable within three months of delivery. Ann gave Dave a typewritten document setting out this arrangement, at the bottom right-hand corner of which appeared the name 'The Wino Company' and directly underneath that, also typed, 'Ann Appleby'.

In December 1993 Ann and Betty formed a company with the name 'Bokay Ltd' (having changed their minds about the desirability of the name 'Wino Ltd'). They each subscribed for 500,000 £1 fully paid shares. In January 1994 Ann sold Grapeacre to Bokay Ltd for £600,000 (its true market value at that time). In July 1994 Ann and Betty sold all their shares in Bokay Ltd to Eric Endacott who has since found out all the above facts. Dave has never been paid for the grape press he supplied.

Discuss.

University of London LLB Examination
(for External Students) Company Law June 1995 Q8

General Comment

Here, consideration must be given to the circumstances in which promoters may be held liable for breach of duty towards the company, and some analysis of the nature of the duty is called for. The position of director/shareholders who deal with their own company must be taken into account, and also the status and effects of pre-incorporation contracts upon company and promoter.

Skeleton Solution

Nature of promoters' duties – importance of chronological order of dealings – nature of breach; remedies available and purpose of damages – Ann as director/shareholder; disclosure requirement – liability of company for pre-incorporation agreements – novation possibility – personal liability for Ann.

Suggested Solution

There are three principal points raised by the question: first, the duties that are owed by promoters towards the company itself; second, Ann's profitable transaction while director or shadow director; and, third, the question of rights or obligations arising from arrangements made prior to incorporation but in contemplation of it.

The duties owed by promoters

This matter is relevant because of Eric's awareness of Ann's profit of £400,000 from Grapeacre. He may feel that as she was a promoter of Bokay Ltd that the company has some claim to this profit. Ann will be viewed as a promoter, having the aspect of one who undertakes to form a company for a given project and who does all that is necessary for that purpose (*Twycross v Grant* (1877) 2 CPD 469), although there is no statutory definition. The promoter is seen as owing a fiduciary duty towards the company analogous to that of an agent, but the courts have developed a particular approach towards promoters. The vice for the promoter is to make secret profits from the promotion as did many professional promoters in the last century. Everything depends upon when the initial purchase or transaction creating the potential for profit takes place. If it is after the first active steps towards promotion have taken place then disclosure to everyone else subscribing for the capital is necessary (*Re Cape Breton Co* (1885) 29 Ch D 795). Conversely, if the transaction takes place before any active steps are taken, when only an intention to promote exists, he will owe no duty to account (*Erlanger v New Sombrero Phosphate Co* (1878) 3 App Cas 1218). Although there is some artificiality about this temporal distinction, it is applied. He will, however, still owe a duty to disclose, as distinct from a duty to account, even in the latter situation, ie where the purchase took place before active steps were taken (*Re Lady Forrest (Murchison) Gold Mine Co Ltd* [1901] 1 Ch 582).

Applying these principles to the Grapeacre transaction, Ann purchased before any active steps were taken so she will not owe a duty to account to the company, but she will have a duty to disclose fully to Betty in January 1994, assuming that she is the only other member and director. If there were no disclosure, the company would have had the right to rescission but, possibly, the right to rescission had been lost because of passage of time, or restitutio in integrum is neither possible nor desired. The case law indicates that damages may be sued for by the company (*Re Leeds and Hanley Theatre of Varieties* [1902] 2 Ch 809), provided that the true market value at the time of the company's purchase is ascertainable (*Re Cape Breton Co*). This raises the question of the measure of damages; will it be the difference between the purchase price of £500,000 and £200,000 or between £500,000 and the true market value of £400,000 or is there, in fact, any loss at all? This is not a case of a duty to account, it is merely for the loss caused to company by a failure to disclose, and the loss to the company appears to be nil. On this basis it is difficult to see how the company could get more than nominal damages.

Ann must have been either a director or, at least, a shadow director at the time of the purchase of Grapeacre and there will be possibilities under the director duty to account to the company for profits, unless authorised by the company, where the opportunity to profit arose through the directorship (*Regal (Hastings) Ltd v Gulliver* [1967] 2 AC 134n). Nevertheless the company in general meeting can consent to the retention of profits, provided full disclosure of the matter had been made in the notice convening the meeting. It sounds as if this may have occurred and, in any case, *North-West*

Transportation Co Ltd v *Beatty* (1887) 12 App Cas 589 is authority for the proposition that a director acting in the capacity of shareholder can deal with the company in his own interest, provided there is no fraud or oppression. It sounds as if it could be difficult to require Ann to account for her profits on this basis.

The supply of the grape press

This sounds as if an agreement was concluded in November 1993, before Bokay Ltd was incorporated, and the question becomes one of whether there was a contract at all for the press and, if so, who has rights or obligations under it. Bokay had no legal existence and could not contract for itself or via an agent (*Kelner* v *Baxter* (1866) LR 2 CP 174). It could not adopt or ratify the contract after it was incorporated (*Natal Land and Colonization Co Ltd* v *Pauline Colliery and Development Syndicate* [1904] AC 120). For a company to be party to an agreement concluded prior to its incorporation, that agreement must be incorporated into a new contract agreed post-incorporation when the company had become a legal person. The *Natal Land* case shows that mere performance of pre-incorporation agreements does not amount to evidence of a new contract, but is restrictively viewed as the 'offer' in a conventional offer/acceptance analysis in which the other party to the original agreement must then supply some 'acceptance', without which there is no contract with the company. This situation looks less like a novation than an attempted adoption of the old agreement which will not make the company a party to it (*Re Northumberland Avenue Hotel Co* (1886) 33 Ch D 16). Nevertheless, if there is some evidence of fresh terms this will point towards a fresh agreement made after incorporation (*Howard* v *Patent Ivory Manufacturing Co* (1888) 38 Ch D 156), and it might be argued here that as Dave originally entered into agreement with Wino Ltd but subsequently delivered, and presumably invoiced, to Bokay Ltd, that he has entered a new contract with the company. The existence and terms of such a contract would be a matter of evidence. Even if no such contract can be shown, Dave should be entitled to a quantum valebant against the company (*Rover International Ltd* v *Cannon Film Sales Ltd (No 3)* [1989] 1 WLR 912).

If there was no post-incorporation contract, and the company has not used the press or made itself liable to Dave, the question is whether Ann can be personally liable to Dave on the agreement. Both under the common law (*Kelner* v *Baxter* (1866) LR 2 CP 174), and by s36C(1) Companies Act 1985, persons who purport to act for the company, or as its agent on pre-incorporation contracts, are personally liable (*Phonogram* v *Lane* [1982] QB 938), and the level of awareness of the parties is not relevant at all, although express agreement to the contrary will protect. Ann could be personally liable.

QUESTION THREE

'Section 36C of the Companies Act 1985 has done much to improve the position of third parties who enter into contracts with promoters of a company prior to the incorporation of the company; but s36C has not resolved all the problems for the promoter and for the third parties.'

Discuss.

University of London LLB Examination
(for External Students) Company Law June 1999 Q3

General Comment

This answer does not require an historical essay on the common law and development of s36C. It does, however, require an analysis of the drafting of the section and the problems that have arisen. Students should also be aware that s36C applies to events taking place during pre-incorporation negotiations and should not confuse this with ultra vires issues which apply after incorporation.

Skeleton Solution

Position of promoters prior to the Companies Act 1985 – effect of s36C on pre-incorporation contracts – what does s36C cover? – personal liability of the promoter by s36C for contracts entered into by him on behalf of a company before its incorporation (but it is not apparent that the promoter has the same right to enforce a contract) – s36C subject to an agreement to the contrary (must be express) – limitations of s36C – lack of case law – s36C improved life for promoters and pre-incorporation contracts?

Suggested Solution

At common law if a company attempts to enter into a contract before it is incorporated it will be of no effect as the company is non-existent and so cannot be a party to a contract. However, the promoter or agent who made a contract on behalf of an unincorporated company could be liable on the contract. The law before 1985 was set out in the cases of *Kelner* v *Baxter* (1866) LR 2 CP 174, where the promoters who signed an agreement 'on behalf of' a company which was about to be formed were held to be personally liable on the contracts as principals in place of the non-existent company, and *Newborne* v *Sensolid (Great Britain) Ltd* [1954] 1 QB 45, where the contract was held to have been made by the non-existent company and the agent's name was added to authenticate it and neither the company nor the agent could sue on the contract.

The law relating to pre-incorporation contracts was changed when the European Communities Act 1972 came into force, implementing the First Company Law directive. This became s36C Companies Act 1985 which states:

> 'A contract which purports to be made by or on behalf of a company at a time when the company has not been formed has effect, subject to any agreement to the contrary, as one made with the person purporting to act for the company or as agent for it, and he is personally liable on the contract accordingly.'

This section removes the distinction between *Kelner* v *Baxter* and *Newborne* v *Sensolid (Great Britain) Ltd* [1954] 1 QB 45 and has the effect that if an agent's name is appended to a company's name to authenticate it then the agent will become personally liable.

The case of *Phonogram* v *Lane* [1982] QB 938 was the first case to consider the wording of this section and the court concluded that promoters would now be personally liable for all pre-incorporation contracts made by them on behalf of an unformed company. If a promoter wishes to exclude personal liability this must be clearly stated as an express term of the contract.

In the case of buying a company off the shelf, what matters is the date on which the company came into existence. The name of the company at the time is not relevant: *Oshkosh B'Gosh Inc* v *Dan Marbel Inc and Craze* (1988) 4 BCC 795. If a company is in existence at the time a promoter makes a contract then s36C will not apply and the company can ratify the contract, provided the promoter made it clear that they were acting as agents for the company.

A problem arose in the case of *Cotronic (UK) Ltd* v *Dezonie* [1991] BCC 200 where Mr Dezonie signed a contract for and behalf of his company, which unbeknown to him had been struck off the company register five years previously. As soon as Mr Dezonie realised this he incorporated a new company with the same name and sought to rely on the contract. This created a problem as the company did not exist at the time the contract was entered into, nor did Mr Dezonie have the intention to form a company when the contract was entered into, so again s36C did not apply.

From the decisions it is clear that s36C will only protect third parties where the contract identifies a specific company as the contracting party and that company has not yet been incorporated.

Also, the wording of the statute is silent as to whether a promoter can enforce a contract as well as having a contract enforced against him or her. The case of *Cotronic (UK) Ltd* v *Dezonie* raised this issue, but the court did not consider it as they decided that s36C did not apply. The lack of further cases in this area means that this issue is yet to be resolved.

Conclusion

It would seem that s36C has done little to resolve the problems for the promoter and third parties. It has removed the uncertainties caused by the cases of *Kelner* v *Baxter* (1866) LR 2 CP 174 and *Newborne* v *Sensolid (Great Britain) Ltd* [1954] 1 QB 45, but has left further uncertainties. In addition, full novation of a contract will still be required when a company does come into existence to release the promoter from the burden to any contract entered into on behalf of the unformed company.

QUESTION FOUR

'It may have taken over a hundred years, but the Financial Services Act 1986 has finally solved the problem of providing an adequate remedy for someone who suffers damage through an investment in a public company and who was induced to make that investment by a material misrepresentation.'

Discuss.

University of London LLB Examination
(for External Students) Company Law June 1992 Q3

General Comment

This is quite a difficult question in that it requires critical analysis of the solution offered by the Financial Services Act 1986 to the problem of compensating those misled into investing in a public company. This basic objective of investor protection is one with which company law has long been preoccupied and as capital markets become more complicated it becomes in turn more complex to fulfil. It should be noted that this question was written prior to the passing of the Public Offer of Securities Regulations 1995, but is included because a similar question in modified form could well be set in the future.

Skeleton Solution

Gaps in 'old law' – s67 Companies Act 1985 – definition of 'prospectus' – new statutory regimes for public offers of listed securities (Pt IV FSA) and unlisted securities (Public Offer of Securities Regulations 1995) – new statutory remedies; s150 FSA – persons liable to pay compensation – defences available to responsible persons – measure of damages – continuing common law remedies preserved.

Suggested Solution

Prior to the Financial Services Act (FSA) 1986 the Companies Act (CA) 1985 requirements relating to public issues and prospectuses did not apply at all to the listed securities markets ie those securities admitted to the Stock Exchange's official list – the tightest and most difficult to enter UK public capital market. The Companies Act 1985 (Pt III, ss56–79, the prospectus provisions) only applied to the Unlisted Securities Market and the 'over the counter' market for securities. This meant that there were disparities in the different regimes for public issues and defects arose such as the fact that the prospectus provisions of the Companies Act 1985 were interpreted to apply only to offers for the subscription or purchase of securities for cash. Since most takeover offers are structured for non-cash consideration they fell outside the investor protection regime. Part III CA 1985 has been replaced by the Public Offer of Securities Regulations 1995 (see below).

The Financial Services Act 1986 aims to rationalise and put on a more level footing the disclosure and compensation provisions relating to the Stock Exchange's official listed market and the other markets in which the public is induced to part with its money by way of investing in company shares. Historically investor protection in the former had been good whereas it left much to be desired in the latter.

Part IV FSA 1986 deals with the admission of securities of a public company to the official list of the Stock Exchange. It designates the Stock Exchange as the competent authority for the purposes of making listing rules, and applying them to determine whether a company fulfils the criteria contained therein. The Act talks of prescribed listing particulars rather than using the term 'prospectus', the Stock Exchange should ensure that its listing rules require in particular that listing particulars contain enough information pertaining to the financial position and prospects of the company issuing securities as well as information on rights attaching to those securities to enable an investor to make a reasonably informed assessment of those matters (s146 FSA 1986). They must be approved by the Stock Exchange and then registered with the Registrar of Companies.

What remedies exist then if despite apparent compliance with these statutory requirements, the relevant listing particulars or prospectus contain information which adds up to a material misrepresentation of the true position, so that an investor is misled into investing his monies where he otherwise would not have done, and thereby suffers loss? The principal statutory remedies are contained in s150 FSA 1986 which governs compensation for false or misleading listing particulars and s166 which governs compensation for false or misleading prospectuses and replaces s67 Companies Act 1985. Section 150 FSA 1986 imposes civil liability on the persons responsible for any listing particulars which contain false or misleading statements or omissions which in turn cause loss to any person who has acquired the securities to which the particulars relate. It is worth noting that compensation is payable under s150 to anyone who bought the securities in question even if he bought on the secondary market and did not rely directly on the listing particulars. It might perhaps be thought that s150 would award a misled investor his loss of expectation of gain as a result of the misleading statement as a measure of damages. However the Act is not clear here; in using the words 'suffers a loss' it seems that the basic tort measure of damages, viz out of pocket expenses, is being employed. This seems strange and less than satisfactory in an investment context. The persons liable to pay compensation to a misled investor are enumerated in s152 FSA 1986 as the issuer, every director or person who has given his authority to be named as a director in the listing particulars, others who have expressly assumed responsibility for the contents of the particulars, and lastly others who authorised their contents. Section 151 FSA 1986 provides defences available in a s150 compensation action which are broadly similar to those contained in the old prospectus provisions of the Companies Act (s68 CA 1985) namely, reasonable belief in the veracity of the statement, reasonable reliance on the authority of an expert, acting in an official capacity etc. It is arguable that an investor who has suffered loss and cannot proceed against any of the persons liable under s150 could proceed against the Stock Exchange itself for breach of statutory duty. Part V FSA 1986, which applied mirror provisions to unlisted securities was never implemented. Instead, in response to the EC 'Prospectus Directive', the Public Offer of Securities Regulations 1995 were passed and implemented in June 1995. These provide in respect of all offers of unlisted securities (save those exempted in regulation 7) for a prospectus with the form and content specified (regulation 8 and Sch 1) to be published and made freely available, and registered at the Companies Registry prior to publication. Persons responsible for the prospectus (as defined in regulation 13) may uncur liability for false or misleading prospectuses (regulation 14) and have available to them the defences in regulation 15, broadly similar to those in s151 FSA 1986 and formerly (in relation to unlisted securities) in s68 CA 1985. With unlisted securities, it may also be possible to invoke remedies enjoyed by the Securities and Investments Board (SIB) under the FSA on behalf of the investor. Of particular value are s61 (restitution orders) and ss53 and 54 (access to the SIB compensation scheme).

Finally whether the securities are listed or unlisted, the misled investor may have a common law right to rescind the contract of allotment for the securities on the basis that a material misrepresentation has been made; rights to damages which may exist under the Misrepresentation Act 1967; and an action for deceit.

In order to be able to rescind the contract of allotment the misrepresentation must be shown to be the responsibility of the company, ie made by the directors or the company's agents: *Lynde* v *Anglo-Italian Hemp Spinning Co Ltd* [1896] 1 Ch 178 and the investor must not have lost his right to rescind by affirming the contract in any way, eg acting as a member, attending and voting at meetings etc. Rescission does not equal compensation although it will help the investor to avoid other possible liabilities (further calls to pay if shares part paid etc). Section 2(2) Misrepresentation Act 1967 may give the investor damages instead of rescission in the case of the material misrepresentation being an innocent one, and s2(1) affords a remedy in damages for negligent misrepresentation. The usual difficulties with the application of the Misrepresentation Act 1967 and ascertaining damages under it apply but there is nothing to indicate that the Act does not apply to public offers of shares. Regardless of an action against the company the investor can proceed against the promoters, directors, issuers and experts responsible for the prospectus if it can be shown they acted fraudulently. The difficulties of establishing fraud at common law are legendary, however.

The statutory framework provided for investor compensation by Pt IV FSA 1986 and the Public Offer of Securities Regulations 1995 in the event of misleading prospectus and listing particulars statements is likely to be clearer and more certain in operation than the general common law remedies and more rational and wider in application than the pre-existing Companies Act 1985 provisions, although it is not likely to be without its own difficulties for judicial interpretation.

QUESTION FIVE

Ice Rinks plc was until recently a private company controlled by its founders, Jane and Chris. It has had an outstanding history of growth and now manages ten ice rinks under lease from various local authorities. Jane and Chris wanted to increase the scale of their operations and on the advice of Londonbank, a leading merchant bank, they decided to raise fresh capital for the expansion by issuing four million £1 shares and by obtaining a listing on the Stock Exchange. Accordingly, in March 1994, Londonbank made an offer for sale of four million ordinary shares. This was accompanied by an application to the Stock Exchange for listing. The application was successful.

Listing Particulars were published which stated that the turnover of Ice Rinks plc was likely to increase by 50 per cent in 1994 and 1995 because of the Winter Olympics generating publicity for the sport. This statement was not referred to in the accounts and was not taken into account in the profit forecast.

The issue price was 150 pence per share and the flotation was a great success with the price of shares rising steadily to 250 pence after the first month of trading.

The Listing Particulars omitted to mention that the leases on seven of the ten ice rinks held on lease were due to expire in April 1994 and the respective local authorities were refusing to renew the leases.

The Winter Olympics has not resulted in the hoped-for increase in turnover for the ice rink industry and the fact that the leases were not being renewed has also come to light. It has now been learned that a proposed EC Directive with the stated aim of rendering the ice rink industry environmentally friendly will require costly changes in the ice-making plants at ice rinks. The price of shares in Ice Rinks plc has now fallen by 90 per cent.

Advise Slippy who bought shares in Ice Rinks plc on flotation by application from Londonbank, and advise Slide who purchased shares one month later when the shares were at their peak in the market.

[In answering this question, candidates are not required to display a detailed knowledge of the contents of the Stock Exchange's Listing Rules – 'The Yellow Book'.]

University of London LLB Examination
(for External Students) Company Law June 1994 Q8

General Comment

This question deals with problems which arise when listing particulars contain untrue or misleading particulars. The position under the Financial Services Act 1986 must be considered, but so too must the common law remedies. Mention could also be made of possible criminal sanctions to complete the picture.

Skeleton Solution

The flotation and the offer for sale – listing particulars – persons responsible for false or misleading particulars – defences – FSA 1986 remedies – common law remedies – criminal sanctions.

Suggested Solution

Financial Services Act 1986 provisions

Ice Rinks plc ('the company') is a listed company on the London stock exchange. Like the vast majority of listed companies, it started out as a private company and was later 'floated' on the stock exchange by means of an offer for sale. Under this procedure the company allots a block of new shares to the issuing house (Londonbank) and the latter re-sells the shares by offering them to the public. Londonbank will also have agreed to underwrite the issue, promising to buy up any unsold shares.

The law on listed issues is now contained in Pt IV of the Financial Services Act (FSA) 1986, implementing a number of EC Directives. A document known as the Listing Particulars (formerly prospectuses) must be prepared and made available to the public. The content of the Listing Particulars is broadly specified in the FSA 1986, with the detailed content being supplied by the stock exchange's rule book, called the Listing Rules ('The Yellow Book').

Section 146(1) FSA 1986 contains a general duty of disclosure. The Listing Particulars ('particulars') must contain all the information that investors would reasonably require to make an informed decision on whether or not to buy the shares. The information should relate to the assets, liabilities, financial position, profits and losses and prospects of the issuer, and the rights attaching to the shares.

Section 146(2) goes on to provide that only information which is known or which would have been reasonable to obtain by making enquiries need be included. Section 146(3) gives further guidance on what needs to be included, saying that regard must be had to:

a) the nature of the issuer and of the securities;

b) the nature of the persons likely to consider acquiring the securities;

c) matters which may reasonably be within the knowledge of professional advisors.

The statement that there is a likelihood of a 50 per cent increase in turnover falls within s146(1) as it relates to the issuer's prospects. The particulars should also have included the information that the local authorities were refusing to renew the leases on seven of the ice rinks. Section 148 exempts disclosure of certain information but it does not apply here.

It is not clear if and when the proposed EC Directive came into existence. If it was in existence when the particulars were being prepared, then it is submitted that it is information which could have been reasonably discovered by making enquiries under s146(2). It should therefore have been included in the particulars. If it came into existence after the preparation of the particulars and before dealing commenced then supplementary listing particulars should have been submitted to the stock exchange under s147, as the proposed directive probably amounts to a 'significant new matter'.

Section 150 provides that compensation is payable by 'persons responsible' for 'untrue or misleading' statements in the particulars, which includes omissions. So the failure to mention the proposed directive and the refusal to renew seven of the leases would be covered.

The omissions are 'untrue or misleading'. Forecasts such as the turnover prediction are also likely to be considered to be untrue or misleading. In a different context, a duty of care was held to be owed to the purchaser of shares who bought on the strength of a profit forecast in a takeover document: *Morgan Crucible Co plc v Hill Samuel Bank Ltd* [1991] 1 All ER 148. In the present case it is said that there is a 'likelihood' of an increase in turnover, which may not be strong enough to be misleading.

Section 152 says that the persons responsible for the particulars are:

a) the issuer of the securities (the company);

b) the directors;

c) every person who has accepted responsibility for all or part of the particulars;

d) any other person who has authorised the contents of the particulars or part of them.

Remedies under the FSA 1986: Slippy

Subject to the defences in s151 FSA 1986, the company and its directors, presumably Chris and Jane, would be liable to compensate Slippy. Londonbank would also incur liability for those parts of the particulars for which they have accepted responsibility, or authorised. The range of persons responsible is wider than the previous statutory regime (s67 Companies Act (CA) 1985), and now includes the company itself.

Exemptions from liability to pay compensation are contained in s151. In respect of the turnover prediction, 151(1) provides a defence where it was 'reasonably believed, having made such enquiries (if any) as were reasonable, that the statement was true and not misleading'. Another available defence might be contained in s151(2), where a statement is made by an expert. The turnover prediction, however, does not appear in the accounts and was not referred to in the profit forecast, which tends to suggest that is not the view of an expert.

There do not appear to be any defences available covering the omission to state the refusals by the local authorities to renew seven out of ten leases on the ice rinks. It is unlikely that those responsible for the particulars did not know about the refusal of the local authorities to renew the leases.

As mentioned earlier, in relation to the proposed directive much depends on if and when it came into existence. The 'reasonable belief' defence might again be available under s151(1). The onus of proof is on the person claiming to fall within one of the exemptions in s151.

The measure of damages under s150 will probably be assessed according to tortious principles, ie to restore Slippy to his original position. This is not entirely free from doubt but it is supported by Gower (*Principles of Modern Company Law*, 5th ed, p345).

Remedies under the FSA 1986: Slide

Slide's position is similar to that of Slippy. He too will be able to claim compensation. Compensation is not limited to those who purchased shares from the company and extends to those who, like Slide, purchase the shares in the market after dealing has commenced. This is an improvement on the former provision in s67 CA 1985.

Slide will have to show a causal connection between the misstatement/omission and the loss. This will be difficult if there has been a lapse of time such that the particulars can be said to have had an influence on the market price. The lapse of time in Slide's case is one month and it is probably not long enough to bar a claim by Slide for compensation.

Common law remedies

Section 150(4) FSA 1986 expressly preserves existing common law remedies available to an investor who suffers loss as a result of a misrepresentation.

Slippy may be available to rescind his contract with Londonbank. The issue here is whether there has been a misrepresentation. An omission is not usually regarded as a misrepresentation unless it can be regarded as a positive statement. Not mentioning the EC Directive and the refusal to renew the leases might be equivalent to a positive statement that there is no proposed directive in existence and that all the leases are renewable. The difficulty with the turnover prediction is that it may be regarded as a statement of opinion rather than one of fact.

If rescission is available, Slide will be able to rescind against his vendor, as he purchased in the market. The usual bars to rescission apply, such as lapse of time etc.

If the misrepresentations are fraudulent damages may be available under the tort of deceit: *Derry* v *Peek* (1889) 14 App Cas 337. In the present case, the facts do not really suggest fraud.

If the misrepresentation is negligent or innocent then there may be a claim for damages under the Misrepresentation Act 1967. It used to be the rule that the investor had to rescind his contract before a claim for damages could be made: *Houldsworth* v *City of Glasgow Bank* (1880) 5 App Cas 317. This is no longer necessary due to s111A CA 1985.

Damages may be available for negligent misstatements under the principles established in *Caparo Industries plc* v *Dickman* [1990] 2 WLR 358. Under this rule those responsible for the Listing Particulars will owe a duty of care to those investors who apply for shares on the basis of the particulars, but not to subsequent purchasers in the market: *Al-Nakib Investments (Jersey) Ltd* v *Longcroft* [1990] 1 WLR 1390. Applying this to the present case, Slippy may have a remedy under this heading, but Slide will not as he is a subsequent purchaser in the market. This shows the advantages of claiming compensation under the FSA 1986, which does extend to subsequent purchasers.

Criminal liabilty

Under s47(1) FSA 1986 it is an offence for any person to knowingly or recklessly make a statement, promise or forecast which is misleading, false or deceptive or to dishonestly conceal any material fact. The purpose must be to induce another to enter into an investment agreement, such as to buy shares in a company.

Under s19 Theft Act 1968, the officers of the company (directors) will be liable for statements which to their knowledge may be false, misleading or deceptive, if made with intent to deceive a member or creditor of the company: *R v Lord Kylsant* [1932] 1 KB 442.

Slippy and Slide will not gain any personal compensation from these criminal prosecutions, unless the court awards them compensation as the victims of an offence under s35 Powers of Criminal Courts Act 1973.

Chapter 5

Capital

5.1 Introduction

The word 'capital' has several meanings and students should become familiar with the various types of capital. It is a fundamental principle that a company's capital (by which is sometimes meant nominal capital, sometimes issued, sometimes both together) be maintained to provide a measure of security for creditors and investors. Thus the nominal capital may be increased, consolidated, subdivided or converted into stock, but may not be reduced except by following the procedure in ss135–138 Companies Act (CA) 1985, which includes the requirement to obtain court approval.

5.2 Key points

General

Capital might be reduced indirectly by paying dividends out of capital, by the company purchasing its own shares or giving financial assistance to others to do so. All these have therefore been prohibited or tightly controlled by law. In general, public companies are more strictly constrained in this regard and, in addition, are required to have a minimum nominal capital of which a specified proportion is paid up (see Chapter 6) and must call a general meeting if their net assets fall to half or less of their called-up share capital (s142 CA 1985).

Dividends

A company must not pay dividends except out of profits available for the purpose (s263 CA 1985). Profits available for the purpose are accumulated realised profits less accumulated realised losses.

Whether profits are to be treated as accumulated is decided according to the principles of good accounting practice (CA 1985, Sch 4, paras 88–91).

Part VIII CA 1985 contains detailed rules relating to the treatment of revaluations of assets, and to the use of interim and initial accounts as the basis for a dividend.

Where an unlawful dividend is paid, a shareholder who knows of the unlawfulness may be required to repay the dividend to the company (s277 CA 1985).

Public companies are subject to a further restriction in that they may not pay a dividend if the result of doing so would be to reduce their net assets below the value of their called-up capital plus undistributable reserves (s264 CA 1985).

Purchase of own shares

It has long been established that for a company to purchase its own shares is a capital reduction and thus forbidden (*Trevor* v *Whitworth* (1887) 12 App Cas 409). This general rule is now contained in s143(1) CA 1985, but is relaxed by a number of other provisions.

By s159 company may issue redeemable shares, ie shares which are expressed on the face of them to be redeemable, and these will then be redeemable in accordance with the terms and conditions attached to them at the time of issue. However, a company must always have some shares which are not expressed to be redeemable.

Shares not issued as redeemable may also be purchased by the company (s162 CA 1985). The articles must permit the redemption or purchase, and the relevant procedure (which differs according to whether it is a 'market purchase' (s166) or 'off-market purchase' (s164)) must be followed. Any company may pay for its shares out of distributable profits or out of the proceeds of a fresh issue of shares made for that purpose. Private companies only may also use capital subject to the safeguards in ss171–177. These include a statutory declaration by the directors, supported by an auditors' report, to the effect that the company is solvent and will remain so for the coming year. Declarations without reasonable grounds give rise to an offence for which directors are personally liable.

Assistance for purchase of own shares

Sections 151–154 CA 1985 impose a general prohibition on a company providing financial assistance, whether directly or indirectly, for the purchase of its own shares.

At the same time s153 provides exemptions from the prohibition where the assistance is given as an incidental part of some larger purpose of the company and is given in good faith in the best interests of the company. The difficulty of applying this section is shown by the case of *Brady* v *Brady* [1989] AC 755.

Section 151 additionally provides exemptions from the general prohibition which apply only to private companies. This section contains the relaxation of the rules introduced by the 1985 Act. Essentially private companies are exempt from the prohibition so long as they follow certain procedures (specified in ss155–158). These involve a statutory declaration and auditors' report similar to those required for direct purchase.

If the net assets of the company are to be reduced by the giving of the assistance, then the funds used must be distributable profits of the company (s155(2)).

Finally, the proposal must be approved by a special resolution of the General Meeting, except where the company proposing to give the assistance is a wholly-owned subsidiary of the company which is to receive the assistance.

Proposed changes

The Final Report of the Company Law Review published in July 2001 recommended simplification of the capital maintenance regime for all private companies with , in particular, repeal of the present obscure, complex and costly rules on financial assistance in connection with share acquisitions.

5.3 Key cases and statute

- *Acatos and Hutchinson* v *Watson* [1995] 1 BCLC 218
  Purchase of a company's entire share capital was not a breach of s143 CA 1985

- *Brady* v *Brady* [1989] AC 755
  Complexities of financial assistance provisions

- *Parlett* v *Guppys (Bridport) Ltd* [1996] 2 BCLC 34
  To be unlawful, financial assistance under s151(1) CA 1985, the company's net assets must be reduced to a material extent

- *Trevor* v *Whitworth* (1877) 12 App Cas 409
  Rule against company purchase of own shares

- Companies Act 1985

  - ss135 to 138 – contains procedure for reducing capital

  - s142 – requirement to call a general meeting when assets fall to less than half called-up share capital

  - s143(1) – statutory recognition of rule in *Trevor* v *Whitworth*

  - ss151 to 154 – general prohibition on provision of financial assistance

  - ss155 to 158 – relaxation of the provision for private companies

  - s159 – possibility to issue redeemable shares

  - s162 – purchase of shares by company

  - ss171 to 177 – private companies may use some capital to finance repurchase

  - s263 – requirement to pay dividends out of profits

  - s264 – further restrictions on plc's rights to pay dividends

- s277 – where shareholder is aware that dividend is unlawful they become liable
- Sch 4, paras 88 to 91 – contain good accounting practice

5.4 Questions and suggested solutions

QUESTION ONE

Blue plc is a major conglomerate which has several wholly owned subsidiaries. One of these subsidiary companies is Sky Ltd. Sky Ltd specialises in the lending of money. Blue plc wished to further expand its operation and were in negotiations with Red plc to merge some of their operations. As part of this reconstruction, Red plc were proposing to acquire a substantial number of shares in Blue plc but due to an unexpected delay in obtaining finance from their bank, Red plc proposed delaying the purchase of the shares until July 1996. Blue plc were unhappy about the delay because the share price of Blue plc was falling and this was having an adverse affect on the financing of several other takeovers which were based on Blue plc's share price. The board of directors ('the board') of Blue plc proposed that they should give Red plc some help to purchase the share immediately. The Board procured a loan from Sky Ltd arguing that the loan 'was in good faith in the interests of Sky Ltd'. The directors of Sky Ltd were concerned about their future employment and felt unable to refuse making the substantial loan, despite the fact that the loan breached their normal rules of business on lending.

Advise the directors of Sky Ltd.

University of London LLB Examination
(for External Students) Company Law June 1996 Q6

General Comment

The question has two aspects which must both be addressed. The first aspect is the question of the extent to which a company can assist in the purchase of its own share capital and how this fits in with the notion of holding companies and wholly-owned subsidiaries. The second aspect concerns the limits for the purposes for which directors can exercise their powers and the relationship with their fiduciary duties towards the company.

Skeleton Solution

The maintenance of capital principle, rationale, scope and mechanisms – the emotional circumstances where assistance is allowed – the position of Sky Ltd – the position of Sky Ltd directors in agreeing to the loan – consequences and sanction.

Suggested Solution

The problem that is posed for Blue plc and Sky Ltd here is that the proposed actions may be seen as offending against the long-established company law principle that the share capital base of a company must be jealously guarded and maintained for the protection of creditors and all persons dealing with the company, and any reduction of that capital must be carried out in accordance with the Companies Acts. The current provisions can be found in Pt V, ss151–158 Companies Act (CA) 1985 and the relevant provisions are ss151–158, which deal with companies providing financial assistance for the purchase of their own shares or the shares of a company's holding company to another person. The general rule is that such transactions are unlawful: s151(1) CA 1985. This is, however, subject to numerous exceptions that are set out in s153 CA 1985 and a special regime is given in s155 CA 1985 for private companies who provide assistance. Section 155 CA 1985 recognises the more relaxed approach that can be taken for private companies and those with private holding companies in situations where it is clear that net assets are not reduced by the financial assistance or the assistance is provided out of distributable profits.

The question is, therefore, whether Sky Ltd can be seen to fall within any of the excepted circumstances. Section 155 cannot help here because, although Sky Ltd seems to fall within the section, it has no application at all where the assistance is provided for purchasing shares in a public holding company or where, in a chain of holding companies, there is one which is public: s155(1) and (3) CA 1985. Another possibility is seen in s153(1) CA 1985 which exempts the situation where the providing company's principal purpose in assisting is not the giving of the assistance but is 'an incidental part of some larger purpose of the company' and the assistance is given in good faith in the interests of the company: s153(1)(a) and (b) CA 1985. The problem for Sky Ltd's directors is that they will have some difficulty in showing such a larger purpose (it is Blue plc which has a 'larger purpose') and their concern is not bona fide in the interests of the company but is really about their own future employment prospects as they cannot hold shares in what is a wholly owned subsidiary company.

The question becomes one of whether the Sky Ltd directors can properly take the view that as Blue plc really own Sky Ltd, does Blue plc's 'larger purpose' constitute a larger purpose of Sky Ltd? In other words, can a company have a 'purpose' which is not that of its shareholders? It is submitted that it cannot, and that the larger purpose of Blue plc in expansion of the group as a whole is also the larger purpose of Sky Ltd. The problem with this provision is that the case decided on the point, *Brady* v *Brady* [1989] AC 755 shows a strict construction given to 'purpose' and difficult distinctions are drawn between the reasons why assistance may be given and the purpose of giving the assistance. In this situation the reasons are those of expansion and reconstruction of the group. On a strict construction of 'purpose', the purpose is purely to assist in purchasing shares, a prohibited matter.

Another possible exception can be seen in s153(4)(a) CA 1985 where the 'lending of money is part of the ordinary business of the company, the lending of money by the company in the ordinary course of its business' is not prohibited. The problem here is whether the breaching of Sky Ltd's normal rules of business is enough to take the loan outside 'the ordinary course of its business'. This is probably more a question of fact than of law. If the breach was of a fairly minor procedural rule, the exception might be available but if the breach is more serious the subsection will not protect Sky Ltd. As Sky Ltd is obviously an English company there is no assistance to be gained from the recent first instance decision in *Arab Bank plc v Mercantile Holdings Ltd and Another* [1993] BCC 816 which held that the prohibition does not apply to foreign subsidiaries of English holding companies .

The position for the directors of Sky Ltd is clearly very difficult. If they decide that they might rely upon the 'larger purpose' argument in s151(1)(a) CA 1985, the point may be raised as to whether they were acting 'in good faith in the interests of the company'. It does seem that in many respects, the 'company', if viewed as being really Blue plc, has an interest in making the loan. The directors, in going along with this, are incidentally observing their own best personal interests but provided that there is no conflict of these interests, the directors will not breach their fiduciary duties towards Sky Ltd. The vice for any director is to put himself in the position where his interests and the company's may conflict, as in *Industrial Development Consultants Ltd v Cooley* [1972] 2 All ER 162.

If the directors put their faith in s153(4)(a) CA 1985, the lending of money in the ordinary course of business, they will have to be able to explain to the court why the breach of rules does not take the matter outside the ordinary course of business. If it did so, they might be in the unenviable position of being in breach of the prohibition in s151 CA 1985 and also in breach of their fiduciary duty towards Sky Ltd itself for which they could be required to account. This would involve an investigation as to the extent of the directors' powers, as given by the memorandum and articles of association, to disregard lending rules.

The directors of Sky Ltd should be made aware that any company acting in contravention of s151 CA 1985 is liable to a fine and every officer of it is liable to imprisonment or fine or both: s151(3) CA 1985. The consequence of all this is that Sky Ltd's directors should begin to question themselves as to how closely they investigated the claim by the Blue plc board of directors to be speaking in the name of the members of Sky Ltd. If they failed to address this point, the matter may come back to given them difficulties in the future. One course of action that might help the directors is to show their bona fides in respect of s153(1) CA 1985 and to protect them from charges of breach of fiduciary duty towards Sky Ltd by calling an EGM of Sky Ltd and seeking ratification of their acts by ordinary resolution as in *Bamford v Bamford* [1970] Ch 212 or, if the breach of rules was an ultra vires act, by special resolution along with a separate special resolution relieving the directors from liability under s35(3) CA 1985 as substituted by s108 CA 1989.

QUESTION TWO

a) Success plc has an issued share capital of £1 million divided into 800,000 £1 ordinary shares and 200,000 £1 preference shares. The articles of association of the company provide that the holders of the preference shares 'shall be entitled to an annual dividend of 18 per cent in preference to the ordinary shareholders'. The articles further provide that 'the rights attached to any shares shall be deemed to be varied by the reduction of capital paid up on those shares'.

You are asked to advise the board of directors who feel that the company has too much capital and wish to pay off the preference shares at par in reduction of capital. The preference shares stand at £1.26 in the market.

b) York Ltd has an issued share capital of 12,000 £1 shares. Four brothers, Andrew, Bill, Colin and David are the directors of the company and each of them holds 3,000 shares. Andrew wishes to sell all his shares and is prepared to let his brothers buy 1,000 shares each. His brothers are anxious to purchase the shares since they want the ownership of the company to remain in the family. The Beano Bank plc is prepared to lend the necessary money to Bill, Colin and David, provided that the company guarantees the loans with a floating charge over its assets. However, the directors have now been told that the floating charge would infringe s151 of the Companies Act 1985.

Advise the directors.

University of London LLB Examination
(for External Students) Company Law June 1995 Q7

General Comment

The first part of the question requires a review of the case law on the relationship between reduction of capital, cancellation of capital and variation of class rights, as well as the statutory provisions covering permitted reductions. The second part needs detailed analysis of the giving of financial assistance by a company towards transactions in its own shares, the rationale behind the general prohibition and knowledge of the exempt situations.

Skeleton Solution

a) Class rights question – whether cancellation is 'reduction' – statutory requirements for reduction – special situation of preference shares.

b) Rationale of statutory rules concerning acquisition of own shares – 'larger purpose'; employees exception – private company relaxation; statutory requirements.

Suggested Solution

a) This part of the question raises points of company law which must be separately addressed.

The effect upon the class rights of the preference shareholders

The express provision in the articles that a reduction of capital is deemed to be a variation raises the question that has troubled the courts many times, whether a cancellation of the class amounts to a 'reduction' or 'variation'. In *Re Northern Engineering Industries plc* [1994] BCC 618 a very similar situation occurred and the Court of Appeal had little sympathy for the argument that a 'reduction' was different to or less than a cancellation of the class. The directors must look at the rest of the articles and consider carefully the requirements imposed there or under the Companies Act (CA) 1985 regarding class consents, or they may face a challenge on a class rights basis.

The statutory provision for reduction of capital in public companies

The directors will need to bear in mind the requirements of ss135 to 141 CA 1985 concerning the circumstances and processes required for a valid reduction of share capital. The directors will, of course, have to rely upon authority in the articles to reduce capital – Table A art 34 will suffice if no other article covers the matter. The director's purpose seems to be well within s135(2)(c) as a disposal of surplus and unnecessary capital as in *Prudential Assurance Co Ltd v Chatterley-Whitfield Collieries Ltd* [1949] AC 512. This case is also authority for the point that the directors may repay the shares at par rather than at £1.26 provided that there is nothing in the rights attached to the shares which would entitle the preference holders to share in a distribution of surplus assets of the company (*Re Saltdean Estate Co Ltd* [1968] 1 WLR 1844). The reduction will have to be done by special resolution (s135(1)), and is subject to confirmation by the court (s136)), which means that other creditors may be allowed to object (s136(3)). There really seems no problem in this and there is no danger of the capital being reduced below the authorised minimum level for a public company which would activate s139. The order and minute of reduction, and the court order in confirmation, must be delivered to the Registrar of Companies, and the resolution will only take effect upon registration and not before (s138(2)). This is, of course, a statutory exception to the general rule against company self purchase (s143(1)(b)).

b) This part of the question concerns the extent to which a company can take part in the acquisition of its own shares by way of providing financial assistance. Sections 151–158 CA 85 provide a regulatory mechanism to prevent abuses by the controller of a company which, effectively, allowed companies to provide the means of purchasing themselves as in *Re VGM Holdings Ltd* [1942] Ch 235 and *Belmont Finance Corporation Ltd v Williams Furniture Ltd* [1979] Ch 250. The assistance here is by way of the provision of a guarantee in the form of a floating charge. This is clearly within 'financial assistance given … by way of security' in s152(1)(a)(ii), so the directors must proceed with care. There is an important exception in s153(1) if the transaction is such that the company's primary purpose lies not in the acquisition by the brothers or assisting the acquisition but, instead, is an 'incidental part of some larger purpose of the company' (s153(1)(a)), and the assistance is given 'in good faith in the interests of the company' (s153(1)(b)). This question of 'larger purpose' was looked at by the House of Lords in *Brady* v *Brady* [1989] AC 755 and also in the case of *Plant* v *Steiner* (1988) 5 BCC 352, and it does seem that this 'larger purpose' must be distinguished from the motive or reason for the transaction. The maintenance of share control within a family is much more likely to be viewed as a motive as it is difficult to see what larger purpose is served as the company acquires no new benefit, service or asset. Even a freedom from deadlock is not viewed as such on the basis of *Brady* v *Brady*. It seems that this will not help the directors here.

It may be that the directors can take advantage of s153(4)(bb) which allows for exemption for share transactions between employees. If this could not be complied with because the directors were not employees within the section, there is a general relaxation of s151 for private companies under s155 and this might be applicable here. There would be no reduction of net assets as no payment is made here (s155(2)), special resolution of the general meeting is required (s155(4)), and the directors would have to make a statutory declaration of solvency (s156). The special resolution would need to be passed within a week at the latest of the making of the statutory declaration (s157(11)). There is also a timetable given by s158 so that the assistance cannot be given before four weeks have elapsed following the special resolution. No assistance can be given later than eight weeks after the statutory declaration unless the court orders otherwise (s158(4)). A copy of the special resolution, the statutory declaration and an auditor's report must be sent to the Registrar within 15 days of the special resolution (s156(5)), but failure to observe these formalities did not breach s151 or invalidate the resolution in *Re NL Electrical Ltd* [1994] 1 BCLC 22.

From all of the above it is clear that the directors must fall within the employee exception or must take great care to observe the private company requirements, otherwise they will breach s151. The consequence of this is that the company would face a fine and 'every officer of it who is in default' faces imprisonment or fine or both by s151(3).

QUESTION THREE

The share capital of Rose Ltd is composed of the following shares.

a) 10,000, 5 per cent £1 preference shares which are also preferential as to the return of capital.

b) 10,000, 7 per cent £2 preference shares.

c) 30,000, £2 ordinary shares.

All shares carry equal voting rights. The articles are silent as to the capital rights attached to the 7 per cent preference shares but are otherwise in the form of Table A.

Rose Ltd now proposes to make the following alterations in its capital structure.

a) To reduce its capital by paying off the 5 per cent £1 preference shares at par. It intends to borrow money from its Bank to finance this transaction.

b) To reduce the par value of the 7 per cent £2 preference shares and the ordinary shares by £1 because of the depreciation in the value of assets of Rose Ltd.

c) To sub-divide the ordinary shares into 25 pence shares, each share carrying one vote.

Some minority shareholders of the 5 per cent £1 preference shares and the 7 per cent £2 shares object to these proposals and now seek your advice as to what, if anything, they can do. They are also concerned about the procedures adopted by Rose Ltd to implement these proposals.

Advise the minority shareholders accordingly.

University of London LLB Examination
(for External Students) Company Law June 1999 Q7

General Comment

The principle of maintenance of capital is probably one of the most misunderstood areas of company law, as assets of a company are often below the amount of its issued capital. The requirement to maintain capital is an obligation not to return cash or assets to members and provides a minimum standard to protect creditors from members withdrawing their capital from a company. This is a general question on the reduction of capital and the variation of class rights. Students should consider the procedures to be adopted for both these transactions, and also the rights of the minority to challenge any proposals put forward. As it is a general question candidates should not find it a particularly complicated one to answer.

Skeleton Solution

General rule; reduction of capital illegal unless permitted by statute – ss135 to 141 Companies Act 1985 – *Trevor* v *Whitworth* – procedure for shareholders to determine, but court must approve the method used – variation of class rights – company procedures – minority shareholders' rights.

Suggested Solution

Reduction of capital is covered by ss135–141 Companies Act (CA) 1985. By *Trevor* v *Whitworth* (1877) 12 AC 409 the general rule is that a reduction of capital is illegal, unless it is permitted by the statute. Section 135 CA 1985 gives this permission for a company to reduce its capital, but there must be the authority in the articles of association to do this and the court must sanction the reduction. Although the section gives the members the power to reduce the capital in any way, s135(2) CA 1985 provides specific things that a company may do. It may extinguish or reduce liability on any of its shares in respect of unpaid share capital; it may cancel any paid up capital which is lost or not represented by the available assets; and it may pay off any paid-up share capital which is in excess of the wants of the company.

However, it is for the members to decide just how the reduction in capital should be carried out, and the court can confirm any method that the shareholders propose. However, the court will need to be satisfied that the interests of the existing creditors are protected by any proposals. Care should be taken that the company does not enter into illegal transactions whilst reducing its share capital.

The company will need to obtain a special resolution to reduce the capital and the court will need to be assured that the reasons for the reduction were clearly explained to the members before they voted.

The question does not explain why Rose Ltd is carrying out these alterations. If it is because the company has suffered a loss of capital then the preference shares should be the last group of shares to be reduced. Because these alterations also vary the class rights of some of the shareholders, this variation must be approved by a three quarter majority of the class.

Once the special resolution for the reduction of the capital has been passed, the company must send a petition to the court for the reduction to be confirmed. It is possible that the court may require the company to add 'and reduced' to its title, but this is now very uncommon. Once the court has confirmed the reduction, a copy of the order showing how the capital has altered must be lodged with the Registrar and the reduction of capital takes effect at the time the paperwork is registered.

The court will consider three factors before confirming the reduction. It needs to be satisfied that the reduction is fair and equitable between the different classes of shareholders in the company, even though there is no rule that a reduction of capital must affect different classes equally and that the proposal affects all shareholders of the same class in a similar way, unless those who are treated differently are fully aware of what is happening and have agreed to it, and finally that the reasons for the reduction were properly explained to the shareholders so that they were able to make an informed decision.

If Rose Ltd is returning capital in excess of the company's requirements then the preference shares which have priority on return of capital should be paid off first, whereas if the reduction is because Rose Ltd has suffered losses, it is the ordinary shares that should be paid off first. We are not told if the preference shareholders have rights of participation in surplus assets on a winding-up, which might give them a cause of action if their rights are not being strictly observed.

With regard to variation of class rights in connection with a reduction of capital, s125 CA 1985 requires the agreement of three quarters of the class affected. The court will not confirm a variation which they consider to be improper. Where the agreement of the class has been obtained, the class rights may be changed to a substantial degree. The Law Commission is considering reform for this procedure, which is complicated and expensive.

Where a variation in class rights has adversely affected a minority of shareholders, provided that minority equals 15 per cent of the issued shares of the class affected and they have not voted in favour of the variation, they may apply to the court to have the variation cancelled. Section 127 CA 1985 has a narrow scope and there is little case authority on its application. There are House of Lords' dicta in *Carruth* v *Imperial Chemical Industries Ltd* [1937] AC 707 and *Re Holder's Investment Trust Ltd* [1971] 1 WLR 583 which suggest that a minority shareholder in a particular class has a right to challenge a class resolution on the ground of lack of good faith.

QUESTION FOUR

In 1979 Excelsior plc made a net trading loss of £1,500,000 and in 1980 another loss of £1,000,000. In 1981, however, it made a profit of £1,000,000 and entered into negotiations to purchase a factory from Henry. The price was eventually agreed at £500,000 despite the fact that valuers appointed by Excelsior assessed the factory's value at £400,000. The directors of Excelsior decided to pay the price asked by Henry because they considered that the factory would considerably increase the company's profitability over the next few years. The purchase price was paid partly in cash (£200,000) and partly by the issue to Henry of 300,000 £1 shares, which issue was made concurrently with a rights issue made by the company to its existing shareholders of 1 share at par for each share held. James, one of the directors of Excelsior, who held 100,000 shares wanted to take up the rights issue, but was unable to raise the cash. He therefore negotiated with the company to defer payment in respect of his acceptance of the rights issue pending the declaration by the company of a dividend. At the end of 1982 the company in fact declared a dividend in respect of the entire profit made in 1981 and this enabled James to pay the company the amount owing in respect of the rights issue. In 1983, the company was compulsorily wound up.

Advise the liquidator.

University of London LLB Examination
(for External Students) Company Law June 1984 Q8

General Comment

This question is somewthing of a rarity – a problem question on the maintenance of capital.

Skeleton Solution

Purchase of factory – valuation rules – consequences of breach – duty to pay in cash.

Dividends – losses of previous years must be made good before dividend can be paid – this has not been done – liquidator can require repayment from any shareholder who was aware of this.

Financial assistance – disguised return of capital prohibited – there has probably been a breach here – liquidator should be advised to sue James.

Suggested Solution

Three issues arise in this problem: the provision of financial assistance for the purchase of a company's shares, the declaration of dividends and payment for shares.

The factory has been purchased from Henry in cash and through the issue of 300,000 £1 shares. Under s103 Companies Act (CA) 1985 a company is forbidden to allot shares as fully or partly paid-up for non-cash consideration unless the consideration has been valued by an independent expert within the past six months and a copy of the report has been served on the company and the proposed allottee. If this requirement is contravened the allottee is liable to the company for an amount equal to the nominal value of the shares plus any premium thereon (a subsequent holder of the shares will be similarly liable unless he is a bona fide purchaser for value without notice of the contravention of s103). The fact that the directors paid an extra £100,000 for the factory in the belief that it would be a profitable acquisition does not necessarily involve them in liability – this may have been a perfectly proper decision – but the expert's report must state the extent to which the par value of the shares and any premium are to be treated as paid up (a) by the consideration and (b) in cash (s108(4)).

The second problem concerns the declaration of dividends at the end of 1982. Before 1980 the only significant rule was that dividends must not be paid out of capital (*Flitcroft's Case* (1882) 21 Ch D 519), and this allowed the payment of a dividend where there was a surplus on revenue account for the current year even though losses of previous years had not been made good. An unrealised profit generated by a revaluation of fixed assets could also be used to fund a dividend or a bonus issue: *Dimbula Valley (Ceylon) Tea Co Ltd* v *Laurie* [1961] Ch 353. New rules were introduced in 1980 (see now CA 1985, Pt VIII). Dividends may be paid only out of profits available for the purpose, and the profits available for the purpose are accumulated realised profits less accumulated realised losses so far as not previously written off in a reduction or reorganisation of capital duly made. One very important consequence of this is that accounting periods are no longer treated in isolation – thus losses of previous years must be made good before any dividend can be paid. In the case of public companies such as this one there are further restrictions under s264. Plcs may not make distributions if the result would be to reduce the net assets below the sum of the called-up capital and the undistributable reserves (share premium account, capital redemption reserve).

In the present case it is clear that previous losses have not been made good, so that the distribution is unlawful. Under s277 a member who receives a wrongful distribution with actual or constructive knowledge that it is unlawful is liable to repay it to the company. Thus the liquidator could sue for repayment of the dividend.

The third point is the provision of financial assistance to James in respect of the rights issue. It should be observed that the financial assistance here consists not of declaring a dividend but of agreeing to defer the payment for shares. The rules in this area were relaxed somewhat by the 1981 Act (see now CA 1985, ss151–157) but there are still restrictions on what is effectively a disguised return of capital. The general rule is still that it is unlawful for a company or any of its subsidiaries to give assistance for the purchase of that company's shares. There are exceptions (if the assistance was not given for the purpose of assisting in the purchase or if it was merely incidental to some broader purpose), but these exceptions, which are couched in regrettably vague and subjective terms, do not appear to apply here. Other exceptions allow the giving of assistance where the directors have made a statutory declaration as to the company's solvency and the transaction has been approved by the General Meeting, but these also are not relevant here.

Breach of s151 is a criminal offence, but there will also be civil liability on James (*Steen v Law* [1964] AC 287), and the liquidator should therefore be advised that it may be worthwhile bringing an action against James.

QUESTION FIVE

To what extent, if at all, is the law on financial assistance [contained in ss151–158 of the Companies Act 1985] still destructive of genuine commercial transactions? Is there any rational policy running through the legislation or case law? How could the law in this area be improved?

University of London LLB Examination
(for External Students) Company Law June 1994 Q2

General Comment

This is a demanding question in that it requires a critical analysis of the provisions dealing with the prohibition against a company giving financial assistance for the acquisition of its shares. It also requires a fairly detailed knowledge and understanding of the case law, especially the complex case of *Brady* v *Brady* [1989] AC 755. Consideration also needs to be given to recent proposals for reform. Students generally find this a difficult area, as indeed it is, and the question should only be attempted if you fully understand the topic and have read around it.

Skeleton Solution

Capital maintenance doctrine – prohibition against financial assistance – examples of financial assistance with reference to case law – the destruction of genuine commercial transactions – *Brady* v *Brady* – reform proposals – consideration of DTI's suggested two-tier structure – company law reform has now proposed simplification of the rules relating to capital maintenance for all private companies.

Suggested Solution

Under the capital maintenance doctrine, a company's share capital must be kept intact for the benefit of the creditors. While it cannot be guaranteed that the fund will be intact when the creditors come to rely on it, case law has established that the share capital cannot be paid out of the company except in the legitimate course of its business or under a recognised procedure in the legislation: *Trevor* v *Whitworth* (1887) 12 App Cas 409.

One way in which the capital of a company may be reduced is where the company gives financial assistance to another person for the purchase of its shares. Section 151 of the Companies Act (CA) 1985 lays down a general prohibition against this and it implements Article 23 of the Second Company Law Directive which contains a similar prohibition, but only in relation to public companies.

Financial assistance is prohibited if given before, at the same time as, or after the acquisition of a company's shares and covers gifts, guarantees, securities, indemnities, loans etc: s151(2) CA 1985. The courts will not try to strain the meaning of the term 'financial assistance' in order to bring an arrangement within the meaning of the section. Instead, they will look at the commercial realities of the case: *Charterhouse Investment Trust Ltd* v *Tempest Diesels Ltd* [1986] BCLC 1.

A number of exceptions to the prohibition are contained in s153 CA 1985, and there is a total relaxation of the prohibition for private companies, provided they comply with the procedure laid down in ss155–158 CA 1985.

The original prohibition was contained in s45 CA 1929. This became s54 CA 1948 which was reworded in CA 1981 due to problems of interpretation. The current provisions are now contained in ss151–158 CA 1985. The policy running through the legislation has always been to stop abuses by the giving of financial assistance but, at the same time, trying to ensure that genuine commercial transactions are not caught. So, if company A lends money to company B so that B can purchase shares in A, this will clearly be in breach of s151 CA: *Steen* v *Law* [1964] AC 287.

The original provisions were enacted to stop a common abuse, whereby a takeover bidder would borrow money from a bank and then repay the bank out of the company's funds after the takeover was complete: *Selangor United Rubber Estates* v *Cradock (No 3)* [1968] 1 WLR 1555.

While the previous and current legislation on financial assistance may be said to have a rational policy, it appears that the courts have struggled to interpret and apply it in such a way as to allow genuine commercial transactions. A good example, although decided under the old provisions, is *Belmont Finance Corporation Ltd* v *Williams Furniture Ltd (No 2)* [1980] 1 All ER 393. Here, company A purchased an asset from company B. Company B then purchased shares in company A. Had company A provided financial assistance? The Court of Appeal held that it was an artificial transaction designed to put company B in funds so that it could purchase A's shares. The directors of A had to account for the assistance, amounting to £500,000, as constructive trustees. The directors of company A argued, unsuccessfully, that the asset was purchased at a fair price and that it was a genuine commercial transaction in the company's interests.

In *Belmont*, Buckley LJ left open the position where a company puts a third party in funds, partly to allow it to purchase its shares, and partly as a result of a bona fide commercial transaction.

The uncertainty which the *Belmont* decision caused led to the introduction of rules allowing private companies to give financial assistance within ss155–158 CA 1985 and also to allow financial assistance, under s153(1) and (2) CA 1985, for the acquisition of shares where:

> 'a) ... the company's principal purpose in giving that assistance is not to give it for the purpose of any such acquisition, or the giving of the assistance for that purpose is but an incidental part of some larger purpose of the company, and
> b) the assistance is given in good faith in the interests of the company.'

This 'principal purpose' exemption was considered by the House of Lords in *Brady* v *Brady* [1989] AC 755. The facts are extremely complex, but in outline the business of Brady was that of a soft drinks' manufacturer and road haulier. It was run by two brothers, Bob and Jack. The company began to make losses as a result of the breakdown in the relationship between Bob and Jack. A plan was devised whereby the business would be split up, with Jack taking the haulage side, and Bob the drinks side of the business. To off set the difference in value between the two sides of the business, it was agreed that Jack's new company, M Ltd, would receive assets from Brady Ltd to help pay for the shares in Brady Ltd.

It was accepted that this amounted to financial assistance by Brady Ltd and this was relied on by Bob when he was sued by Jack, who wanted specific performance of their agreement. Jack claimed the transaction fell within the larger purpose exemption in s153 CA 1985.

The House of Lords held that the transaction did not fall within s153, but granted specific performance on the ground that it fell within the private company exemption in ss155–158.

Despite finding that the scheme was in good faith and in the interests of the company, Lord Oliver was unable to find some larger purpose to which the financial assistance was merely incidental. He said that it was necessary to distinguish between the purpose and the reason for giving the assistance. In this case the only purpose of the assistance was to enable Jack to acquire the shares in Brady. The reason was to promote the re-organisation of the family business so that it could be split between Jack and Bob and allow them to go their separate ways. Their Lordships felt that the advantages which the scheme produced were mere 'by-products'.

Lord Oliver justified this approach by saying that any other result would deprive s151 of 'any useful application'. However, most commentators agree that this is a very narrow interpretation of the wording in s153, as it failed to take into account the wider commercial considerations of the scheme. It is now very difficult to think of a clear example of when the larger purpose exemption would apply and its scope is very uncertain.

The result of *Brady* v *Brady* [1989] AC 755 is that genuine commercial transactions will probably continue to be caught by the financial assistance provisions.

It is suggested that the law in this area could be improved along the following lines.

a) The 'larger purpose' exemption could be amended so that financial assistance would not be prohibited where the 'predominant reason' for the transaction is for the benefit of the company. If this test is adopted then the problems in *Brady* would be overcome.

b) It is difficult to understand why the penalties contained in s151(3) make the company itself liable to a fine, for this will reduce a company's capital still further. Consideration should be given to repealing this sanction.

c) The procedure allowing private companies to give financial assistance could be simplified. For example, the requirement to pass a special resolution could be replaced by the requirement simply to pass an ordinary resolution.

d) It is arguable that financial assistance which does not materially reduce the net assets of the company should be allowed by way of a 'de minimis' exemption. This would help clear up a doubt about whether or not a company has provided financial assistance when it pays the expenses and costs incurred by a person who has subscribed for its shares.

e) Some commentators have suggested the complete abolition of the financial assistance rules in relation to private companies. They have done so arguing that companies can guarantee another's debt without any formality, but that if the guarantee relates to the acquisition of its shares, then it has to comply with the procedure in ss155–158. They argue that it is arbitrary to have no formalities for the first type of guarantee, while imposing a strict procedure on the second type. Complete abolition is, however, only a remote possibility.

The DTI in its consultative document 'Company Law Review: Proposals for Reform of ss151–158 of the Companies Act (October 1993)' suggested three types of possible reform. However, despite the DTI's consultation document and the call for reform by practitioners and by such bodies as the Law Society, the reforms have not yet happened and the uncertainty surrounding the provisions as evidenced by the decision in *Brady* still continues.

However, the Steering Group on Company Law Reform has recognised that the capital maintenance regime is stifling the development of many companies. They have proposed a repeal of the rules relating to the provision of financial assistance in connection with share acquisitions for all private companies.

Finally, mention should be made of *Arab Bank plc* v *Mercantile Holdings Ltd and Another* [1993] BCC 816. In this case, Millet J has cleared up an uncertainty in the law by holding that s151 does not apply if financial assistance is given by a foreign subsidiary of an English parent company, for the purpose of purchasing the parent company's shares. Presumably, any reform will not now have to consider the question of whether or not a foreign subsidiary is within the financial assistance provisions.

Chapter 6
Shares

6.1 Introduction

The subject of shares is a large one, which is in many ways fundamental to the structure and theory of company law; as appears below, some matters related to it are in this book dealt with in other chapters. Students therefore need to be aware that it is not sufficient to be familiar with the material in this chapter, for questions commonly overlap with Chapter 5: *Capital* and Chapter 8: *Meetings*, as well as occasionally with Chapter 9: *Directors* and Chapter 11: *Minorities*.

6.2 Key points

Issuing shares

Every company must have an authorised capital, and shares may not be issued beyond the limits of that capital. A public company must have the minimum authorised capital prescribed by s118(1) Companies Act (CA) 1985.

No shares may be allotted unless the directors have been authorised to allot (s80 CA 1985). Such authority may be given in the articles or may be conferred by an ordinary resolution of the general meeting. In the latter event it may be valid for a period not exceeding five years. A private company may only take advantage of the elective resolution procedure under s379A CA 1985. This substitutes the provisions of s80A for those of subss 80(4) and (5), and authority may be given for any fixed period or indefinitely, although it is revocable at any time. On an elective resolution ceasing to have effect, the authority takes effect as if for a fixed period of five years or, if it has already run for five years, it ceases immediately.

It is a criminal offence to make an allotment without s80 authority, but this does not affect the validity of the allotment.

Section 89 CA 1985 provides that in private companies shares issued for cash must initially be offered to existing members in proportion to their shareholdings. A shareholder who suffers loss as a result of a breach of this rule can claim compensation from the company (s95 CA 1985) but the violation does not appear to affect the validity of the allotment.

In all cases the power to issue shares must be exercised bona fide in the best interests of the company. Thus it is not proper to issue shares solely in order to defeat a motion for the removal of a director, nor to defeat an attempted takeover. Where it appears that an issue of shares has been made for an improper purpose, the issue can still be ratified by the general meeting (GM). In such cases the court will order the matter to be referred to the GM for a decision, on the basis that the shares whose issue is disputed may not be voted at that GM.

In addition to the above, the issue of shares for an improper purpose may in some cases be evidence of a course of conduct unfairly oppressive to the minority, so as to bring s459 CA 1985 into consideration. As to this section see Chapter 11: *Minorities*.

Class rights

Where there are different classes of shares further special problems arise. A modification of the rights attaching to that class of shares normally requires the consent of the holders of the shares of that class at a special meeting as well as a resolution of the GM of the company.

Such resolutions are in any event open to challenge as not having been made in good faith. It is not wholly clear what test is to be applied, but the better view seems to be that the resolution must be for the benefit of holders of that class of shares as a whole. This can cause difficulties where some (but not all) holders of eg preference shares are also holders of ordinary shares, and it is desired to reduce the privileges attaching to the preference shares, thereby benefitting holders of ordinary shares). There have been judicial suggestions that it must be for the benefit of all members of that class including the objectors, but it is thought that this would give too much veto power to a small minority (see, eg, *Re Holders Investment Trust* [1971] 1 WLR 583).

Rules as to payment for shares

Shares may not be issued at a discount (s100 CA 1985) but may be issued at a premium subject to s130. A non-cash consideration may be accepted although, in the case of public companies, subject to special rules concerning acceptance of undertakings and valuation of non-cash consideration. Furthermore, a public company cannot commence business unless it has allotted shares to a nominal value not less than the authorised minimum (see above) and those shares are paid up as to at least one-quarter and the whole of any premium. Public companies which do not satisfy these requirements may have to re-register as private.

Voting rights

This topic is dealt with in Chapter 8: *Meetings*.

Transfer of shares

It is common in small private companies for the articles of association to contain restrictions on the freedom to transfer shares. These are considered desirable because of the need to control who becomes a member.

The provisions come in a number of common forms. One form gives the directors an absolute discretion to refuse to register any transfer of shares. A modified version of this removes the discretion where the transfer is to a member of the transferor's family. Another version allows the directors rights of pre-emption on any shares which are to be offered for sale.

Such restrictions are in principle valid, but the power given to the directors must in all cases be exercised bona fide in the best interests of the company.

Maintenance of capital

Important topics which overlap with those discussed in this chapter include the rules as to payment for shares, reductions in capital, purchase by a company of, or giving financial assistance for the purchase of, its own shares, and dividend rules, are all dealt with in Chapter 5: *Capital*.

6.3 Key cases and statute

* *Birch* v *Cropper* (1889) 14 App Cas 525
  Class rights – in absence of express provision, all shares are presumed to be equal

* *Holder's Investment Trust Ltd, Re* [1971] 1 WLR 583
  Concerns over power of veto in hands of small minority

* *Smith and Fawcett Ltd, Re* [1942] Ch 304
  Discretion to refuse to register transfer of shares may be absolute and uncontrolled so long as it is exercised bona fide in the company's best interests

* *Tett* v *Phoenix Property and Investment Co Ltd* [1986] BCLC 149
  Deals with procedure for refusing registration

* *Thundercrest Ltd, Re* [1994] BCC 857
  A company was not entitled to allot shares in a rights issue to another when they knew the original allottee wanted the shares but had not received the offer letter

* *White* v *Bristol Aeroplane Co* [1953] Ch 65
  The issues of new shares does not affect the class rights of preference shareholders

- Companies Act 1985

  - s80 – no shares may be allotted by the directors without authorisation

  - s89 – pre-emption rights in private companies

  - s95 – right to compensation by shareholder

  - s100 – shares may not be issued at a discount

  - s118(1) – plc must have minimum amount of authorised share capital

  - s130 – shares may be offered at a premium

  - s379A – elective resolution procedure for private companies

  - s459 – conduct which is unfairly oppressive to the minority

6.4 Questions and suggested solutions

QUESTION ONE

Berle and Means had an optimistic view of the significance of the separation of ownership and control in the company structure. They were of the view that corporate managers would be public-spirited and would manage the company as statesmen, orchestrating the firm to meet public needs.

What are the consequences of the separation and control of the company for the shareholders and for the directors of the company? How is director behaviour regulated and do these systems for the regulation of director behaviour achieve the ideal envisaged by Berle and Means?

University of London LLB Examination
(for External Students) Company Law June 1999 Q1

General Comment

The tension that exists in a company between the shareholders and the directors is a fertile area for discussion. Historically the boundaries have moved considerably and the European influence on the shifting of these boundaries is worth considering. Of greater importance internally is the combined code of best practice which guides directors of listed companies. However, the code also provides useful general guidance to directors of all companies. This general idea of separation of ownership and control is not without its critics and there are those who believe that directors should be subject to shareholders' control. The courts generally accept the principle of separation of powers, but debate still continues with the academics.

Skeleton Solution

The shareholders, although they own the company, generally do not manage it –

management of the company takes place through the directors who are required to act bona fide on behalf of the company in what they consider to be the best interests of the company – directors' duties; specific statutory duties imposed by law; the memorandum and articles of association; combined code on corporate governance – do these controls meet the views of Berle and Means?

Suggested Solution

The principle of separation and control refers mostly to public companies where the shareholders are not the same people as the directors. In the majority of private companies, where shareholders and directors are the same people, this principle does not apply.

The directors derive their authority to manage the company from the articles of association, Table A, art 70 which states:

> 'Subject to the provisions of the Companies Act 1985 as amended, the memorandum and the articles and to any directions given by special resolution, the business of the company shall be managed by the directors who may exercise all the powers of the company.'

The shareholders cannot tell the directors how to exercise that power. In *Howard Smith Ltd* v *Ampol Petroleum Ltd* [1974] AC 821 the directors of the defendant company resolved to issue shares to raise capital and to reduce the holding of the defendant company to a minority to enable the plaintiff company's takeover bid to succeed. It was held that the shares had been allotted for an improper purpose. This is the principle of separation and control referred to in the question. This general power of management is subject to anything else that is contained in the articles, so in *Quinn & Axtens* v *Salmon* [1909] 1 Ch 311 the articles of *Quinn & Axtens* provided that the business of the company was to be managed by the directors subject to such regulations as may be prescribed by the company in a general meeting. One of the articles provided that no resolution of the directors on certain important matters would be valid if either of the managing directors voted against the resolution. One director voted against a resolution and the company tried to ratify the resolution by a simple majority. The House of Lords gave effect to the articles even though this had the effect of enforcing rights given to a member in his capacity as a director. Lord Wedderburn argues that this supports his view that every member has a personal right under s14 Companies Act (CA) 1985 to see that the company is run according to the articles, as the articles constitute a contract between the company and it members.

Directors' fiduciary duty

The directors exercise of authority is granted to them as fiduciaries, and as they are employed by the company they must act bona fide for the best interests of the company. That is they must act in honesty and good faith. They must exercise their powers for the purpose for which they were given, but it is for the directors to decide what they consider to be bona fide, not what a court would consider to be bona fide, so the exercise of these powers is subjective. In *Re Smith and Fawcett Ltd* [1942] Ch 304 it was held that a discretion to refuse to register transfers of shares may be absolute and uncontrolled as long as it is exercised bona fide in the company's interests.

The issue of what constitutes the interests of the company needs to be examined. There has been a move towards adopting a stakeholder approach to the running of a company which includes the interests of shareholders, employees , customers and creditors as interests of the company. This is a practical management approach, but the legal approach is to consider the company as the economic entity which comprises the present and future shareholders. However, by s309 CA 1985 the directors must have regard to the interests of employees as well, and in an insolvency situation, regard must be paid to the interests of the creditors.

Protection of shareholders

The protection given to the shareholders is that they can dismiss a director by virtue of s303 CA 1985, by an ordinary resolution on special notice of 28 days.

Table A of the Companies Regulations 1985 recognizes that shareholders could require the directors to alter the articles of association by special resolution, but this does not seem popular with the judiciary. However, most of the cases on this point are commonwealth cases and are therefore only of persuasive authority.

If the directors act outside the provisions of the Companies Act 1985 then it is only the shareholders that can ratify their unauthorised acts. Ratification must be by way of special resolution passed in a general meeting and this can only happen if the act was outside the company's objects. If the act was illegal there will be no possibility to ratify.

If the directors will not or are unable to exercise their powers of management, by reason of situations such as deadlock or demise of the whole board, those powers of management will revert to the shareholders who can then exercise them: *Barron* v *Potter* [1914] 1 Ch 895; *Alexander Ward & Co Ltd* v *Samyang Navigation Co Ltd* [1975] 1 WLR 673.

Liability for negligence – the duty of care and skill

The statement of a director's duty of care is to be found in *Re City Equitable Fire Insurance Co Ltd* [1925] Ch 407 which states:

> 'A director need not exhibit in the performance of his duties a greater degree of skill than may reasonably be expected from a person of his knowledge and experience.'

The most important aspect of this duty is that directors are not required to have any specific qualifications, but will be judged on the knowledge and experience they actually have: *Re Brazilian Rubber Plantations and Estates Ltd* [1911] 1 Ch 425. However, in the case of *Norman* v *Theodore Goddard* [1992] BCC 14 Hoffman J, as he then was, introduced an element of subjectivity into the test of the standard of care by looking at s214 Insolvency Act 1986. This test states that the degree of care is that which would be taken by a reasonably diligent person having both (a) the general knowledge, skill and experience that may reasonably be expected of a person carrying out the same functions as are carried out by that director in relation to the company, and (b) the general knowledge, skill and experience that that director has. This test has now become both subjective as at (b) and objective as at (a) but its use may be open to question as it is a test for wrongful trading that has been incorporated as a wider test for directors' care and skill. Lord Hoffman followed this decision in *Re D'Jan of London* [1994] 1 BCLC 561.

The Law commission is looking at the duty of care and skill and has asked whether a statutory statement on the duty of care might be more consumer friendly than the present state of the law. Their draft legislation favours the subjective/objective approach as used by Lord Hoffman in the two cases mentioned.

Corporate governance

This area is concerned with how the company is directed and the relationship between the board of directors, management and shareholders and has been developed by the Cadbury Committee, the Greenbury Committee, the Hampel Committee and the Turnbull Committee. The Combined Code was produced by the Hampel Committee in 1998 and it focuses on several issues including the relations between the board and shareholders. The aim of the combines code is to allow companies to create and establish their own governance policies in a flexible manner. The codes are not legally binding, but are part of a self regulatory system that operates for listed companies through the Stock Exchange.

Conclusion

Although there are controls that exist as discussed above, they do not go as far as Berle and Mean's ideal situation.

QUESTION TWO

Violet, Red and Blue are shareholders/directors of Rainbow Ltd, each holding 250 of the issued £1 ordinary shares in the company. Green, who is not a director and has a rival business, holds the other 250 shares, and there is a further £1,000 of nominal capital unissued. The articles of Rainbow Ltd contain a provision that any member wishing to transfer his shares must first offer them to the other members.

Violet and Red are approached by Black, who offers them a very good price for their shares in Rainbow Ltd. Without telling Blue or Green about this, at a directors' meeting Violet and Red propose issuing all the unissued capital to the directors, telling Blue it would be useful to have more shares in case they ever had to fight off a takeover bid. Blue objects that they do not have the authority to issue the shares and, after a heated argument leaves the meeting. Violet and Red then go ahead with issuing the remaining capital to themselves. They then propose calling a general meeting to pass a resolution removing the pre-emption clause from the company's articles.

Before the meeting can be held, Blue dies, leaving his shares to Green. Although his executor executes a share transfer in favour of Green, Violet and Red refuse to register it, saying that, because of the pre-emption clause, Blue's shares now belong to them. They then decide that since they now hold all but 12.5 per cent of the issued share capital, they can change the articles without holding a meeting and so they write to Green saying that as they have inserted a clause in the articles which says that competitors are not allowed to be members of the company, he must transfer his shares to them. They then execute a contract to sell all the issued shares in the company, including Green's and Blue's to Black.

Advise Green

Written by the Editor

General Comment

This is a complex question which centres on directors' powers in connection with the issue and transfer of shares, although other topics are touched on. The first thing to do in any question of this nature is to work out in what proportions the shares are held and how the proposed changes affect these proportions. Only then is it possible to evaluate whether resolutions effecting the changes will be valid.

Skeleton Solution

No duty to disclose self-interest – authority to allot: s80 – proper purpose rule – transmission of shares on death – director's power to refuse to register – reasons – alteration to articles – special resolution – whether meeting can be dispensed with – remedies open to minority shareholder.

Suggested Solution

It is usual and acceptable for articles of small private companies to contain a pre-emption clause of the type in this question, since it is reasonable in a small company for the members to wish to restrict membership. There seems no reason why Violet and Red should feel obliged to tell the other shareholders about the approach from Black, even though they are also directors, since they owe no duty to them as individuals (*Percival* v *Wright* [1902] 2 Ch 421). Directors must be given specific authority by the general meeting, or by the articles, to allot shares (s80 Companies Act (CA) 1985). From Blue's reaction, it does not seem that the directors have the appropriate authority. Even if they did have the authority, Blue would be right to be concerned about the purpose of the issue since the 'proper purpose rule' states that directors may only use their powers for the purpose for which they are granted. The true reason – to make a profit for the directors – would certainly be an improper purpose, and even their given reason was considered to be an improper purpose in *Hogg* v *Cramphorn* [1967] Ch 254.

Furthermore, s89 CA 1985 provides that companies proposing to allot shares must first offer them on the same or more favourable terms to existing members. Private companies may exclude these statutory pre-emption rights by a provision in the articles disapplying the relevant sections, but Table A does not provide such a disapplication. Unless the articles of Rainbow specifically disapply s89, it may be that these rights apply and Green and Blue are entitled to part of the newly allotted shareholding in proportion to their existing holdings.

Contravention of s80 does not affect the validity of any allotment made, but any director who 'knowingly and wilfully' permits it is liable to a fine (s80(9)). Under the proper purpose rule, the directors concerned would be in breach of their fiduciary duties and the allotment would be invalid unless ratified by the general meeting (*Bamford* v *Bamford* [1970] Ch 212). The new shares would not be counted in the votes at the general meeting and, since Violet and Red validly hold only 50 per cent of the issued capital, they could be outvoted by the combined efforts of Blue and Green. It would then be a matter of whether one of them was chairman with a casting vote which would either sanction or invalidate the allotment. Contravention of s89 gives rise to a joint and several liability on the company and every officer who knowingly authorised or permitted the contravention to compensate any person to whom an offer should have been made.

Assuming, however, that the allotment was valid, the additional shares give Violet and Red 75 per cent of the voting power at a general meeting which would be sufficient for them to pass a resolution removing the pre-emption clause from the articles. Section 9 CA 1985 provides that the articles may always be altered by special resolution (a 75 per cent majority at a general meeting of which 21 days' notice has been given). The only objection that a dissenting minority shareholder can raise is that the alteration is not in the interests of the company as a whole. However, case law suggests that the court will not interfere unless fraud can be proved (*Shuttleworth* v *Cox Bros & Co (Maidenhead) Ltd* [1927] 2 KB 9). Possibly the court may consider it sufficiently 'fraudulent' if the majority has not considered the effect on the minority (under the extended definition of 'fraud' to be found in *Estmanco (Kilner House) Ltd* v *Greater London Council* [1982] 1 All ER 437 and *Clemens* v *Clemens* [1976] 2 All ER 268.

The directors' right to refuse to register a transfer depends on the articles. A right of refusal is often contained in the articles of small private companies for the same reason as they contain pre-emption rights. If the articles do not require the directors to give their reasons, they do not have to do so (*Re Smith and Fawcett Ltd* [1942] Ch 304), but if the directors do give their reasons, the court is allowed to examine them and decide whether they are in fact reasonable. A refusal by Red and Violet to register on the ground that Blue's shares belong to them is, it is submitted, unreasonable. They cannot simply appropriate Blue's shares since even when there is transmission on death, a proper instrument of transfer is required (*Re Greene* [1949] Ch 333) and the proper procedures for pre-emption must be followed, ie offering the shares to all the members.

Green is doing nothing wrong by being involved in a rival company as a shareholder owes no duties to a company in this regard. Even a director may be involved in a competing business (*Bell* v *Lever Brothers* [1933] AC 161). However, alterations to the articles which have the effect of expelling a member who is competing have been permitted by the court in the past (*Dafen Tinplate Co* v *Llanelly Steel Co* [1920] 2 Ch 124). Nevertheless, even if Violet and Red do validly hold 87.5 per cent of the voting capital, as they claim, there is still a need formally to pass a special resolution at a properly convened general meeting. A written resolution is only valid if all the members entitled to attend and vote at the general meeting consent to it.

Green is luckier than his predecessors in earlier decades since s459 CA 1985 provides a remedy in respect of conduct unfairly prejudicial to members of a company. This is considerably wider and more satisfactory than the remedy provided by the 'fraud on the minority' exception to the rule in *Foss* v *Harbottle* (1843) 2 Hare 461 on which he would formerly have had to rely. Provided that he can show a case for unfairly prejudicial conduct, the court is able to afford him almost unlimited remedies and, in this particular case, orders for rectification of the register to perfect the transfer to him of Blue's shares, for compensation for loss of s89 pre-emption righs (if applicable) and for the purchase of his shares at a fair price, would be the remedies he should seek.

QUESTION THREE

The share capital of Valhalla Limited ('the company') consists of 60,000 £1 shares which are held as to 15,000 by Alan, 12,500 each by Barry, Colin and Donald (all four of whom are directors) and 7,500 spread among five different investors who take no interest in the affairs of the company but who may be relied upon to vote as instructed by Barry. Originally the company was carried on by Barry, Colin and Donald, but when they arranged for the company to buy Alan's business, this was paid for by the issue to Alan of 15,000 shares. On this occasion as part of the agreement under which Alan's business was purchased, the articles of association of the company were altered so as to include the following clause:

'No resolution by the board of directors of the company, or by the company itself, which concerns the acquisition or disposition of property for a price in excess of £100,000, shall be valid unless agreed to by any shareholder holding more than 20 per cent of the issued share capital of the company.'

Barry, Colin and Donald are now anxious to expand the property development operations of the company and recently proposed the purchase of a corner site for £1m for redevelopment. Alan voted against this proposal. Barry, Colin and Donald are concerned that Alan will veto the proposed expansion of the company's business and have been searching for ways in which Alan's entrenched veto might be eliminated.

Advise them.

University of London LLB Examination
(for External Students) Company Law June 1992 Q8

General Comment

A question involving the position of minority shareholders is always a strong candidate for inclusion in the paper. Whether the question is set in the guise of to what extent the majority can lawfully make life uncomfortable for the minority, or advising the minority how fair the position is, the basic legal material requiring discussion is still the same.

Skeleton Solution

Division of share capital – votes and resolutions – clause in articles – alterability of articles – restraints on alterability – terms of contract for sale of business – possible claim for breach of contract – class rights – variation of class rights.

Suggested Solution

Alan holds one quarter of the issued shares, the other directors between them hold over 60 per cent, and the remaining shareholders will vote as instructed by Barry. Hence (assuming each share holds only one vote as appears to be the case) the other directors will not only be able to carry a resolution voted on by a show of hands at a general meeting but can also do so on a poll (where there is one vote per share held), which Alan as holder of one tenth of the voting rights would, under the Companies Act (CA) 1985, s373, be able to demand. An ordinary resolution will suffice (subject to the power of veto) to authorise the purchase.

A resolution to acquire the site could instead be passed at a meeting of the board of directors, where Alan is a minority. Despite the resolutions Alan would (as a holder of more than 20 per cent of the shares) exercise his veto under the articles; the veto is effective despite a resolution passed in general meeting approving the acquisition: *Quinn & Axtens* v *Salmon* [1909] 1 Ch 311.

The other directors may seek to alter the articles and delete the veto by special resolution in general meeting under s9. They (plus the small shareholders who would support them) command the 75 per cent of the votes which is the minimum necessary for its passing (see s378). At least 21 days' notice specifying the intention to propose the resolution as a special resolution must first have been given to the members. Neither waiver of notice nor written resolution procedure are plausible here.

There are, however, certain constraints upon a company's ability to alter its articles. The most relevant is that the alteration must not constitute a fraud on the minority and must be bona fide intended to benefit the company as a whole. Otherwise the fact that the alteration is productive of hardship to the minority appears to be unimportant: *Allen* v *Gold Reefs of West Africa* [1900] 1 Ch 656. 'Intended to benefit the company as a whole' seems here to relate to the intended benefit of the shareholders as a collective body: *Greenhalgh* v *Arderne Cinemas Ltd* [1951] Ch 286. There appears to be no evidence of malice towards Alan, the majority do not appear to be acting other than in the general interest, and their view is not obviously unreasonable. The resolution should therefore be valid.

We are not, however, informed of the precise terms of the contract for sale of Alan's business; did the contract itself provide that Alan, as any shareholder with at least 20 per cent of the shares, should have the right of veto? If so, mere alteration of the articles would not of itself be effective to eliminate a right contained in a contract itself quite separate from the articles. In *Baily* v *British Equitable Assurance Co* [1904] 1 Ch 374 the Court of Appeal stated that it would be dangerous to hold that a company had any greater power to breach contracts than a private individual would have. But it is not clear what remedies can successfully be invoked to protect the contract right. In *British Murac Syndicate* v *Alperton Rubber Co* [1915] 2 Ch 186 the court granted an injunction to restrain the company from altering its articles to insert provisions inconsistent with the separate contract, while in *Punt* v *Symons and Co* [1903] 2 Ch 506 it was suggested that it might be appropriate to enjoin the company from breaking the separate contract rather than from altering its articles. Or the remedy might be damages only, a position seemingly supported by a dictum of Lord Porter in *Southern Foundries Ltd* v *Shirlaw* [1940] AC 701. However, any agreement by a company to fetter its right to alter its articles is void (*Russell* v *Northern Bank Development Corporation Ltd* [1992] 1 WLR 588).

It could further be argued that the rights of each holder of 20 per cent or more of the shares are, under the present articles, different from each shareholder with less than that quantity, and thus constitute a separate class of shares. In *Cumbrian Newspapers Group Ltd* v *Cumberland and Westmorland Herald Newspaper and Printing Co Ltd* [1986] 3 WLR 26 it was held that rights conferred on a shareholder as such by the company's constitution are class rights even though not attached to any particular class of shares. This, if correct, would appear to be the case here. If so, it is suggested that it is far from clear that the variation of class rights provisions in s125 would apply, since these refer to variations where the rights attach to a class of shares. But if s125 did apply, a holder of at least 15 per cent of the shares could apply to the court within 21 days to disallow a variation, on the basis that the variation would be unfairly prejudicial; such a plea would, however, be very likely to fail on the merits.

QUESTION FOUR

'Although the class rights concept has important consequences in many different areas of company law the reality is that it is more likely to lead to confusion and to obstruct desirable change than to provide any real measure of protection for shareholders or creditors.'

Discuss.

University of London LLB Examination
(for External Students) Company Law June 1995 Q2

General Comment

The question involves consideration of the difficulties surrounding the source and nature of class rights, both for the member and for the courts. These problems must be set against whatever perceived protection can arise for members and creditors, followed by a conclusion as to whether the protection is real or illusory.

Skeleton Solution

Outline problem of ascertaining nature and source of rights – indicate possible sources of the rights – methods and difficulties of altering class rights according to source – class consents for certain types of alteration – changes that do or do not amount to variation of rights – protection of creditors – conclusion.

Suggested Solution

The class rights concept does, indeed, provide some safeguards for both members and creditors but it does seem that some of the protection is more illusory than real. This is illustrated by considering the position of members and creditors separately.

The position of shareholders

The essence of the class rights concept is that a member holding shares of a particular class is entitled to the rights and priorities (or lack of them) that attach to his shares, and to be treated by the company and its controllers in strict accordance with those rights. That is the basis upon which he acquired those shares and the degree of protection given to the member is dictated by his ability to prevent changes to the rights against his wishes. The problem that most commonly presents itself for the member is to ascertain, with certainty, just what his rights are, from where they arise and who or what may change them. This is a major problem because the rights might derive from one or any combination of the company's memorandum, the articles, the shareholders in general meeting, the board of directors or even from statements made in listing particulars for new share issues. When one adds to this problem of source the fact that the method required to alter the rights will vary according to their source, the complexity becomes great.

Theoretically, it should always be possible to find out the source and nature of class rights by reference to the Registrar of Companies. Any rights set out in the memorandum or the articles will be able to be seen but it may be that shares have been issued under the power in, or similar to, Table A art 2, which allows the issue of shares with such rights as the Board attaches when deciding to issue them. Here, the class member will need to look at the particular resolution of the Board or the General Meeting, as the case may be, to ascertain his rights. Even then, he may not be sure of the position because if there is any conflict between the rights given by resolution and any rights in that or any other class of shares given by the memorandum, or the articles, the resolution is, to that extent, ineffective: *Hogg* v *Cramphorn Ltd* [1967] Ch 254. Section 128 Companies Act (CA) 1985 provides some help in that upon any allotment of shares with rights that are not set out in either memorandum or articles or in any special resolution of the general meeting and which differ from the rights attaching to previously issued shares, a statement of the share class rights must be sent to the Registrar within one month of the allotment: s128(1) CA 1985. This also applies to any naming of the new class created by the differential rights attached to the new allotment. Despite this, there is still a possibility of missing additional rights which might attach to the rights by reason of being set out in listing particulars or similar documents, as happened in *Jacobs* v *Batavia & General Plantation Trust Ltd* [1924] 2 Ch 329.

The next problem for the prospective or actual class member is to establish just how his rights would need to be altered procedurally. This is often a complex matter as everything depends upon the source of the rights. If given by the memorandum, they can only be altered if the memorandum so provides (s267 CA 1985), or if the memorandum itself contemplates alterations in a way set out in the articles so that the article becomes incorporated by reference into the memorandum (*Re Welsbach Incandescent Gas Light Co Ltd* [1904] 1 Ch 87), or by the consent of all the members of the company (s125(5) CA 1985). If, on the other hand, the rights are given by the articles or by the resolution of the Board or the General Meeting, the method of alteration and conditions for validity of the alteration depend upon whatever provision, if any, is made in the articles themselves. With the exception of an article providing for alteration of rights by resolution of the General Meeting, CA 1985 requires class consents to the alteration. If there is no provision in the articles for alteration the rights may only be altered with the consent of 3/4 in nominal value of the issued shares in the class or by an extraordinary resolution having a majority of 3/4 of the votes cast at a separate class meeting: s125(2) CA 1985. These last consents also apply where there is provision in the articles or memorandum for alteration of rights but where the purpose of the alteration is in any way connected to directors' authority to issue shares or to reduce share capital: s125(3) CA 1985.

If the class member gets through the maze outlined above he may then face the further problem of trying to ascertain just what it is that amounts to an alteration of his rights. The law on this point makes a strong distinction between changes that materially affect the rights of a class and changes which have no effect beyond altering the value of the shares. In the latter case, the position of the class member is greatly changed but it will not amount to an alteration by which rights are 'affected, modified, dealt with or abrogated': *White* v *Bristol Aeroplane Co* [1953] Ch 65. Here existing preference shareholders who could have exercised voting rights to prevent such alterations were held by the court to have been properly prevented from voting against the issue of new fully-paid preference shares to ordinary shareholders. The result was a serious dilution of the existing preference class so that their prospects on a repayment of capital and their limited voting powers in General Meetings or class meetings were both greatly reduced. The court concluded that what was altered was not the class rights but the enjoyment of those rights in the sense of the capacity to turn them to personal advantage.

Similar difficulties are to be seen in the question of whether the cancellation of a class of shares, usually preference, amounts to an alteration of class rights. There are cases that point both ways in this area and much depends upon whether there is an ultimate right to participation in surplus assets after repayment of all shares of every class, as in *Re Old Silkstone Collieries Ltd* [1954] Ch 169 and *House of Fraser plc* v *AGCE Investments Ltd* [1987] AC 387. In *Re Northern Engineering Industries plc* [1994] BCC 618, the Court of Appeal held that the complete cancellation of a class of preference shares would equate to a reduction of capital which, by the articles of association, constituted a deemed variation of class rights, but the case only serves to illustrate the difficulties where such express deeming provisions are absent.

The position of creditors

The position of creditors of the company is as full of uncertainty as that of the shareholder. They can be no more sure of the continuation of the existing capital structure, share classes and control of the company than anyone else. The creditor might, in certain circumstances, be allowed by the court to object to an alteration of class rights which consisted of a reduction in capital (s136 CA 1985), but objections will not be heard in most alteration situations.

In summary, it is submitted that the unwieldy and obscure position on class rights is such that any perceived protection offered to either member or creditor is likely to be outweighed by the difficulties in ascertaining the true extent of the rights in question.

Chapter 7
Debentures

7.1   Introduction

7.2   Key points

7.3   Key cases and statute

7.4   Questions and suggested solutions

7.1 Introduction

This chapter examines the problems which arise in connection with the taking of loans by the company in return for a debenture (any document which acknowledges a company's indebtedness). Debentures may be unsecured but are more often secured by a charge on the company's assets.

7.2 Key points

Fixed charges

A fixed charge attaches to specific assets of the company. If the asset includes land, it may be referred to as a mortgage, and the charge may need to be registered at the Land Registry (registered land) or Land Charges Registry (unregistered).

Floating charges

A floating charge (which can only be given by a company) attaches to present and future assets which by their nature are changing all the time, eg stock, but it is inherent in the nature of a floating charge that the company can deal freely with the assets until 'crystallisation' (see below) (*Re Yorkshire Woolcombers' Association Ltd* [1903] 2 Ch 284). Thus, if the company is prevented by the charge from doing so, the charge must be fixed even though the assets are 'floating' (*Siebe Gorman & Co Ltd* v *Barclays Bank Ltd* [1979] 2 Lloyd's Rep 142).

Crystallisation of floating charges

'Crystallisation' means that the charge becomes fixed and attaches to specific assets. It occurs on the happening of certain events – at common law, default or liquidation – which are often specified in the debenture. 'Automatic crystallisation' is sometimes attempted by a clause in the debenture which is triggered when a fixed charge is created ranking in priority to the floating charge. As this type of clause subverts the principle that fixed charges take precedence over floating charges, there is some doubt as to its validity, although there are dicta in support (see *Davey* v *Williamson* [1898] 2 QB 194; *Evans* v *Rival Granite Quarries Ltd* [1910] 2 KB 979; and *Re Brightlife Ltd* [1986] BCLC 418), and such a clause has been upheld in New Zealand (*Re Manurewa* [1971] NZLR 909).

Registration

Any charge or debenture must be registered at Companies House within 21 days of its creation. Failure to comply with this requirement renders the security void, though it does not invalidate the loan. The court may permit registration after the 21-day period has expired and the charge takes effect subject to any charges registered in the meantime. A certificate of registration is conclusive evidence of the date of registration.

Priority of charges

Fixed charges take priority over floating charges for repayment, and legal over equitable charges. Where there is more than one charge of the same rank, the first in time of creation prevails provided it is properly registered. The chargees themselves may agree to alter the order of priority (*Re Automatic Bottle Makers Ltd* [1926] Ch 421). A clause may be included prohibiting the creation of a later charge having priority (a 'negative pledge' clause). The present position is that this is effective only if the later chargee has actual knowledge both of the existence of the earlier charge and the negative pledge clause. Constructive notice, by mere registration of the earlier charge alone is insufficient (*Wilson* v *Kelland* [1910] 2 Ch 30).

Receivership

A debenture or charge usually contains a power for the debenture holder to appoint a receiver in the case of default. If it does not, application may be made to the court to make an appointment. An administrative receiver, appointed under a floating charge, must be a qualified insolvency practitioner. The receiver takes over the management of the business for a time in order to obtain payment for his own debenture-holder, but he has first to pay the costs of the receivership and holders of charges having priority to his own. Section 44 Insolvency Act (IA) 1986 makes him an agent of the company. The administrative receiver has extensive powers to manage the company.

7.3 Key cases and statute

* *Agnew* v *Inland Revenue Commissioners* [2001] 2 AC 710
  In determining whether a charge is fixed or floating the court's task is to discover what rights the parties intended to create and then to decide whether, as a matter of law, those rights create a fixed or floating charge

- *ASRS Establishment Ltd, Re* [2000] 2 BCLC 631
  The courts will not accept the label the parties attach to a contract as a conclusive statement of its legal nature

- *Automatic Bottle Makers, Re* [1926] Ch 412
  Chargees may agree to alter order of priority

- *Brightlife Ltd, Re* [1986] BCLC 418
  Triggering of automatic crystallisation

- *Pearl Maintenance Services, Re* [1995] 1 BCLC 449
  Whether a charge over book debts was fixed or floating

- *Real Meat Co Ltd (In Receivership), Re* [1996] BCC 254
  Priority of charges

- *Siebe Gorman & Co Ltd* v *Barclays Bank Ltd* [1979] 2 Lloyd's Rep 142
  If a charge cannot crystallise it must be fixed and not floating

- *Wilson* v *Kelland* [1910] 2 Ch 30
  Mere registration of the earlier charge is not sufficient for constructive notice

- *Yorkshire Woolcombers' Association Ltd, Re* [1903] 2 Ch 284
  Contains definition of a floating charge

- Insolvency Act 1986

  - s44 – makes receiver the agent fo the company

  - s239 – giving of a preference

  - s245 – invalid charge

7.4 Questions and suggested solutions

QUESTION ONE

Henry is the majority shareholder and managing director of Bat and Ball Ltd ('the company'), whose business consists of selling sports equipment. Owing to the recession, Henry lent the company £50,000 on 1 January 1989, but by the middle of 1989 business had hardly improved and Henry, worried about his loan, caused the company to grant him a fixed charge over its shop and book debts as security for a further loan of £50,000. In November 1989 the Midwest bank, where the company's overdraft was £75,000, threatened to petition for the winding-up of the company unless it was given some form of security. As a result, Henry caused the company to grant a floating charge to the bank over all the company's assets.

Although the position looked increasingly hopeless, Henry, on the advice of his accountant, continued trading because an end to the recession was widely forecast. In fact, this turned out to be too optimistic a forecast and in November 1990, a petition was presented for the winding-up of the company and a winding-up order was granted in March 1991. For the six months prior to the grant of the winding-up order, Henry only drew half his agreed salary (ie £1,500 per month instead of £3,000).

The company's fixed assets and book debts are valued at £50,000 and the company's other assets would yield £10,000.

Advise the liquidator.

University of London LLB Examination
(for External Students) Company Law June 1991 Q5

General Comment

Debentures is a fairly popular topic; however there is a twist to the question in that Henry, the main shareholder in Bat and Ball Ltd has been granted a fixed charge. Essentially the principles remain the same. Distinction has to be made between fixed and floating charges. The concept of crystallisation, registration of charges and priority of charges. Fraudulent and wrongful trading are also relevant though fraud maybe difficult to prove.

Skeleton Solution

Liquidation retrospective to date of petition – distinguish between fixed and floating charges and registration of charges – concept of crystallisation – fixed charge takes priority unless caught by automatic crystallisation clause, only happens if later chargee has actual notice of earlier clauses – IA 1986, s245 may invalidate floating charge, not applicable to fixed charges – fraudulent and wrongful trading relevant – order of payment.

Suggested Solution

In a liquidation money must be paid out in a strict order of priority. The first payment is the costs and expenses of liquidation, then the fixed chargees, followed by preferential creditors and lastly floating chargees and any payment due to unsecured creditors. The liquidation is deemed to have commenced on the date of the petition ie November 1990. The liquidator will be concerned to establish the priority of payment to be made in the liquidation.

It is clear that Henry has a fixed charge since this charge was created in the middle of 1989. This fixed charge created by the company is registrable under Companies Act (CA) 1985, s396, and it is valid if duly registered within 21 days. However, in so far as the charge relates to land it also requires to be registered under the Land Charges Act 1972. Failure to comply with this requirement will render the charge void against the liquidator and a subsequent purchaser for value of the legal estate. If this criterion is not met both the company and any officer in default is liable to a fine. This is because most companies obtain much of their finance from debentures secured by charges and it is important that people dealing with the company are able to find out which assets are subject to charges.

There is a possibility that Henry's fixed charge has priority over Midwest Bank's floating charge which would only have become a fixed charge on the date of the petition. However, in causing the company to grant him a fixed charge, Henry is clearly infringing Insolvency Act (IA) 1986, s239, by giving a preference to one creditor of the company (ie himself) ahead of other creditors. Such a preference will accordingly be void, and Henry may be required to repay the money to the company.

The liquidator should also be advised to bear in mind ss213 and 214 IA 1986 where a director of a company incurs personal liability for 'fraudulent trading' ie trading in such a way as fraudulently to prefer one creditor over another. The provisions also deal with 'wrongful trading' ie continuing to trade knowing that the company is insolvent. There is sufficient evidence to indicate that Henry will find himself liable under both these provisions. Under the statutory predecessors of these provisions, a narrow view was taken of the concepts of 'defrauding' and 'fraudulent purpose': *Re Patrick and Lyon* [1933] All ER 590, but it should not be assumed that the same approach would be taken at the present day, as the courts' attitude seems to have hardened somewhat with regard to such indiscretions. A misfeasance summons may be taken through the company by the liquidator under s212 IA 1986 against the accountant as he has a contractual relationship with the company and owes it a duty of care and was negligent in advising Henry to continue trading, when there was clear evidence that Bat and Ball Ltd was tottering on insolvency. However, success as to the outcome of such an action is debatable.

The floating charge granted in favour of Midwest Bank requires consideration. The general concept of a floating charge was explained in *Re Yorkshire Woolcombers' Association Ltd* [1903] 2 Ch 284 as a charge over assets present and future. Because these assets would in the ordinary course of business change, the charge to remain floating until some event occurs which causes crystallisation. The events which are normally regarded as causing crystallisation are the appointment of a receiver and the commencement of a winding-up: *Re Victoria Steamboats Co* [1897] 1 Ch 158. The difficulty is to decide on the validity of express clauses which make crystallisation happen on the occurrence of certain specified events, ie automatic crystallisation clauses. The point does not seem to be settled in English law, but the decision of Hoffmann J in *Re Brightlife Ltd* [1987] Ch 200 gives some support for the recognition of these clauses in English law.

In any event there is a possibility that Midwest Bank's charge is invalidated by IA 1986, s245. This provides that where in the twelve months before the commencement of a winding-up, a floating charge is created and the company was insolvent immediately after the creation, the charge will be invalid except to the extent that fresh consideration was given for it. In other words such a charge cannot be used to secure pre-existing borrowing. It is arguable that no fresh consideration was provided by Midwest Bank as the floating charge was merely the re-financing of the company's debts to the bank. If this argument is accepted, then s245 will apply, and the charge will be invalidated.

Thus the payout in the liquidation are (in order): costs and expenses of the liquidation, the preferential creditors (including Henry's wages in the previous four months preceding the liquidation, the Inland Revenue, DSS and others), then the floating charge to Midwest Bank, followed by Henry's charge to the extent that they have not been invalidated.

QUESTION TWO

Sam Sandcastle was the sole director and shareholder (apart from one share held by his wife) of Grand Illusions Limited ('the company'), a company which specialised in the manufacture and sale of jewellery. Some of this jewellery was manufactured by Sam himself under an agreement between himself and the company, some was manufactured by jewellers who sold their items to the company and some was imported by the company from abroad. The company had also entered into agreements with Denis Diamond and Pearl Pond to take their entire output of manufactured jewellery.

The company has been badly hit by the recession and the overdraft with the Bank of Cash and Credit ('the bank') climbed to £300,000 by the end of 1991. The bank demanded security and in February Sam caused the company to grant a floating charge over all its undertaking to the bank as well as a fixed charge over all its book debts. Despite hectic trading in the period from February to May, the company's fortunes continued to decline.

In May, the Bank undertook an investigation of the company's affairs and discovered:

a) that the company had a substantial amount of manufactured jewellery which when the economy improves will probably be saleable at substantial profits;

b) that the company had taken delivery of large quantities of the raw material necessary for the manufacture of jewellery, but that much of this had been supplied under contracts with retention of title provisions;

c) that Sam had caused the company to pay him £50,000 in part reduction of a loan made by Sam to the company in 1990 and in part payment for jewellery made by Sam and sold to the company;

d) that the company owed Pearl and Denis each about £10,000;

e) that the Inland Revenue was pressing for payment of Corporation Tax arrears of some £50,000;

f) that in 1991 the company entered into an agreement with the Easy Financing Company, in terms of which all sales abroad by the company were to go through the Finance Company in exchange for 90 per cent of the invoiced price and that all payments made to the company in respect of such sales were to be received by the company as agent for the Finance Company.

A petition has now been presented for the appointment of an administrator to the Company. The company's total assets are probably not worth more than £100,000 but there are signs of considerable improvement in the economy. Advise the bank whether:

a) to accede to this petition, or

b) to appoint an administrative receiver, or

c) to oppose the petition in favour of a winding-up petition.

University of London LLB Examination
(for External Students) Company Law June 1992 Q5

General Comment

The question poses a good many issues concerning priority of claims to the assets of an insolvent company and the validity of its recent transactions, coupled with some comparison of administration, receivership and liquidation. Thus it could not be answered satisfactorily without insolvency as a whole having been studied.

Skeleton Solution

Assets of insolvent company – avoidance of certain transactions – *Romalpa* – priority of claimants – aspects of administration, administrative receivership and liquidation compared.

Suggested Solution

The validity of the charges to the bank should first be checked. There is unlikely to have been any failure to register under the Companies Act (CA) 1985, s398, nor is there any likelihood of a preference under s239 Insolvency Act (IA) 1986. But if the company were to commence liquidation, or a petition on which an administration order was made were to be presented, within 12 months of the creation of the floating charge, and had been unable to pay its debts at the date the charge was created, the charge would be invalidated except for money paid, or the value of goods and services supplied, at or after creation of the charge (s245 IA 1986). Although the decision in *Re Yeovil Glove Co Ltd* [1965] Ch 148 could reduce the impact of s245 upon the floating charge to the bank, yet insofar as s245 poses a threat to the bank's position it would obviously benefit the bank to avert liquidation or the appointment of an administrator at present.

As regards the raw material supplied under the *Romalpa*-type (see *Aluminium Industrie Vaassen BV v Romalpa Aluminium Ltd* [1976] 2 All ER 552) reservation of title clauses, such clauses usually succeed insofar as the raw material is still clearly identifiable and unused; the clause may also be so worded as to succeed if the raw material has been incorporated into a larger article, provided the raw material is still readily identifiable and can be physically identified (*Hendy Lennox (Industrial Engines) Ltd v Graham Puttick*

Ltd [1984] 1 All ER 152), but not if they have been blended into other goods in such a manner as to lose their identity (*Borden (UK) Ltd v Scottish Timber Products Ltd* [1981] Ch 25). The raw material, therefore, may well not be an asset of the company, but much will turn on the facts and the precise wording of the *Romalpa*-type clauses.

With regard to the payment of £50,000 made by the company to Sam, this may be a preference under s239. If a company has at a relevant time given a person a preference, the administrator or liquidator may apply to the court for an order restoring the position prior to the preference. The court is also given wide powers under s241. A creditor such as Sam is preferred if the company does anything which has the effect of putting the creditor in a better position should the company go into insolvent liquidation, but only if, also, the company was, when deciding to give the preference, influenced by a desire to better his position. Since Sam is, by virtue of his being a director of the company, a person 'connected' with it, the time of the preference will not be a 'relevant time' unless given within two years of the commencement of liquidation or the presentation of the petition on which an administration order was made, as the case may be.

The Revenue is no longer a preferential creditor, and Sam, Pearl and Denis are also ordinary creditors as to the sums listed as still owed to them. Hence the bank, insofar as it is a valid secured creditor, ranks in priority to them. A liquidator or administrative receiver must however pay any preferential creditors in priority to the holder of a floating charge.

The arrangement with Easy Financing Company appears to be neither a preference nor a security. The assignment would appear to be absolute. If so, the company could presumably only assign to Easy Financing such interest in the book debts as the company then had.

As indicated, the appointment of a liquidator or administrator may invalidate the floating charge to the bank wholly or in part; conversely a liquidator or administrator could seek court orders setting aside preferences. Appointment of an administrative receiver would not endanger the security conferred by the floating charge, but an administrative receiver is not empowered to have preferences set aside. The bank must choose its course according to the relative sums, dates and risks involved.

QUESTION THREE

Pip Ltd is a manufacturing company which has in recent years run into financial difficulties. On 1 January 1992 the company borrowed £100,000 from Quinn (who is not connected with the company) and issued a debenture to him for that amount. The debenture was expressed to be secured by a floating charge over all the property and undertaking of the company and the company was prohibited from creating any other charge ranking in priority to or pari passu with the floating charge. The debenture also provided that the floating charge was to crystallise automatically without necessity for the appointment of a receiver or other intervention by the chargee if the amount of its liabilities should at any time in fact become greater than the value of its assets. On 15 August 1992 the company's liabilities, for the first time ever, exceeded the value of its assets and it did not become solvent again for three weeks.

On 6 September 1992 the company borrowed £100,000 from Rob (who is not connected with the company) and issued a debenture to him for that amount. This debenture was expressed to be secured by a 'fixed charge over all book debts and other debts now or at any time during the continuance of this security due or owing to Pip Ltd'.

On 1 March 1994 a petition for the winding-up of Pip Ltd was presented by a creditor and a winding-up order was made on 2 May 1994. The liabilities of the company exceed its assets.

Advise the liquidator as to the order of priority of the above charges, on the assumption that each was duly registered.

University of London LLB Examination
(for External Students) Company Law June 1994 Q5

General Comment

This question is a fairly standard one. The authorities on automatic crystallisation of floating charges are sparse. The candidate is therefore required to give some critical analysis of the relevant principles/doctrine.

Skeleton Solution

Floating charges – characteristics – negative pledge clauses – validity of, notice/knowledge of – automatic crystallisation clauses – validity of – desirability of – failure to intervene upon crystallisation – estoppel.

Suggested Solution

But for the 'negative pledge' and 'automatic crystallisation' clauses contained in the charge granted to Quinn, Rob's fixed charge would have priority. This consequence flows from the very nature of a floating charge. Of the three (non-exhaustive) criteria set out by Romer LJ in *Re Yorkshire Woolcombers' Association Ltd* [1903] 2 Ch 284 (where he explained the nature of a floating charge), perhaps the most significant is the management autonomy that is afforded to the company pending crystallisation. The company retains authority to deal with the property subject to a floating charge 'in the ordinary course of business'. This involves the consequence that a floating charge will not generally take priority over a fixed charge created subsequent to it: see *Re Castell & Brown* [1898] 1 Ch 315. The creation of fixed charges is part of the ordinary course of business.

'Crystallisation' is the metaphor used to describe the transition from floating charge into fixed charge. Once crystallisation has taken place, the company must have the consent of the debentureholder if it is to deal with the property subject to the charge.

To shore up the relatively poor priority of floating charges, it has become common for companies to insert negative pledge clauses, similar to that given in favour of Quinn. The validity of negative pledge clauses has been largely assumed in the decided authorities. It is worth pointing out, however, that negative pledge clauses should always be strictly construed because they limit the company's actual authority to deal with the charged asset/s. For that reason they are arguably inconsistent with the management autonomy which is one of the hallmarks of a floating charge (above). The question is whether or not Rob is bound by the negative pledge clause.

To be bound by the clause, Rob must have knowledge or notice of it. The simple fact that the debenture was duly registered does not suffice. Since there is no requirement to register particulars of any negative pledge clause when registering the charge (see s397 Companies Act (CA) 1985), there can be no constructive notice of it: see *Wilson* v *Kelland* [1910] 2 Ch 30. To be bound by the negative pledge clause, Rob must have actual knowledge of it or have been wilfully blind as to its existence, eg he may have been put on notice as to the existence of the negative pledge but failed to ascertain its precise effect. We are given no information as to the state of Rob's knowledge and so will assume that he did not, in fact, know of the negative pledge in favour of Quinn. (It is worth mentioning that the 1989 amendments to the 1985 Act, see s416(2)(c), which are yet to be enacted, provide for the registration of negative pledge clauses.)

What about the purported automatic crystallisation of the floating charge? There is no decided appellate authority in which the validity of automatic crystallisation clauses has been upheld. Such clauses are of doubtful validity because it is possible that a charge will crystallise upon the occurrence of a particular event, without either the company or the chargee knowing that crystallisation has taken place. Prejudice might therefore occur to a subsequent fixed chargee who thinks that his fixed charge has priority over the earlier floating charge, which he does not know has, in fact, become a fixed charge. This is exactly the problem faced by Rob. The Cork Committee (1982) were against the introduction of automatic crystallisation clauses.

The validity of such clauses has been upheld in New Zealand in *Re Manuwera* [1971] NZLR 909 but doubted in the Canadian case of *R* v *Consolidated Churchill Copper Corporation Ltd* [1978] 5 WWR 652. Further, Hoffmann J in *Re Brightlife Ltd* [1987] Ch 200 remarked obiter that such clauses should, in his view, be upheld on the policy ground of general freedom to contract. Rob might argue with force that the clause is not valid for the above reasons. In addition, he might argue that both Quinn and Pip Ltd are estopped from denying the priority of his charge, on the basis that neither took any steps upon crystallisation occurring in August 1992. It is arguable that this failure constitutes an implied representation by Quinn and Pip Ltd that the floating charge had not crystallised.

Whether or not the court would be prepared to uphold the validity of the automatic crystallisation clause, it is submitted that Rob's charge would have priority on the basis of estoppel by representation.

QUESTION FOUR

Bill and Bob are the directors of Bank Finances plc ('the company') which is a long established merchant bank which trades globally. In order to finance margin calls required by their Singapore office they agreed on 1 January 1994 to create a floating charge over the company's entire undertaking (in England) in favour of Ratfink Bank Ltd in return for a loan of £1,000,000,000. The floating charge contained a clause providing that it would crystallise in the event of any default or enforcement proceedings being taken against the company. This charge was registered on 21 January 1994.

On 14 January 1994 the company refurbished their head office in London. In order to finance the interior design project Bill and Bob withheld money due to the Government in the form of VAT and PAYE and also obtained a loan from Beckley's Bank for £1,000,000. This loan was secured over the book debts of the company. The charge was registered on the 17 January 1994.

On 15 February, John demanded payment for the office furniture that his firm had supplied to the company. Following advice from the company's finance director the board secured the amount outstanding to John by a fixed charge over the company's factory. The finance director also advised the board 'that the company is in a position whereby it is unlikely to pay all its creditors and this financial situation is unlikely to be resolved'.

The company continued to trade until November 1994 when it went into liquidation.

Advise the liquidator.

University of London LLB Examination
(for External Students) Company Law June 1995 Q6

General Comment

It is necessary here to consider the characteristics of fixed and floating charges, and the factors which establish priority both between such charges and also as against other company creditors, unsecured or preferential. The question of voidable preferences is also significant here, and detailed knowledge of statute and common law is necessary in such a question.

Skeleton Solution

Ratfink's charge; outline of floating charges – Beckley's charge; analysis – registration and priorities – John's preferences – priority between fixed and floating charges – voidable preferences – priority between floating charges and automatic crystallisation – avoidance of floating charges by liquidator – final order of priority for liquidator.

Suggested Solution

The liquidator will need to consider the order of priorities created by the transactions entered into by the company during 1994. This requires consideration of the nature of the particular charges and the respective circumstances of their creation and registration.

The Ratfink Bank Ltd charge

This is expressed to be a floating charge and, as it is over the company's entire undertaking in England and contains express provision for crystallising events, this seems to be a true floating charge, applying the tests in *Illingworth v Houldsworth* [1904] AC 355. A charge on the company's 'undertaking' was held to be a floating charge in *Re Panama, New Zealand and Australian Royal Mail Co* (1870) 5 Ch App 318. The charge was properly registered and the particulars delivered within the 21 days allowed by s398(1) Companies Act (CA) 1985. Provided that this charge was also entered into the company's own register of charges, all that was necessary seems to have been done.

The Beckley's Bank charge

This is secured on the book debts of the company, but it is not expressed to be either floating or fixed so it is vital to ascertain which it is. The nature of book debts is to change rapidly and there is necessity for the company to have freedom to deal with its book debts within the normal course of business, like any other asset. The general rule about book debts charges is that they exhibit the characteristics of floating charges as explained by Romer LJ in *Re Yorkshire Woolcombers' Association Ltd* [1903] 2 Ch 284 and also in *Re Brightlife Ltd* [1986] BCLC 418. There seems to be nothing of the specific and exceptional circumstances seen in *Siebe Gorman & Co Ltd v Barclays Bank Ltd* [1979] 2 Lloyd's Rep 142, which pointed towards a fixed charge, although *Re New Bullas Trading Ltd* [1994] BCC 36 indicates that if the true intention of the parties is of a fixed charge, the courts will uphold this position, particularly if the charge is expressed to be fixed. As shown in *Agnew v Inland Revenue Commissioners* [2001] 2 AC 710 in determining whether a charge is fixed or floating the court's task is to discover what rights the parties intended to create and then to decide whether, as a matter of law, those rights create a fixed or floating charge. This charge, in the absence of good evidence to the contrary, seems to be intended to be a floating charge. This charge also seems to have been properly registered.

As between these two charges, both properly registered, it becomes necessary to consider the effect of registration. Prima facie, the first created of these equally valid charges will take preference (*Re Benjamin Cope & Co Ltd* [1914] 1 Ch 800), but the problem is that the taking of a floating charge over the entire undertaking of the company in England necessarily contemplates a freedom for the company to deal with its assets within the course of business, and a later floating charge over a substantially narrower range of assets, such as book debts, may achieve priority as happened in *Re Automatic Bottle Makers* [1926] Ch 421. Much will depend upon whether the earlier charge contains any prohibition upon the creation of subsequent charges having parity or priority, whether the later one was expressed to be subordinate to the earlier one and, if there was no reference to priorities in the later charge, whether Beckleys could be in the position of 'equity's darling' having no actual or constructive knowledge of the earlier prohibition. The registration of the earlier charge gives constructive notice of its existence to Beckleys, but not of any prohibition on creation of later charges ranking in priority, (*Siebe Gorman & Co Ltd* v *Barclays Bank Ltd* [1979] 2 Lloyd's Rep 142). There is provision in ss414, 415 CA 1985, as inserted by s103 CA 1989, for the Secretary of State for Trade and Industry to make rules requiring such prohibiting clauses to be a necessary particular for registration, so as to cause a later chargee to have constructive notice of them, but at present this is not the case. Unless Beckleys have actual notice, they will not be bound by such a clause, if one exists. On balance, as between these two charges it seems that Beckleys may have priority. The question of priority between the floating charges and the preferential creditors is considered below.

John's fixed charge

This charge, over the factory, must observe the general rules of formality for creating such a charge over land, and there seems to be no obstacle to creating a fixed charge subsequent to the floating ones. Even an express prohibition in the earlier charges would not make the fixed charge invalid, it would be merely a breach of contract (*Griffiths* v *Yorkshire Bank plc* [1994] 1 WLR 1427). Provided that neither of the earlier charges had crystallised by the time of creation, John would seem to get priority over both as only crystallisation can convert them into a fixed charge having priority. The difficulty for John is that the security was created at a time when the company was heading into trouble, and it does not seem to have been registered. Lack of registration within the statutory 21 days would cause the charge to become void as against a liquidator of the company (s399(1) CA 1985) and, provided the 'relevant event' of the beginning of insolvency proceedings took place after the creation of the charge, as seems to be the case here (s399(2)(a)), he would simply be an unsecured creditor. If, in fact the charge was registered, John should be entitled to priority against any other creditor, preferential or not. A possible difficulty for John is that the company seemed already to be in trouble at the time of his charge being given. He might be seen as having been given a 'preference' within s239 Insolvency Act (IA) 1986 if the charge was created within the 'relevant time' under s240 IA 1986. This means within two years of the onset of insolvency if he is 'connected', or six months otherwise. He may just escape this on the given facts but, even if he was within a relevant period, if the company did not intend to create a preference and the charge was granted for good commercial reasons it will not be a preference (*Re Paragaussu Steam Tramway Co; Adamson's Case* (1874) LR 18 Eq 670).

The next question for the liquidator is the priority between the floating charges and the preferential creditors. It seems, in the absence of further information, that both charges are likely to be crystallised into fixed charges by the events leading up to the liquidation. Probably what it is that constitutes the express crystallisation event seems to depend upon the established law on automatic crystallisation, under which the 'going into liquidation' will be the event. It may be, of course, that Beckleys had put in a common form of clause providing automatic crystallisation immediately before any act by the company entitling Beckleys to enforce its security (*Re ELS Ltd* [1994] 3 WLR 616).

Assuming that the priority between the two charges is established by their crystallising events, the question is whether these charges will bind the liquidator. Section 245 IA 1986 makes such floating charges void if created within 12 months before the onset of insolvency. Both charges were within this period but there is statutory validity, provided that the moneys were paid as consideration for the charge and paid at the same time or after the creation of the charge (s245(2) IA 1986). This seems to be the situation here so the charges will bind the liquidator.

The final priority to decide is that of the preferential creditors for VAT and PAYE. By s40 IA 1986 these will get priority over the floating charges, even though these will have been crystallised into fixed charges (s40(1)). Thus, the order of priority for the liquidator will be first, John's fixed charge over the factory, which seems to be created too early to be caught as a voidable preference, and will take precedence over the liquidator, next the preferential creditors and, finally, the floating charges. These will be in order of crystallisation or, if at the same time, rank equally.

Chapter 8

Meetings

8.1   Introduction

8.2   Key points

8.3   Key cases and statute

8.4   Questions and suggested solutions

8.1 Introduction

This chapter examines the problems which may arise in connection with the conduct of a company's general meeting. Questions usually concern the validity of a resolution passed at a general meeting. (The related topic of a member's standing to challenge an invalid resolution is dealt with in Chapter 11: *Minorities*, and the two topics should be learned together as problems typically feature both.) A resolution may be invalid because the majority by which it was passed was insufficient, the procedure under which it was passed was defective, or the meeting at which it was passed was invalid. Annual General Meetings (AGMs) must be held, the first within 18 months of incorporation, and subsequent AGMs within 15 months of the last (s366 Companies Act (CA) 1985), unless the company is a private company which has elected to dispense with the requirement (s366A). A general meeting which is not an AGM is an EGM (Extraordinary General Meeting).

8.2 Key points

Notice of meetings

A meeting will be invalid if proper notice is not given. This will be 21 days in the case of an AGM, and 14 days in the case of an EGM (Extraordinary General Meeting) (unless a special resolution is proposed, in which case the notice must be 21 days also). All the members entitled to attend and vote may agree in writing to accept shorter notice of an AGM (95 per cent of the membership for an EGM) (s369).

Notice must be given to all those entitled to attend and failure to do this will invalidate the meeting, but there is usually a saving in the articles for accidental omissions. Notice will be invalid unless it contains certain information (including the date and place and the fact that the member is entitled to appoint a proxy to attend and vote in his stead) and states the business to be transacted with sufficient particularity to enable members to decide whether or not to attend. The full text or substance of special, extraordinary or elective resolutions must be included (*Re Moorgate Mercantile Holdings Ltd* [1980] 1 WLR 227). If directors are to benefit personally from the resolution, this should also be clear (*Baillie* v *Oriental Telephone Co* [1915] 1 Ch 503).

While the board usually calls a meeting, holders of 10 per cent of the voting capital may require the board to call an EGM (s368), and the court has power to call a meeting if the directors at any time wrongfully fail to do so (s371).

Quorum

A meeting will be invalid if it is not quorate. A quorum is the minimum number of persons who must be present in person or by proxy. The articles usually specify a quorum (Table A states two members or proxies). Sometimes one person may be a valid quorum (see eg s370A CA 1985 – single member companies, and the court's power to call meetings). An inquorate meeting may be adjourned. (As to adjournment generally, see *Byng* v *London Life Association Ltd* [1990] Ch 170.)

Procedure

Statute says very little about the conduct and procedure at meetings. Table A, however, lays down fairly comprehensive rules and most companies adopt these. Except where noted, the rules which follow are those in Table A, but the relevant articles of association must always be consulted to see whether these rules have been varied.

The meeting will have a chairman who is specified in the articles or elected by the meeting (s370(5) CA 1985). Table A says the chairman of the board or, in his absence, another director is to chair the meeting. The chairman has considerable power in deciding whom to allow to speak and for how long, ruling on amendments to resolutions, deciding whether a poll may be taken, often exercising proxy votes and deciding whether to adjourn the meeting. He will usually have a casting vote and it is important to check how and when it is to be exercised.

The initial vote is usually taken on a show of hands in which the members will have one vote each. In a poll, voting rights will normally be based on the number of shares held so there may be advantage to demanding a poll. Additionally, proxy votes which are not taken into consideration on a show of hands may be included in a poll. The chairman is entitled to insist on a poll and a valid demand may also be made by the holders of at least 10 per cent of the votes, or by any five members of the company present in person.

Resolutions

Resolutions are usually proposed by the directors, but members holding at least one-twentieth of the total voting rights, or 100 members holding shares on which there has been paid up an average sum per member of not less than £100, may propose a resolution and require the board to give notice of it (s376).

An ordinary resolution is passed by a simple majority of votes at a meeting of which at least 14 days' notice is usually required. A special resolution requires 75 per cent and 21 days' notice (s378(2)), while an extraordinary resolution, which also requires 75 per cent of the votes, requires no minimum notice. It should be noted that the majorities are of those voting in person or by proxy (in the case of a poll), not a majority of all the members. Students should familiarise themselves with the occasions on which a special or extrordinary resolution is required.

Certain resolutions (eg a resolution to remove a director) requires 'special notice', even though only a simple majority of votes is needed to pass the resolution. Special notice is a minimum of 28 days.

The CA 1989 introduced two new kinds of resolution for private companies only:

a) Elective resolution

This is available where specified in the 1985 Act to dispense with certain requirements (the most important perhaps being the duration of directors' authority to allot shares under s80A CA 1985 – see Chapter 6: *Shares*). It requires 21 days' notice and agreement at the meeting by all members entitled to vote in person or by proxy.

b) Written resolution

This is an agreement in writing by all the members entitled to attend and vote at a general meeting. It is available for any matter which can be effected by any kind of resolution at a general meeting, save only removal of a director or auditor before expiration of office, and is as effective as a resolution passed at the meeting.

The scope of amendment to resolutions is narrow: amendments proposed prior to a meeting must be given the same notice as the original resolution. At the meeting itself only limited amendments (and none of substance) may be accepted (*Re Moorgate Mercantile Holdings Ltd* [1980] 1 WLR 227).

Proposals for reform

The report on Company Law Reform has suggested that the rules on a company's internal administrative procedures should be simplified so that private companies need no longer hold AGMs, lay accounts in general meeting or appoint auditors annually unless they positively opt to do so. They will no longer be obliged to appoint a company secretary. It should also become easier for private companies to take decisions by written resolution without the need to hold a general meeting.

8.3 Key cases and statute

* *Baillie* v *Oriental Telephone Co* [1915] 1 Ch 503
  It should be made clear if the directors are to benefit from the resolution

- *British Union for the Abolition of Vivisection, Re* (1995) The Times 3 March
  The court exercised its power under s371 CA 1985 to direct the company to hold an EGM in such a way as to avoid potential disruption

- *Byng* v *London Life Association Ltd* [1990] Ch 170
  Gives information about adjourning meetings

- *Harman & Anor* v *BML Group Ltd* [1994] 1 WLR 893
  Exercise of court's power to order a meeting under s371 CA 1985

- *Moorgate Mercantile Holdings Ltd, Re* [1980] 1 WLR 227
  Full text of special or extraordinary or elective resolutions must be included with the notice of the meeting

- Companies Act 1985

  - s366 – timing of the AGM

  - s368 – 10 per cent of voting capital may request an EGM

  - s369 – shorter notice of AGM may be agreed unanimously

  - s370 – procedure for meetings

  - s371 – court can call meeting if directors do not

  - s378(2) – majority required for special resolution

8.4 Questions and suggested solutions

QUESTION ONE

Mace Ltd has articles of association in the form of Table A. It has a nominal and issued share capital of £10,000 divided into 10,000 shares of £1 each. Ginger holds 300 shares, Saffron 200 and Coriander 2,600. None of them are directors but Coriander's husband, Chilli, who owns no shares, is. The balance of the shares are held as to 1,000 by Clove, 1,000 between the chairman and the other directors and 4,900 between a number of small shareholders, most of whom do not attend general meetings.

The board of Mace Ltd gives notice of an EGM on 1 November 1995. It states that the meeting is to take place at the company's registered office on 21 November 1995. The business to be discussed is stated as follows:

'The following resolutions are to be discussed and passed if considered appropriate:

a) a special resolution that the name of the company be changed to Allspice Limited;

b) an ordinary resolution to increase the capital of the company to £15,000 and subdivide the shares into 30,000 shares of 75p each.'

The Secretary fails to send notice to Clove whom he believes to have sold his shares. Clove is, however, told about the meeting by his friend Chilli and attends. Ginger and

Saffron write to the Chairman of Mace Ltd proposing a resolution to remove Chilli as a director. As the Chairman does not like Chilli, he instructs the Secretary to send an amended notice adding a resolution to this effect which goes out on 5 November.

At the meeting, Coriander proposes that resolution (a) be amended to substitute 'Spicerack Limited' for 'Allspice Limited'. The Chairman decides to put both alternatives to the meeting and 'Allspice Limited' is chosen by all but Coriander. Ginger then points out that 30,000 75p shares do not total £15,000. The Chairman blames the Secretary who he says is bad at arithmetic and the corrected resolution (30,000 50p shares) is passed, Coriander voting against. The removal of Chilli is then put to the meeting and, although Coriander and sufficient others present give a majority against, the Chairman says that the resolution is carried by the proxies he holds and his own casting vote.

Advise Coriander who wishes to challenge the resolutions passed at the meeting.

Written by the Editor

General Comment

This question is typical of the kind of problem which might be set on the topic. Candidates need to grasp the provisions of both Companies Act (CA) 1985 and Table A, and be able to apply them to the situation. They must also be aware of the importance of the value of shareholdings given in calculating the necessary majorities and qualifying percentage holdings.

Skeleton Solution

Two areas: validity of notices and resolutions – notices: notice period; to whom to be given; contents – resolutions: majorities and notices required; right of minority to propose; amendments; use of proxies and Chairman's casting vote.

Suggested Solution

For a resolution to be valid it must, first of all, have been passed at a valid meeting. Notice of general meetings must be given to all entitled to attend and vote, otherwise the meeting is invalid (s370(2) Companies Act (CA) 1985). Notice was not given to Clove, which might have invalidated the meeting, but there is a saving in the articles for accidental omissions (Table A, art 39). There may be some doubt as to whether this was an 'accidental omission', however. But, when a member attends a meeting, it is assumed that he received notice of it (Table A, art 113).

The notice itself must conform to certain requirements. It must contain the date, place and time of the meeting and a statement that a proxy (agent) may be appointed to attend and vote in the member's stead. It is not clear whether the notice in this case conforms to the rules in all respects and, if it does not, this might be a ground for challenge.

The notice must also state the business to be transacted sufficiently that members can decide whether or not to attend and set out the text or substance of any special, extraordinary or elective resolution to be proposed (s378 and *Re Moorgate Mercantile Holdings Ltd* [1980] 1 WLR 227). The notice appears to conform with this requirement.

The required notice in this case is 21 days because a special resolution is to be proposed, while 14 days would have been sufficient if only ordinary resolutions were on the agenda (s369). Again the notice appears satisfactory in this respect.

As regards the resolutions themselves, changing a company's name requires a special resolution (a 75 per cent majority of votes of members present in person or by proxy at a general meeting of which at least 21 days' notice has been given (s378(2)). Coriander proposes an amendment. Amendments may be proposed, accepted and voted upon at a general meeting, but not amendments of substance (*Re Moorgate Mercantile Holdings Ltd* [1980] 1 WLR 227). The name is clearly fundamental and this would have been a substantial amendment, so the Chairman was wrong to put it to the meeting. However, the resolution to change the name to 'Allspice' was not validly passed since with Coriander voting against a 75 per cent majority could not have been obtained.

As regards resolution (b), the amendment here may fall within the definition of 'clerical error' and might thus be acceptable. As only an ordinary resolution is needed (s121) to alter the capital (provided a reduction is not proposed), Coriander's 26 per cent would not be sufficient to block it. Thus, it would appear to have been validly passed.

Turning to the resolution to remove Chilli, an ordinary resolution is always sufficient to remove a director (s303(1)). However, although Ginger and Saffron together hold one-twentieth of voting shares and are accordingly able to propose a resolution (s376(1)), their resolution can only be put to an AGM, and in any case a resolution to remove a director is invalid if at least 28 days' notice (special notice) of its proposal are not given. This is required under s303(2) to enable the director to make representations. Possibly it was also wrongly notified, since it appears to have been the Chairman's personal decision to give notice rather than a decision of the board. Finally, for the resolution to be passed on a majority of proxy votes, all of the proxies would need to have been valid and properly lodged in accordance with the articles. If the Chairman's casting vote was needed to attain a majority, it should have been exercised in accordance with the articles, ie there must have been an equality of votes for him to exercise a second vote (Table A, art 50).

It therefore seems that Coriander can challenge resolution 1. Passing a resolution by the wrong majority is an exception to the rule in *Foss v Harbottle* (1843) 2 Hare 461 but this would not mean that her choice of name would take precedence. A separate meeting would have to be requisitioned by Coriander to put this forward. She has sufficient voting capital under s368 to requisition a meeting (only 10 per cent is required) but it seems would have to lobby some support for her resolution.

Coriander apparently has no ground for challenging resolution (b), although this resolution dilutes her voting capital below the 26 per cent required for her to block a special resolution. Although *Clemens* v *Clemens* [1976] 2 All ER 268 suggests that such dilution is inequitable, it may be confined to the particular facts of a quasi-partnership company, and *Greenhalgh* v *Arderne Cinemas Ltd* [1946] 1 All ER 512 might support the view that it is generally acceptable for the majority to use their voting rights in this way. At best, she might try to argue that it is conduct unfairly prejudicial under s459 CA 1985, but such an argument seems unlikely to succeed.

The resolution to remove Chilli would seem to be invalid. However, if it seems likely that were the proper procedure to have been followed (28 days' notice, representations, etc) the resolution would still have been passed, the court may refuse to cancel it.

QUESTION TWO

Outline the formalities required for the calling of a company general meeting. Are the existing requirements sufficient to protect the interests of all concerned?

Written by the Editor

General Comment

For the most part this is a straightforward essay question, which merely requires a through knowledge of the relevant statutory provisions. The final part of the question does, however, call for some critical comment on the present rules, and it is no doubt on this part of the answer that the good student's ability will become apparent.

Skeleton Solution

Distinguish AGMs and EGMs: AGM each year; 21 days' notice required, unless short notice procedure followed – EGM when called by directors or requisitioned by 10 per cent of members; 14 days' notice needed – notice of meeting must specify business to be transacted – rules provide reasonable balance between too many GMs and too few, though creditors are entirely unprotected.

Suggested Solution

Company general meetings fall into two types, the Annual General Meeting (AGM) and Extraordinary General Meetings (EGMs). All meetings other than the AGM are EGMs.

An AGM must be held at least once in every calendar year, and no more than 15 months may elapse between AGMs. However, so long as a company holds its first AGM within 18 months of incorporation, it need not hold an AGM in the year of incorporation or in the following year (s366 Companies Act (CA) 1985). Twenty-one days' notice is required for the AGM, unless the articles provide for a longer period. Short notice is acceptable if consented to by all the members entitled to attend and vote at the AGM (s369(3)). The method of giving notice is specified in the articles, but will normally by by post to all members. However, s366A CA 1985 provides that a private company may dispense with AGMs.

Holders of 10 per cent of the votes may require the board to call an EGM (s368) and the court has power to call a meeting if the directors at any time wrongfully fail to do so (s371).

The notice of the meeting must specify the business to be transacted with sufficient particularity to enable members to decide whether or not to attend.

EGMs by definition do not happen at regular intervals. Normally the calling of them is at the discretion of the board, but attention is drawn to s368 (mentioned above). Only 14 days' notice is required for an EGM.

The question also asks about the protection of relevant interests. This is a difficult issue, since it is not clear that the rules really aim to protect any particular interest. As usual in company law it is possible to identify the shareholders, the directors and the creditors as three groups whose interests must be balanced. The GM is the residual authority within the company, retaining any powers which have not been delegated to the directors. From the directors' point of view it is important not to have too many GMs, since they are liable to interfere with the smooth running of the company. This may explain the rule that the calling of EGMs is normally to be left to me directors. At the same time it is necessary to have some GMs, so that the shareholders can be kept informed and can have the chance to express their views on important matters of company policy. Thus, there must be at least one GM in each year. The s368 power to requisition a meeting is also relevant in this context, since it provides a way in which a disaffected minority can air some of their grievances. In terms of controlling the directors the requirement of giving details of the business may also be mentioned. This operates to prevent unannounced resolutions from being slipped through a GM.

In general, therefore, the conclusion seems to be that the rules provide a reasonable balance between the directors and the shareholders. It is to be observed, though, that the interests of the creditors do not seem to be treated as being of any relevance here. Admittedly, it is hard to see what can be done about this, particularly since creditors have no right to attend the meeting anyway.

Chapter 9

Directors

9.1   **Introduction**

9.2   **Key points**

9.3   **Key cases and statutes**

9.4   **Questions and suggested solutions**

9.1 Introduction

Many of the other topics considered elsewhere involve directors since they are a fundamental part of the company structure. This chapter focuses mainly on the important area of directors' duties and abuse of position. Directors owe their duties to the company (*Percival* v *Wright* [1902] 2 Ch 421), and it is only when there is an exception to the rule in *Foss* v *Harbottle* (1843) 2 Hare 461 (see Chapter 11: *Minorities*) that individual members are entitled to sue them. The company may, however, sue for breach of duty if the majority of members so decide. Further controls include criminal sanctions for a director's failure to comply with statutory obligations, disqualification under the Company Directors Disqualification Act (CDDA) 1986 and the inalienable right of the company to remove a director from office at any time by ordinary resolution (s303 Companies Act (CA) 1985), subject to any compensation rights he may have acquired under his contract of service.

9.2 Key points

Fiduciary duties

Directors were originally regarded as trustees (*Aberdeen Railway Co* v *Blaikie Bros* (1854) 1 Macq 461) and, although it is accepted that they cannot be trustees in the fullest sense, they are still agents and quasi-trustees. As such they have some of the fiduciary duties of trustees, in particular the following.

Not to make a secret profit

Directors are not entitled to remuneration from the company (unless specified in the articles or under their service contract) and must not otherwise profit from their office or from information or opportunities obtained by virtue of their office. Such profits must be disclosed and approved. Otherwise they must be accounted for, even if the directors acted honestly (*Regal (Hastings) Ltd* v *Gulliver (1942)* [1942] 1 All ER 378) or the company could not itself have profited (*Industrial Development Consultants* v *Cooley* [1972] 1 WLR 443). It seems that an opportunity properly considered and rejected by the company can be taken up by a director (*Peso Silver Mines* v *Cropper* (1966) 58 DLR (2d) 1) and, strangely, there is no blanket prohibition against competing with the company (*Bell* v *Lever Brothers* [1933] AC 161). In connection with secret profits, students should note the requirement under s317 CA 1985 for directors to disclose to the board their interest in contracts made by the company, and its relationship with the common law rule against secret profits as discussed in *Guinness plc* v *Saunders and Another* [1988] 2 All ER 940.

The 'proper purpose' rule

Directors have a duty to use their powers only for the purpose for which they were given and not for some collateral purpose (*Hogg* v *Cramphorn* [1967] Ch 254), even though they believe it to be for the benefit of the company (*Howard Smith Ltd* v *Ampol Petroleum Ltd* [1974] AC 821). In both of these cases directors used their power to allot unissued capital for the purpose of defeating a takeover bid and were held to have breached their fiduciary duties. Acts in breach of the proper purpose rule can, however, be ratified by the general meeting (*Bamford* v *Bamford* [1970] Ch 212). For a more modern consideration of the rule, see *Lee Panavision Ltd* v *Lee Lighting Ltd* [1991] BCC 620.

Duties of care and skill

Like anyone else, directors must not act negligently in the performance of their duties. The problem, however, has always been the standard of care, which was fixed artificially low by Romer J in *Re City Equitable Fire Insurance Co Ltd* [1925] Ch 407 when the following rules were formulated:

a) no greater skill is required of a director than may reasonably be expected from someone of his knowledge and experience;

b) a director is not bound to give continuous attention to the affairs of his company, nor bound to attend meetings;

c) in the absence of grounds for suspicion, directors are jusitified in trusting those to whom duties are delegated to perform them honestly.

These principles have been affected by contracts of service, which generally provide for a higher standard. Cases have been few and indecisive, but more recently it has been suggested that a higher standard is required at least from executive directors and professionals such as accountants (*Morgan Crucible Co plc* v *Hill Samuel Bank Ltd* [1991] 1 All ER 148). The Cadbury Report may have affected the situation in relation to non-executive directors also. The attitude of the courts in some of the disqualification cases also suggests that more stringent standards apply nowadays. It is becoming accepted that directors of a company must at least be acquainted with its business. The Listing

Rules require that the directors of a public limited company (plc) must collectively have appropriate expertise and experience for the management of the business. *Re Barings plc (No 5)* [2000] 1 BCLC 523 contains a statement that directors must have, both collectively and individually, a continuing duty to acquire and maintain a sufficient knowledge and understanding of the company's business to enable them to properly discharge their duties as directors. Whilst directors are entitled (subject to the articles of association) to delegate particular functions to those below them in the management chain and to trust their competence and integrity to a reasonable extent, the exercise of the power of delegation does not absolve a director from the duty to supervise the discharge of the delegated functions. No rule of universal application can be formulated as to the duty referred to above. The extent of the duty, and the question of whether it has been discharged, must depend on the facts of each particular case, including the director's role in the management of the company.

Contractual duties

For the most part, the modern director will have a service contract which will regulate his obligations to the company and vice versa. These duties subsist notwithstanding anything in the company's constitution (*Southern Foundries Ltd* v *Shirlaw* [1940] AC 701). However, directors have a duty to manage the affairs of the company in accordance with the memorandum and articles of association (*Quinn & Axtens* v *Salmon* [1909] AC 442).

Statutory duties

The statutory requirements to file accounts and other documentation at the Companies Registry, and otherwise to comply with the provisions of the Companies Acts, fall on the directors. Failure to perform these duties can attract personal liability for fines and even imprisonment, or disqualification under the Company Directors Disqualification Act (CDDA) 1986. Particular note should be taken of s309 CA 1985, which provides that directors must have regard in the performance of their functions to the interests of employees as well as members. Questions are also very often set on on wrongful or fraudulent trading (ss213–214 Insolvency Act 1986), which may be seen in terms of directors' duties, particularly towards creditors, and are dealt with in Chapter 13: *Liquidations*.

Types of director

The law makes no distinction between executive and non-executive directors, although such distinction is of considerable practical importance (see Chapter 15: *External Influences: the EC, Corporate Governance and Human Rights*). In the 1980s, statute introduced the concept of 'shadow directors' (persons 'in accordance with whose directions or instructions the directors of the company are accustomed to act') as an anti-avoidance device, to prevent directors evading their obligations by appointing others in their stead to hold the title but not the power or responsibility.

Property transactions with directors

The scope for directors to abuse their position by using company assets for personal gain is considerable. The fiduciary duties being somewhat limited, statute has forbidden certain transactions (subject to specified exceptions) such as loans by the company to its directors, shadow directors or persons connected with its directors (students should become familiar with the relevant definitions), and imposes stringent requirements regarding disclosure and valuation of others.

Directors' powers

Abuse or excess of power is another important aspect of this topic which has already been dealt with in some detail in Chapter 2: *The Memorandum of Association and Legal Capacity*. The powers of managing the company are given to the directors' collectively (the board), although the board may delegate to individual directors. Usually, a company's articles will give the board all the management powers and, despite an early decision to the contrary (*Isle of Wight* v *Tahourdin* (1883) 25 Ch D 320), the shareholders cannot purport to exercise any of those powers themselves (*Quinn & Axtens* v *Salmon* [1909] AC 442; *Shaw & Sons (Salford) Ltd* v *Shaw* [1935] 2 KB 113), unless the board cannot or will not exercise its powers, eg because of deadlock or where there are no directors able to act.

Disqualification

Disqualification of a person from acting as a director for some specified period may be obtained on one of three grounds under the CDDA 1986.

a) The most serious is misconduct in relation to a company, which includes such matters as conviction of an indictable offence (s2), persistent breaches of companies legislation (s3), and fraudulent trading or other fraud or breach of duty in connection with a winding-up (s4).

b) The second category is 'unfitness'. This is a broader category which attracts a period of disqualification between two and 15 years depending on the seriousness of the case (*Re Sevenoaks Stationers (Retail) Ltd* [1991] Ch 164). The court must make an order if satisfied that the person concerned has been a director of a company which has at any time become insolvent and his conduct was such as to make him unfit to be concerned in the management of a company (s6). Schedule 1 to the Act lists matters for determining unfitness but these are not exhaustive.

c) The residual category includes wrongful trading (s10), being a director while an undischarged bankrupt (s11) and failure to pay under an administration order (s12).

The considerable body of case law deals mainly with the types of conduct which may lead to disqualification and the appropriate periods.

9.3 Key cases and statutes

*   *Aberdeen Railway Co v Blaikie Bros* (1854) 1 Macq 461
    Directors were originally regarded as trustees

*   *Ball v Eden Project Ltd* (2001) The Times 6 June
    Director of Eden project registered 'The Eden Project' as own trademark – held to be breach of fiduciary duty to company

*   *Barings plc (No 5), Re* [2000] 1 BCLC 523
    Knowledge requirement for directors

*   *City Equitable Fire Insurance Co Ltd, Re* [1925] Ch 407
    Formulates standard of care expected of directors

*   *Continental Assurance Co of London plc, Re* (1996) The Times 2 July
    Serious incompetence, such as failing to read the company's accounts, may justify a disqualification order

*   *Duckwari plc v Offerventure Ltd* [1995] BCC 89
    A company entering into an arrangement with a director for acquisition of non-cash assets without obtaining the approval of the general meeting, contrary to s320(1)(d) CA 1985

*   *Gibson Davies Ltd, Re* [1995] BCC 11
    Application under s17 CDDA 1986 for leave to act as a director while disqualified under s6 CDDA 1986

*   *Grayan Building Services Ltd (In Liquidation), Re* [1995] 3 WLR 1 (Court of Appeal)
    In a case of disqualification the court cannot take into account conduct subsequent to that relied on to obtain the order

*   *Guinness plc v Saunders and Anor* [1988] 2 All ER 940
    Disclosure of interest in contracts

*   *Hogg v Cramphorn* [1967] Ch 254
    Directors must use powers only for the purpose for which they were given

*   *Industrial Development Consultants v Cooley* [1972] 1 WLR 443
    Profits must be accounted for even if the company could not have made them itself

*   *Lee Panavision Ltd v Lee Lighting Ltd* [1991] BCC 620
    Acts in breach of proper purpose rule may still be ratified

*   *Living Images Ltd, Re* [1996] BCC 112
    A director of an insolvent company who authorised a preferential transaction could not be disqualified unless he knew the company desired to benefit the creditor and was influenced by that desire

*   *Moorgate Metals Ltd, Re* [1995] BCC 143; *Richborough Furniture Ltd, Re* [1996] BCC 155
    A de facto director may be disqualified, but it must be clearly shown he was the sole

person, or acted with other shadow directors, who directed the affairs of the company, or acted with validly appointed directors

- *Morgan Crucible Co plc v Hill Samuel Bank Ltd* [1991] 1 All ER 148
  Suggestions that a higher standard of care may be required

- *Neptune (Vehicle Washing Equipment) Ltd v Fitzgerald* [1995] BCC 474
  A sole director must still declare any interest in a company's contracts under s317 at a directors' meeting and have it minuted

- *Percival v Wright* [1902] 2 Ch 421
  Directors owe their duty to the company

- *Peskin v Anderson* [2001] 1 BCLC 372
  Changing company's constitutional restrictions on the purposes for which directors may exercise their power is not necessarily an improper purpose

- *Peso Silver Mines v Cropper* (1965) 58 DLR (2d) 1
  An opportunity considered and rejected by the company can be taken up by a director

- *Regal (Hastings) Ltd v Gulliver* (1942) [1967] 2 AC 134n
  Profits must be accounted for even if the directors acted honestly

- *Secretary of State for Trade and Industry v McTighe (No 2)* [1996] 2 BCLC 477
  The court may consider specific examples of unfitness

- *Working Project Ltd, Re* [1995] BCC 197
  Disqualification proceedings may be brought after winding-up concluded

- Companies Act 1985

  - s303 – removal of directors

  - s317 – disclosure by directors of interest in contracts

  - s309 – directors need to have regard to interests of employees as well as those of shareholders

- Company Directors Disqualification Act 1986, ss2 to 11 – deal with the grounds for obtaining a disqualification order

- Insolvency Act 1986, ss213 to 214 – dealing with wrongful and fraudulent trading

9.4 Questions and suggested solutions

QUESTION ONE

The issued, ordinary shares in Daffy Ltd are held as follows: Sam owns 20, Zenon owns 20, Cynthia owns 25 and Cynthia's husband, Billy, owns the remaining 35. Billy is the managing director of Daffy Ltd. Last year Billy and Cynthia used their voting superiority to ensure that Daffy Ltd employed Billy's son, John, as a director. John is a notoriously erratic and unreliable businessman who has avoided personal bankruptcy several times in the past only by being helped out financially by Billy. Since that time, John has committed Daffy Ltd to several apparently ridiculous transactions, which have nonetheless and against all rational prediction proved highly beneficial to Daffy Ltd. However, both Sam and Zenon are concerned that John may ruin Daffy Ltd despite his recent luck. Billy and John are now proposing firstly, to cut the dividend payment on the shares, and secondly, to award John a new service contract with an enhanced profit-related pay element, which will operate retrospectively over the past 12 months so as to award John a large cash bonus.

Advise Sam and Zenon.

University of London LLB Examination
(for External Students) Company Law June 2000 Q6

General Comment

The difficulty with this question is that it concerns a private company and the courts are loath to interfere with the running of private companies unless there is evidence of fraud.

Skeleton Solution

Potential breaches of director's duties – the remedies available to the minority shareholders – s459 Companies Act 1985 – are the directors using their power for an improper purpose and are they being unfairly prejudicial to the members – can the majority shareholders ratify the wrongs of the directors – do the minority shareholders have any power or control in the appointment and removal of directors under s303 Companies Act 1985?

Suggested Solution

The courts have taken the view that a shareholder must take the risk that the directors of a company may turn out to be of poor quality and they have been reluctant to concern themselves with examining commercial decisions that have been taken by directors: *Re Sam Weller and Sons Ltd* [1990] Ch 682. In *Re Elgindata Ltd* [1991] BCLC 959, a case decided under s459 Companies Act (CA) 1985 allegations of bad management against a director failed. However, in the case of *Re Macro (Ipswich) Ltd and Another* [1994] BCC 781 the court held that mismanagement is capable of amounting to unfairly prejudicial conduct, but the mismanagement must be sufficiently serious for the courts to intervene.

A majority of the shareholders can usually relieve directors for breach of their duty to the company unless there has been a fraud, but this might constitute unfair prejudice to a dissenting minority.

Section 459 CA 1985 requires that a petitioner shall demonstrate prejudice to the interests of some part of the members (including himself) and the grievance must be more than a dispute over company policy and management arrangements as the following cases demonstrate. In *Re Jermyn Street Turkish Baths* [1971] 1 WLR 1047 there had been two shareholders, one of whom had been guarantor of the company's bank overdraft at the time of his death. Thereafter the controlling shareholder had restored the financial position of the company and enabled it to pay off the overdraft. She had allotted more shares to herself and under a pre-agreed formula most of the profits went to her as management commission. No dividends were paid. This was held not to be 'oppression' of the estate of the deceased shareholder and it would almost certainly not be treated as 'unfair prejudice'.

In the case of *Re RA Noble Clothing Ltd* [1983] BCLC 273, there were two shareholder directors, one of whom provided most of the capital and the other managed the company's business. It was agreed between them that the managing director would consult the other over important matters of policy, but he failed to do so and the other appeared to acquiesce. However, they then quarrelled and the petitioner alleged that the lack of agreed consultation was unfair prejudice. The petition was dismissed.

In *Re A Company* [1983] 2 All ER 36, the executors of a deceased shareholder proposed that the company should apply its surplus funds to purchase the shares of the deceased, since they urgently needed the money to support dependants of the deceased. The directors, however, used the money to diversify the business. This was not unfair prejudice to the minority. However, it seems that an unduly restrictive policy over a long period in distributing profits as dividends may amount to unfair prejudice. In *Re Carrington Viyella plc* [1983] 1 BCC 98 the petition was founded on the company's failure to approve the chairman's long term service agreement which was not considered to amount to unfair prejudice.

Section 459 CA 1985 provides that any actual or proposed act or omission of the company or on its behalf may be unfairly prejudicial, which means that a petition can be based on a single decision of the company management.

Who may petition?

The right to present a petition under s459 is limited to a member of the company and the DTI. Sam and Zenon are clearly members of the company and so can present a petition.

The court's powers

If the court is of the opinion that the company's affairs are being conducted in a manner unfairly prejudicial to the interests of some part of the members then the court may make such order as it thinks fit for giving relief. The court has very wide-ranging powers in this situation, but the most usual request by petitioners is that the majority purchase their shares at a fair value. If Sam and Zenon are so unhappy with the state of affairs, this may be the best solution for them. Daffy is a private company and its articles of association may well contain limitations on who shares can be transferred to. If the court is minded to make such an order it will have to consider how to value the shares. In a normal valuation of a minority shareholding the valuer values the company as a whole and then makes some deduction from the proportionate value of the minority holding because it does not have control. In this situation the court has an unfettered discretion to decide whether or not to follow that practice, so if the petitioner is not at fault in any way the court might order a valuation on a strictly proportionate ration to the value of the whole company without deduction for lack of control.

Almost all the cases in recent years have related to disputes within small private companies of a quasi-partnership type and Daffy Ltd would appear to be no exception. There is a doubt as to how the court will view the facts of the dispute in relation to the concept of unfair prejudice. If Sam and Zenon wish to sue the controlling shareholders for wrong done they can ask the court in its discretion to authorise them to do so. The problem with s459 proceedings is the length and cost of the proceedings as was mentioned in *Re Unisoft Group Ltd (No 2)* [1994] BCC 766 and this often puts s459 beyond the resources of the smaller private companies. There are also concerns that s459 petitions could be used as tools of oppression to slow down the proper workings of business and the courts are very aware of this use of the petition.

In this case, John has been highly successful in the ventures he has embarked upon for Daffy and the fears are in the minds of Sam and Zenon. It is not certain that they would be successful in a petition under s459. However, by paying John a salary in the form of a cash bonus retrospectively and also cutting the dividend payment, the directors are using their powers for an improper purpose and are carrying on the affairs of the company in a manner which is unfairly prejudicial to the interests of the members. Sections 318 and 319 CA 1985 provide controls on directors' service contracts but do not control bonuses.

Can the majority shareholders ratify the directors acts?

Ratification would need to occur under the rule in *Foss* v *Harbottle* (1843) 2 Hare 461 and Sam and Zenon would need to establish that the rule does not apply in this case because the breach of duty relates to the enforcement of rights conferred upon the shareholder personally and is therefore nothing to do with the company. In addition, the breach relates to the misappropriation of company property and company property is something that all shareholders have a pro rata interest in.

Are there any other remedies which might be available to Sam and Zenon?

It is difficult as they do not command enough votes to pass an ordinary resolution. They do, however, have negative control of the company and can at least stop resolutions being passed which require a special resolution. The cannot remove John from office under the s303 procedures, but they can requisition general meetings and put forward the proposal that John should be removed.

The practical solution to their difficulties would be to ask the other members to buy them out of their shareholding so that they could invest their money elsewhere.

QUESTION TWO

The main business of Elite Properties plc is the acquisition, development, and disposition of property. There are eight directors who own 15m of the company's 25m issued £1 shares. At a meeting of the board of directors about a year ago, a proposal was presented for the purchase of a site adjoining a rubbish dump. Although the price asked was low (£3m for seven acres), it was felt that the situation might make it difficult to develop the site and sell any houses.

The site in question was, in fact, bought by Speculative Enterprises Ltd, whose share capital is held as to 25 per cent by Donald, Edward and Fred all of whom are directors of Elite Properties. Speculative Enterprises paid £2.5m for the site and a few weeks later sold it for £5m.

At a shareholders' meeting of Elite Properties called to discuss the failure by Elite to purchase the site, the directors used their votes to prevent the passing of a resolution (a) calling on the directors to compensate the company for any loss caused by the failure to purchase the site and (b) calling on Donald, Edward and Fred to account for all profit made as shareholders and directors of Speculative Enterprises Ltd.

Discuss.

University of London LLB Examination
(for External Students) Company Law June 1991 Q6

General Comment

The question involves consideration of several areas and covers directors' fiduciary duties. This includes directors avoiding situations of conflict of interest and duty to the company. *Percival* v *Wright* [1902] 2 Ch 421 needs mentioning and contravention of s317 Companies Act (CA) 1985 and accountability of profits made by Donald, Edward and Fred.

Skeleton Solution

Directors duties owed to company only – consider implications of *Percival* v *Wright* – accountability for personal profit by Donald, Edward and Fred – breach of s317 – breach of fiduciary duty to act for the benefit of the company.

Suggested Solution

The fiduciary duties owed by directors are basically similar to those applying to any other fiduciary relationship, eg, between agent and principal or trustee and beneficiary. They are based upon the principle that since the company places its trust with the directors, they must display the utmost good faith towards the company they are dealing with or on its behalf.

Such fiduciary duties are owed to the company alone, in particular he owes no such duty to the shareholder: this was set out in *Percival* v *Wright* [1902] 2 Ch 421. This general principle has been somewhat modified by subsequent authority. Where the shares are held by only a few people as in *Coleman* v *Myers* [1977] 2 NZLR 298, or where there is a special situation such as a takeover (*Briess* v *Woolley* [1954] AC 333), directors may be held to owe a limited duty of care to the shareholder. There is a possibility this approach will be taken in modern law today.

However, the content of this duty must not be such as to create a conflict with the directors' fiduciary duties to the company. Section 309 Companies Act (CA) 1985 states that the directors when performing their functions must have regard to the interests of the members as well as the employees. The members may therefore wish to object to an act which may not be beneficial to them. Nevertheless, the directors may be able to refute this objection as they may consider it as good industrial practice and more advantageous to the company in the long run.

Hence, the resolution passed by the directors of Elite Properties plc preventing the passing of a resolution by the shareholders to discuss the company's failure to purchase the site is within their discretion, as they were concerned that the acquisition of this site might pose long term problems for the company. The directors of Elite do not have to maximise economic benefit to the company, as they felt they were acting for the benefit of the company as a whole. Moreover, the rule in *Foss* v *Harbottle* (1843) 2 Hare 461 would prevent the shareholders from bringing an action, as the wrong is done to the company and it is for the company to decide what action to take. The company would be the proper plaintiff in such an action.

A director who is anyway interested in a contract with the company must declare the nature of his interest at a board meeting: s317 CA 1985. Donald, Edward and Fred would have clearly contravened this requirement and are personally liable to a fine as they made no mention of their interests in the acquisition of the site rejected by Elite Properties plc.

Further, directors have a fiduciary duty not to use either corporate information or opportunity to make an undisclosed personal profit. In *Industrial Development Consultants* v *Cooley* [1972] 1 WLR 443, the managing director of IDC feigned illness in order to secure the termination of his contract. He then took out a contract in his own name which he had unsuccessfully tried to obtain for the company. Courts held he had to account to IDC for his profits. This was also illustrated in the case of *Boston Deep Sea Fishing Co* v *Ansell* (1888) 39 Ch D 339.

There is however a Commonwealth authority supporting the proposition that a director may retain a profit derived from an opportunity that the company has considered and rejected. In the Canadian case of *Peso Silver Mines* v *Cropper* (1966) 58 DLR (2d) 1, Peso's board considered and rejected the chance to purchase prospecting claims near the company's land. One of Peso's directors bought shares in a new company which was subsequently formed to purchasese the claims. Courts held he did not have to account for his profits. This decision has been widely criticised by academics and has been described by Professor Gower as 'unsatisfactory and undesirable'.

The outcome of the call made on Donald, Edward and Fred to account for all the profit made as shareholders and directors of Speculative Enterprises Ltd would be influenced by several factors in light of *Peso Silver Mines* v *Cropper* (1966) 58 DLR (2d) 1. This would include the percentage of shares held by Donald, Edward and Fred in Speculative Enterprises Ltd respectively. Other factors would be the part played by all three in the Board's decision to reject the site and whether there is any link between the two transactions.

It is submitted, however, that Elite Properties plc will have a good cause of action to make Donald, Edward and Fred personally accountable for the percentage of profits made as shareholders cum directors of Speculative Enterprises Ltd. They have clearly taken advantage of a commercial opportunity as a result of being directors of Elite Properties plc.

QUESTION THREE

Basil and Brenda have for many years been active in the business of property development. They are the directors of Alpha Limited and own about 65 per cent of the shares. The remainder of the shares are spread among some seven or eight shareholders who take little or no part in the running of the company. Basil and Brenda were also directors of Delta Limited, a company in which they held all the shares but which was recently placed in creditors' voluntary winding-up and in which there is a substantial deficit such that creditors can expect no more than 15 pence in the pound.

The main business of both companies was (and is) the purchase of suitable property, its redevelopment for either commercial or residential use and then its sale. Despite the downturn in the economy, Basil and Brenda continued throughout 1990 and 1991 with an aggressive purchasing policy. They were advised on several occasions by the companies' auditors to slow down, but they rejected this advice. This policy led directly to the insolvent liquidation of Delta Limited and, although it seems that this will be avoided in the case of Alpha Limited, that company has suffered huge losses. There will be no dividends for years to come.

These problems were increased by the huge donations of £50,000 which Basil and Brenda caused Alpha Limited to make to the Conservative Party in 1989 and again in 1990. Basil and Brenda have considerable private means and the following transaction has also recently come to light. In the middle of 1991, before the liquidation of Delta Limited, Basil and Brenda learned of the sale of a property in North London for £150,000. As it would have been difficult to raise the finance through either Alpha or Delta, Basil and Brenda bought this property in their own names. It now turns out that this property is much more valuable than anticipated since the Local Authority has unexpectedly allowed redevelopment of this property without any restrictions. As a result Basil and Brenda are planning to sell this property for £350,000.

Advise the liquidator of Delta Limited and the minority shareholders of Alpha Limited. (Ignore the statutory remedies under s459 of the Companies Act 1985 and s122(1)(g) of the Insolvency Act 1986.)

University of London LLB Examination
(for External Students) Company Law June 1992 Q4

General Comment

Although this question is concerned with the duties of directors it also embraces aspects which are only marginally within that topic. The wholly separate issue of the rule in *Foss* v *Harbottle* (1843) 2 Hare 461 is also raised. The candidate's ability to summon up material gleaned from quite distinct parts of company law is also tested.

Skeleton Solution

Delta Ltd – possible negligence claim against directors – fraudulent trading – wrongful trading – Alpha Ltd – negligence – ultra vires – fiduciary duty – rule in *Foss* v *Harbottle*.

Suggested Solution

As to Delta Ltd, it is possible that the directors have handled the company's affairs negligently. But the approach taken by the law in determining whether directors have been negligent could be regarded as somewhat lenient. It must first be ascertained what knowledge and experience the individual director has concerning the activity in question; having found what the knowledge and experience is, the director is then expected by law to have made a reasonable exercise of it: *Re Brazilian Rubber Plantations and Estates Ltd* [1911] 1 Ch 425; *Re City Equitable Fire Insurance Co Ltd* [1925] Ch 407. But the subjective test is now seen as too lenient. Directors these days must show that they know what the business of the company is and that the board has the appropriate expertise and experience for the management of its business. Increasingly, directors' competence is being measured on an objective standard. It is therefore possible that one director or both directors would incur liability under this head. If a claim were to be made under this head, the liquidator would sue in the name of and on behalf of the company (s165 and Sch 4, Pt II Insolvency Act (IA) 1986).

If the company is in liquidation as is the case here and it appears that its business has been carried on with intent to defraud creditors or for any fraudulent purpose, the court may on the liquidator's application order anyone who was knowingly party to the fraudulent trading to make such contribution to the company's assets as the court thinks proper (s213 IA 1986). The mental element in fraudulent trading requires '... real dishonesty involving, according to current notions of fair trading among commercial men at the present day, real moral blame': per Maughan J, in *Re Patrick and Lyon* [1933] All ER 590. Claims under this head are difficult to prove and therefore infrequent.

The liquidator is much more likely to make an application under s214 alleging wrongful trading by the directors; if established, the court may order such contribution to company assets as it thinks proper. Wrongful trading is committed, if the company has gone into insolvent liquidation, by any person who at some point in time before the liquidation commenced either knew or ought to have known that there was no reasonable prospect of the company avoiding insolvent liquidation, and who was a director of the company at that time. But it is a defence to the director to show that, from the time he knew or should have known of the pending insolvency, he thereafter took every step he ought to minimise loss to the company's creditors. Moreover the facts which he ought to have known, the conclusions he should have reached and the steps he should have taken are those attributable to a reasonable diligent person having the knowledge and experience which could reasonably be expected of a person carrying on the functions of that director, plus any knowledge and experience which he in fact possessed. It should be noted that, in contrast with a common law negligence action, s214 in effect requires the director to show, as a minimum, the knowledge and experience which could reasonably be expected of a holder of that post, and irrespective of whether he in fact has such knowledge and experience.

As to the principle governing assessment of the amount of the contribution should the wrongful trading claim succeed, *Re Produce Marketing Consortium Ltd* [1989] 1 WLR 745 should be cited and discussed.

As to Alpha Ltd, the possibility that the directors have been negligent is as it was in respect of Beta Ltd but there will be no claim for fraudulent trading or wrongful trading, since the company is not insolvent. As to the huge donations to a political party, the company may act within the objects clause (whose precise terms we do not know) of its memorandum, and is also by implication entitled to do things which are incidental or conducive thereto. Here the company might have express authority from its objects clause to make political gifts, but it is more probable that reliance will have to be placed on implication; in the former case the gift cannot be ultra vires (*Re Horsley & Weight Ltd* [1982] Ch 442), but otherwise the payment must have been for the benefit of the company, reasonably incidental to its business, and made bona fide in the interests of the company: *Re Lee, Behrens & Co Ltd* [1932] 2 Ch 46. Companies not infrequently make gifts to political parties whose programmes the directors regard as favourable to the commercial interests of the company.

The directors hold all their powers as fiduciaries, and must exercise them bona fide for the benefit of the company and for the purposes for which they were conferred, and must not without company authority profit from their position as directors. This will be particularly relevant to the North London land purchase; if the directors learned of the opportunity in their capacity as directors, they have profited from their position without authority to do so and should account to the company for the gains: *Regal (Hastings) Ltd v Gulliver* [1942] 1 All ER 378. Difficulties remain as to which company or companies the directors are accountable to for the gain – it would seem both are in the relevant area of activity – and in what proportion if liable to both, and whether ratification of what has been done in general meeting would be valid, as a dictum in *Regal* suggests.

Should the directors be liable for negligence or accountable for the profit, or both, the wrong is to a corporate body or bodies, hence under the rule in *Foss* v *Harbottle* (1843) 2 Hare 461 the company is the proper plaintiff, and prima facie the only person whom the court will hear as to the merits; since in this case the directors control the company through their shareholdings the company obviously will not resolve to sue. There are exceptions to the rule; these do not extend to claims for negligence (*Pavlides* v *Jensen* [1956] Ch 565) though it may be different where the directors have personally profited from the negligence at the company's expense (*Daniels* v *Daniels* [1978] Ch 406). An exception is also made when the alleged wrongdoers control the company and are alleged to have acted fraudulently; 'fraud' here is used in a wider sense than common law fraud and includes seriously oppressive conduct: *Estmanco (Kilner House) Ltd* v *Greater London Council* [1982] 1 All ER 437.

Where the wrong is to the company but, under an exception to *Foss* v *Harbottle*, a shareholder is permitted to sue, he does so in what is termed a derivative action; he must also make the company a party to the suit as co-defendant, since the right of action is in truth that of the company and the court is thereby enabled to award damages or other relief, should he succeed, to the company. He must also bring a representative action, suing on behalf of himself and all other shareholders except the defendants, with the consequence that all persons involved are bound by the judgment.

QUESTION FOUR

Robber plc has two wholly owned subsidiaries, Sud Ltd and Tot Ltd. Although all three companies satisfactorily function independently of each other, Robber plc is to some extent reliant on the factories of the subsidiaries for supplies of electronic circuitry for its missile factory.

The board of directors of Tot Ltd have decided that it is virtually essential for Tot Ltd to acquire a more powerful computer system for its factory. Tot Ltd can only afford to raise £150,000 for this, but the system needed, the 'Biggerbyte 601' normally costs around £250,000. The board have recently heard, however, that Ven is prepared to supply the 'Biggerbyte 601' for £180,000, and that Sud Ltd would be prepared to lend £30,000 to Tot Ltd to help with this. Ven holds 15 per cent of the shares in Robber plc and is hoping to use the proceeds of sale of the 'Biggerbyte 601' to acquire a further 3 per cent.

At their board meeting last week, the directors of Tot Ltd decided to go ahead with the purchase of the 'Biggerbyte 601' from Ven, partly because of the low price he is offering and also because they would be happy to see him acquire more shares in Robber plc since they believe that Ven's large stake acts as a deterrent to foreign takeover bidders. The directors of Tot Ltd are anxious to go ahead but have heard that there may be legal problems.

Advise the board of directors of Tot Ltd.

University of London LLB Examination
(for External Students) Company Law June 1993 Q8

General Comment

A fairly difficult question requiring the candidate to contemplate precisely the crux of the problem. Not to be undertaken without a very careful reading of and reflection upon the problem.

Skeleton Solution

Financial assistance: definition of; purpose of prohibition – fiduciary duties of directors: duty to act bona fide; duty not to act for any collateral purpose; principal and subsidiary purposes.

Suggested Solution

The directors of Tot Ltd must consider in depth two matters before purchasing the 'Biggerbyte 601'. In view of the fact that Ven intends to acquire further shares in Robber plc the directors must question whether: (a) the purchase might fall foul of the financial assistance provisions in s151 Companies Act (CA) 1985; and (b) whether in deciding whether or not to purchase the computer it is proper for them to have regard to Ven's proposed acquisition of shares in Robber plc.

Dealing with the question of financial assistance, s151(1) CA 1985 prohibits the provision of financial assistance by a company or its subsidiary where a person is proposing to acquire shares in that company. On the facts Ven is quite clearly proposing to acquire shares in Robber plc, the parent of Tot Ltd. The next step therefore is to ask whether there is financial assistance.

The principle underpinning the prohibition on financial assistance is to protect creditors from unlawful reductions of capital. Whilst financial assistance is defined very widely (but not exhaustively) in s152 of the Act it is worth bearing in mind the dictum of Hoffmann J in *Charterhouse Investment Trust Ltd* v *Tempest Diesels Ltd* [1986] BCLC 1, that the prohibition is penal and ought not therefore to receive a strained construction in order to catch transactions not intended to be caught. This Hoffmann J stated required the court to look at the 'realities' of the transaction. Assistance by gift or guarantee is usually fairly easy to recognise. What however where, as in the instant case, there is a straightforward purchase?

Financial assistance is defined in s152 CA 1985 as including the following: assistance by way of loan or any other agreement whereby the obligations of the giver are fulfilled at a time when reciprocal obligations remain unfulfilled. Also 'any other assistance' which reduces the assets of the company. This part of the definition arguably catches any transaction whereby the assistance is not matched by the company acquiring assets of an equivalent value. Applying this to the facts of the instant case it can be seen that Tot Ltd is to pay £180,000 for a computer which is arguably worth £250,000. The assets of Tot Ltd are likely therefore to be swelled rather than reduced and so the transaction does not reduce the company's assets. There is therefore no financial assistance within the meaning of the Act.

In committing Tot Ltd to the purchase, are the directors abusing their fiduciary duty to act in the best interests of the company? It is difficult to discern any consistent thread running through the authorities on this area. The predominance of authorities concern directors' improper allotments eg where at least one of the purposes of the allotment is to destroy an existing majority or to create a new one: *Hogg* v *Cramphorn* [1967] Ch 254. The underlying principle is however the same. Can directors' actions be underpined by a dual purpose or must directors never act for any collateral purpose?

In *Re Smith and Fawcett Ltd* [1942] Ch 304, Lord Greene MR stated that directors should exercise their discretion in what they and not the court consider to be the best interests of the company, and not for any collateral purpose. The difficulty is of course that directors' actions are often motivated by any number of purposes. In *Mills* v *Mills* (1938) 60 CLR 150, Latham CJ stated that where there is more than one purpose, the proper question to be asked is, 'What is the moving cause?'. Provided generally that the moving cause is the benefit of the company then the course of action will not be upset by the court.

This view was subsequently adopted by the Privy Council in *Howard Smith Ltd* v *Ampol Petroleum Ltd* [1974] AC 821. In particular Lord Wilberforce stated that the starting point would be to identify the power under consideration (eg, to allot shares) and then to examine the substantial purpose for which it was exercised. This approach seems at first glance very sensible. There may nevertheless be difficulties with it. It is presumably open to directors to attempt to protect themselves by passing a board resolution in favour of a particular course and to express as the dominant purpose what is in fact the subsidiary purpose. The courts will of course look at the factual reality of the situation as well as the declared intention of the directors. But the dominant purpose will be frequently difficult to ascertain. Once it is admitted that there is more than one purpose underpinning a particular act, how are the courts to determine dominancy? For example, as in the instant case, it may be that a new computer is very desirable (as is Ven's increased shareholding in Robber plc) rather than an absolute necessity.

It is useful to consider briefly the approach of the High Court of Australia in *Whitehouse* v *Carlton Pty Ltd* (1987) 11 ACLR 715. In this case the court preferred to ask whether the exercise of a power was causally connected with collateral purpose ie if the power would not have been exercised 'but for the' collateral purpose then the exercise of that power should not be upheld. This approach arguably avoids the difficulties occasioned by the dominant purpose test but at the same time is a more stringent one. Applying the above to the facts of the problem it would be sensible to advise the directors of Tot Ltd to direct their minds specifically to the dominant purpose of the purchase, and to proceed with it only if they conclude that they are principally motivated by benefit to Tot Ltd.

Chapter 10

Insider Dealing

10.1 Introduction

10.2 Key points

10.3 Key cases and statutes

10.4 Questions and suggested solutions

10.1 Introduction

This chapter deals with the situation where a person who is in possession of unpublished price-sensitive information about a company uses that information to deal in the securities of that company so as to make a profit for himself. In some circumstances this is a criminal offence under Pt V Criminal Justice Act 1993 which came into force on 1 March 1994, repealing and replacing the Company Securities (Insider Dealing) Act (CS(ID)A) 1985.

10.2 Key points

Background

It has been a matter of some dispute whether the law should prohibit insider dealing. It is often referred to as a 'victimless crime' and some have argued that exploitation of inside information provides a useful incentive for directors and other entrepreneurs. On the other hand, it is argued that small investors in particular are at a disadvantage and that regulation is necessary to preserve confidence in the integrity of the market, and these arguments have been accepted. Against this, however, the legislation provides no remedy for those small investors who are disadvantaged, and it may be said they are perenially at a disadvantage when compared with institutional investors who have closer access to company sources and are 'courted' by companies and invited to special briefings. The law does nothing to redress this imbalance nor, at the other end of the scale, does it seem to have succeeded in combatting large-scale organised insider dealing. The first real attempt to control insider dealing, the Company Securities (Insider Dealing) Act 1985 attracted harsh criticism, including charges that the defences were too wide, the definitions too loose and that a civil remedy was not provided, as well as more practical criticisms concerning enforcement and evidence. Part V Criminal Justice Act 1993 was enacted not so much in response to such criticism but to implement Community Directive No 89/592/EEC which requires Member States to regulate insider dealing, and proclaims itself as a 'restatement' of the law. It may be seen, therefore, as having amended the form rather than the substance of the 1985 Act and its main effect has been to tighten the definitions laid down by its predecessor.

The offence

Section 52 provides that an individual who has information as an insider is guilty of insider dealing if he deals in price-affected securities in relation to that information, encourages another to deal or discloses the information otherwise than in the proper performance of his employment, office or profession. The dealing must be on a regulated market or through a professional intermediary.

The defences

Section 53 provides the following defences:

a) the accused did not at the time expect the dealing to result in a profit attributable to the fact that the information was price sensitive;

b) at the time he believed on reasonable grounds that the information had been disclosed widely enough to ensure that no one taking part in the dealing would be prejudiced by not having it;

c) he would have done what he did even if he had not had the information.

The defences to a charge of disclosing inside information are:

a) he did not at the time expect any person to deal in the securities because of the disclosure;

b) he did expect this but not that it would result in a profit attributable to the fact that the information was price sensitive.

Definitions

Sections 56–60 define the terms used in the substantive parts of the legislation. The most important are noted below.

Inside information (s56(1))

This relates to a particular security or issuer of securities and is not general, is specific or precise, has not been made public and if it were would be likely to have a significant effect on the price of any securities.

Insider (s57(1))

A person has information as an insider if, and only if, it is (and he knows it is) inside information, he has it and knows he has it from an inside source.

Inside source (s57(2))

An inside source is someone who: has information through being a director, employee or shareholder of an issuer of securities; or has access to the information by virtue of his employment office or profession; or has been given the information by a director, employee or shareholder of an issuer of securities.

Penalties (s61(1))

On summary conviction, a fine up to the statutory maximum or six months' imprisonment and, on indictment, an unlimited fine and/or seven years' imprisonment.

Market abuse and the Financial Services and Markets Act 2000

The Financial Services and Markets Act 2000 empowers the Financial Services Authority (FSA) to fine persons who engage in market abuse, which is defined as behaviour occurring in relation to certain investments traded on certain markets which is:

a) based on information unavailable to informed participants in the market who are unaware of it, but if they were aware of it would be likely to regard it as relevant in deciding whether or not to enter into transactions involving investments of that kind; and/or

b) likely to give such participants a mistaken impression as to supply of, or demand for, or the price or value of, investments of that kind; and/or

c) likely to distort the market as far as it relates to investments of that kind.

It is also behaviour which (if the circumstances were publicly known or the behaviour became commonplace or both) would be likely to damage the confidence of such informed participants that the market, so far as it relates to relevant investments of that kind, is a true and fair market. Informed participant means a participant in the market who has an understanding of the market, and behaviour includes inaction as well as action. The FSA initially decides whether someone has engaged in market abuse and serves a warning notice on that person, who has then 28 days to make representations. If thereafter the FSA is still minded to fine the person it must serve a decision notice. In limited circumstances, the court may decide whether or not there has been market abuse. The FSA decides on the amount of the fine to be levied and there is no upper limit.

10.3 Key cases and statutes

Most of the convictions obtained under the CS(ID)A 1985 concerned one-off transactions by single persons in relation to small companies. The important reported cases concerned the interpretation of provisions of the Act which are now repealed. There is virtually no case law on the provisions of the new legislation.

- *Attorney-General's Reference (No 1 of 1988)* [1989] AC 971
  Closing of a loophole

- *Chase Manhattan Equities Ltd* v *Goodman* [1991] BCLC 897
  Penalties (but has been reversed by s63(2) Criminal Justice Act 1993)

- *Chez Nico (Restaurants) Ltd, Re* [1991] BCC 736
  Status of city code

- Criminal Justice Act 1993, Pt V

- Financial Services and Markets Act 2000 – empowers Financial Services Authority
  to fine people engaged in market abuse

10.4 Questions and suggested solutions

QUESTION ONE

Sally is a trainee solicitor working in her firm's corporate department. She overhears a senior lawyer from another team in Sally's firm taking a telephone call from the chairman of Target plc during the course of which she learns that a take-over bid for the share capital of Target plc is to be announced by Hungry plc the following week. She tells her boyfriend James that evening about what she has heard. James is a stockbroker and the next day he buys up traded options on the market to acquire Target shares for £1 each. On Monday of the following week, Hungry plc makes public its bid for Target plc shares and Target plc shares rise to £5 each. James exercises his options over Target plc shares and then immediately resells them for £5 each, netting a profit of £4 per share.

Discuss.

University of London LLB Examination
(for External Students) Company Law June 2000 Q4

General Comment

Candidates should be aware that they are asked to discuss this scenario and are not asked to advise one or other of the parties. Therefore, candidates should consider all parties and the ambit of the question becomes slightly more general than it would be if candidates were asked to advise one of the parties.

Skeleton Solution

What information does Sally, as a potential insider, have? – does that information meet the definition of inside information contained in s56 Criminal Justice Act 1993? – if the information is inside information was it obtained as an insider as defined in s57? – are the securities price-affected securities? – has Sally committed any offence? – can any relevant defences be established? – the same questions should be asked about James.

Suggested Solution

The idea that directors are not permitted to make a secret profit extends into the prohibition against insider trading which since the passing of the Criminal Justice Act (CJA) 1993 has been extended to a wider group of people than directors. Generally speaking insider dealing involves the deliberate exploitation of unpublished price-sensitive information obtained through a privileged relationship to make a profit by dealing in the securities of a company when the price of the securities would be altered if the information were to be disclosed.

Is Sally an Insider?

The offence of insider dealing can be committed only by a natural person and not by a company. Sally will be an insider if she has information that she knows is inside information and that she knows is from an inside source. Under s57 CJA 1993 Sally will hold the information as an insider if she knows it to be inside information and she knows that she has received that inside information from an inside source. This is a subjective belief and understanding. Anyone can be an insider, but the information must come from a director of the issuer. Sally has heard the information during the course of her employment and from the way in which the question is phrased she is aware that the information is coming from the Chairman of Target plc.

Is this inside information?

Section 56(1) CJA 1993 describes what constitutes inside information. It has to relate to particular shares or a particular issuer; it cannot be general information. Information relating to a takeover bid is regarded as information relating to a particular issuer. Second, the information must be specific or precise. The information that Sally receives is that there is to be a takeover bid and this is specific information under this section. There is no suggestion that the information is a rumour and it is probably not a casual remark. The information must not have been made public. Section 58 CJA 1993 gives some assistance to understanding what is meant by being made public in this context. The s58 guidance does not equate to publication in the defamation sense but deals with actual publication in the form of information provided to investors or to be found in public records. The facts indicate that this information has not been made public. Finally, to constitute inside information the information has to be of such weight that were it to be made public it would be likely to have a significant impact on the price of the shares. We are told that James buys uptraded options, and these will fall within the Sch 2 definition of securities.

The offence contained in s52 CJA 1993 is that of dealing with price-affected securities in a prohibited way, which means dealing with the securities yourself, encouraging another person to deal in the securities or disclosing information other than in the proper performance of employment. In considering whether Sally has encouraged James to deal in the securities it makes no difference whether she stands to make any gain from the deal. We are not given sufficient information about the conversation between Sally and James regarding the takeover. Exactly what sort of behaviour is covered by the expression 'encouragement' is unclear. It will therefore be difficult to conclude that Sally has in fact encouraged James to deal in the shares. However, on the facts it would appear that Sally will be guilty of insider dealing as she has disclosed the information otherwise than in the proper performance of her employment and in this situation it is irrelevant whether Sally intends James to act on the information or suspects that he might.

Defences

We now need to consider if any defences may be available to Sally. By virtue of s53 CJA 1993 Sally will have a defence if she can show that she did not expect the dealing in the shares to result in a profit. Again, this may be difficult to prove to the satisfaction of the court as James is a stockbroker and would be presumed to know that a profit would result from such a transaction. The second possible defence is that Sally believed that this information had been widely disclosed. This defence may be open to Sally to use, but we are not given sufficient information to reach a conclusion on this point.

James' interests

James has received the information and knows that it is inside information. He will be an insider by virtue of being tipped off by Sally and so will fall under s57(2)(b) CJA 1993. He has dealt with securities that are price-affected securities and so has committed an offence under s52(1) CJA 1993. Are any defences available to James? The only possible defence might be the use of market information under Sch 1, para 2(1), which provides that a person who has market information as an insider has a defence to a charge of insider dealing if they can show that it was reasonable for them to have acted as they did despite being in possession of the information as an insider. However, para 2(2) states that account must be taken of the circumstances and capacity in which the individual first had the information so it looks as though there will be no defence available to James.

QUESTION TWO

'There are many examples of conduct in the administration of companies which are controlled both by being criminalised by statute as well as being remediable by civil suit at the instance of the victim. Yet in the case of insider trading, there is only a criminal penalty. If insider trading is to be effectively brought to an end, it is essential that a civil remedy should be provided.'

Discuss.

University of London LLB Examination
(for External Students) Company Law June 1992 Q2

General Comment

This question is not, as it may seem to some, simply asking for a straightforward exposition of the law on insider dealing. Such an answer, while it might pass if comprehensive and accurate, would not earn a good mark. Instead it is asking you to think more deeply and critically about the market phenomenon of insider dealing and how the law should best (if at all) control it and prevent it.

Skeleton Solution

Examples of conduct statutorily criminalised and also remediable civilly – outline of criminal penalty for insider trading – assessment of efficacy – arguments for and against proscription of insider trading – utility of a civil remedy for 'victim'.

Suggested Solution

Company law is awash with instances of multiple layers of legal protection in that the Companies Act (CA) 1985 renders criminal many specific acts and omissions of directors (imposing fines and in some cases the possibility of imprisonment) which will also be of relevance in a civil action by the company itself against the directors. An example is the prohibited loans to directors' provisions in s330 CA 1985, contravention of which by a director can result in criminal liability under s342 and civil liability under s341 in that a director must account for any gain to the company and indemnify the company against any loss or damage. A general action for breach of fiduciary duty will also be available for a company against its directors in many cases where they have committed other specific statutory offences – for example s206 Insolvency Act (IA) 1986 (fraud in anticipation of winding-up).

The criminal prohibition on insider dealing, however, although it is wide in the category of persons to whom it can apply (including not just directors but also a number of others concerned in the administration of companies including recipients of inside information or 'tippees'), is not specifically backed up with any civil remedy to compensate the victim of an insider trader. The prohibition is contained in the Criminal Justice Act 1993, Pt V, and applies to dealing in securities on a recognised stock exchange on the basis of unpublished price-sensitive information. The offence also extends to encouraging someone else to deal on the basis of such information and communicating such information to another person expecting that person to deal in the securities resulting in a profit due to the price sensitivity of the information. Thus rings and networks of insiders are technically within the legislation. It is not just persons connected with the company (most obviously directors, officers and advisers privy to sensitive information) who are within the scope of the offence. The consequences of contravention of the Act are purely criminal though s61 imposes up to seven years imprisonment and/or a fine. In fact s61 expressly provides there are to be no effects on the validity of transactions in contravention of the Act and nowhere does the Act provide for any specific civil remedy for the victim(s) of an insider trader.

The enforcement and efficacy of the Act have been strongly criticised. It is sometimes argued that the courts have been hesitant to use their power of imprisonment and fines have been too light, and that a civil remedy which somehow required the insider to disgorge his profits (as pertains in the USA) would have an additional deterrent effect. However, the whole idea of a specific civil remedy calls for closer analysis, for who exactly is the victim of an insider trader? Is it his market counterparty? If so then couldn't it be argued that they suffered no actual loss since they were willing to make the trade when they bought from or sold to the insider at that price? Is the victim the company whose securities are the subject of insider trading? If so then what is the actual damage suffered by that company for listed securities are bought and sold daily for a thousand different reasons? Some commentators have even argued that insider trading is efficient since it improves the rate of dissemination of new information to the market and hence benefits efficiency. At the moment the only sustainable legal argument that a civil remedy exists can be made in the limited circumstances where the insider owes a fiduciary duty to Company A (eg he is a director of Company A) and in the course of the discharge and performance of his duty he comes into possession of unpublished price sensitive information about the securities of Company B. If he deals on his own behalf on the basis of that information then it can be argued that he is liable to account for any gain he makes to Company A in action for breach of fiduciary duty brought by Company A against him: *Regal (Hastings) Ltd* v *Gulliver* [1942] 1 All ER 378 and *Phipps* v *Boardman* [1964] 2 All ER 187. In addition a counter-party to an insider trade could always try to argue fraudulent misrepresentation.

Chapter 11

Minorities

11.1 **Introduction**

11.2 **Key points**

11.3 **Key cases and statutes**

11.4 **Questions and suggested solutions**

11.1 Introduction

The general meeting is where shareholders exercise such power as remains with them. This comprises those matters for which statute prescribes a resolution of the general meeting, together with any powers reserved to the membership by the articles, ratification of otherwise improper acts by the directors, and a residual power to act where the board cannot or will not (see Chapter 9: *Directors*).

As noted in Chapter 8: *Meetings*, the general meeting operates on democratic lines. The concern, however, is that a group of 'wrongdoers' may gain control of the majority of votes and operate the company for their own benefit. This is more likely to happen in a small private company. Generally, the court has been reluctant to interfere with the exercise by the majority of their voting rights, unless there is clear bad faith, but there have been exceptions.

11.2 Key points

The rule in Foss v Harbottle

Fundamental to an understanding of minority protection is a grasp of the rule first formulated in *Foss v Harbottle* (1843) 2 Hare 461. The rule states that when a wrong is done to a company, the proper plaintiff is the company. Thus, the board will usually initiate an action. If the action is against the directors, the majority of shareholders must initiate it on behalf of the company. The minority cannot.

Personal and derivative actions

There are the following exceptions to the rule.

a) Ultra vires or illegal acts (see Chapter 2: *The Memorandum of Association and Legal Capacity*).

b) Resolutions passed by an incorrect majority (*Edwards* v *Halliwell* [1950] 2 All ER 1064).

c) Personal rights of individual members (*Pender* v *Lushington* (1877) 6 Ch D 70).

d) Fraud on the minority.

In these cases, the minority may be able to bring an action. Where his personal rights are involved, the plaintiff brings a 'personal action', but where the right of action belongs to the company and he is the one to bring it because wrongdoers control the company, it is termed a 'minority shareholders' action' or 'derivative action'. A derivative action is, however, brought at the court's discretion and will be disallowed if the plaintiff is a wrongdoer himself, or if the company has gone into liquidation. The plaintiff need not have been a member of the company when the wrong was committed. Although the right of action belongs to the company, an order for costs may now be made in the plaintiff shareholder's favour (*Wallersteiner* v *Moir (No 1)* [1974] 3 All ER 217).

Fraud on the minority

As noted above, the court will interfere where there is obvious bad faith, but it is difficult to find clear distinctions in the older decisions (contrast *Brown* v *British Abrasive Wheel Co* [1919] 1 Ch 290 with *Sidebotham* v *Kershaw, Leese & Co* [1920] 1 Ch 154). The general view of fraud is that it must involve actual dishonesty (*Derry* v *Peek* (1889) 14 App Cas 337). Misappropriation of company assets will certainly found a minority action on this ground (*Cook* v *Deeks* [1916] 1 AC 554) as being clearly dishonest, but there is doubt as to whether negligence, even if self-serving, is sufficient basis for an action (see *Pavlides* v *Jensen* [1956] Ch 565 which suggests it is not, and *Daniels* v *Daniels* [1978] Ch 406 in which a contrary view was taken). In *Clemens* v *Clemens* [1976] 2 All ER 268 the definition of fraud in this context was broadened to include the situation where a majority shareholder used her voting rights to increase the capital and dilute the minority shareholder's equity below 26 per cent. This case may be viewed on its particular merits and contrasts uneasily with the earlier decision in *Greenhalgh* v *Arderne Cinemas Ltd* [1951] Ch 286 where the fundamental point was not dissimilar but minority action was disallowed.

The plaintiff must usually show that the 'wrongdoers' are in control of the general meeting. In *Prudential Assurance Co Ltd* v *Newman Industries Ltd* [1980] 2 WLR 339 'control' was interpreted liberally to include de facto as well as de jure control.

Companies Act 1985: s459

This section confers a more general protection on minority shareholders than is mentioned above. It gives the court discretion to relieve against any course of conduct in the running of the affairs of a company which is unfairly prejudicial to the interests of some or all of its members, including at least the petitioning shareholder. 'Unfairly prejudicial' has been widely interpreted, and may include serious mismanagement

(*Re Elgindata Ltd* [1991] BCLC 959). Section 461 gives the court power to make such order for relief as it thinks fit. Actions under this section have proved popular.

The courts' interpretation of this section has hitherto been liberal in comparison with its earlier restrictive attitude to s210 Companies Act (CA) 1948. However, the recent decision of the Court of Appeal in *Re Saul D Harrison & Sons plc* [1995] 1 BCLC 14 suggests a narrowing of its scope. Here the court held that for a company to be wound up on grounds of directors acting for their own benefit, unless the directors had acted contrary to the company's constitution, it must be shown that they had acted wholly unreasonably or in bad faith.

Winding-up petitions

A more drastic remedy which may be available to an aggrieved member is to petition for the winding-up of the company. Under s122 Insolvency Act (IA) 1986 the court has a general discretion to make such an order if it thinks it just and equitable to do so. The usual basis for petitions of this kind has been the breach of the equitable obligations arising in quasi-partnerships. The leading case is *Ebrahimi v Westbourne Galleries Ltd* [1973] AC 360, where a minority shareholder/director removed from office by the other two shareholder/ directors was awarded a winding-up order. In other cases it has been held that the company should be wound up because the substratum of it has failed: *Re German Date Coffee Co Ltd* (1882) 20 Ch D 169. This is obviously a drastic remedy. It will not lightly be granted, and indeed an aggrieved shareholder should consider carefully before he seeks it. If the company is profitable, then winding-up is unlikely to be the most appropriate solution to the problem. It may be that this remedy is used less now than it used to be, because of the greater availability of lesser remedies under s459 CA 1985.

11.3 Key cases and statutes

- *Barrett v Duckett and Others* [1995] BCC 362
  Fifty per cent shareholder complaining about behaviour of other 50 per cent director/shareholder was allowed to begin derivative action because in same position as minority shareholder in that as a practical matter it would not have been possible for her to set the company in motion to bring an action

- *Clemens v Clemens* [1976] 2 All ER 268
  Broadened the definition of fraud

- *Cook v Deeks* [1916] 1 AC 554
  Misappropriation of company assets

- *Derry v Peek* (1889) 14 App Cas 337
  The general view of fraud is that it must involve actual dishonesty

- *Ebrahimi v Westbourne Galleries Ltd* [1973] AC 360
  Minority shareholder removed from office obtained a winding-up order

- *Edwards v Halliwell* [1950] 2 All ER 1064
  Contains a useful list of the exceptions to the rule in *Foss v Harbottle*

- *Foss v Harbottle* (1843) 2 Hare 461
  Where a wrong is done to a company, the company is the proper plaintiff

- *George Fischer (Great Britain) Ltd v Multi-Construction Ltd* [1995] BCC 310
  Loss in value of shares – a shareholder in subsidiaries could sue for losses incurred by subsidiaries as there was an unquestionable and admitted right of action

- *Little Olympian Each-Ways Ltd (No 3), Re* [1995] 1 BCLC 636
  Whether conduct is unfairly prejudicial must be decided objectively

- *Macro (Ipswich) Ltd and Another, Re* [1994] BCC 781
  Mismanagement as unfairly prejudicial conduct

- *O'Neill v Phillips* [1999] BCC 600
  Reliance on strict legal powers by those conducting the affairs of the company could be a breach of good faith and it would be inequitable to allow them to rely on those rights

- *Pavlides v Jensen* [1956] Ch 565; *Daniels v Daniels* [1978] Ch 406
  Gross negligence may or may not be a basis for an action

- *Pender v Lushington* (1877) 6 Ch D 70
  One of the exceptions to the rule in *Foss v Harbottle*, involving personal rights of individual members

- *Prudential Assurance Co Ltd v Newman Industries Ltd (No 2)* [1982] Ch 204
  Wrongdoers must be in control of the meeting

- *Saul D Harrison & Sons plc, Re* [1995] 1 BCLC 14
  Unfair prejudice – reasonable bystander test is not the most precise test, should look to see whether there has been an infringement of articles or whether powers of management have been used for improper purposes

- *Supreme Travels Ltd v Little Olympian Each-Ways Ltd* [1994] BCC 947
  Section 459 relief sought against non-member

- *Thomas v Maxwell* (1999) The Times 23 March
  Refusal to sign an undertaking not to disclose information put to defendant during questioning could not be regarded as breach of obligation to give all reasonable assistance to inspectors under s436 CA 1985

- *Tottenham Hotspur plc, Re* [1994] 1 BCLC 655
  Unfairly prejudicial conduct – dismissed chief executive remaining as director

- *Wallersteiner v Moir (No 2)* [1975] 1 All ER 849
  An order for costs may be made to the member

- Companies Act 1985

  - s459 – gives general protection to minority shareholders

  - s461 – gives the court wide powers in granting relief

- Insolvency Act 1986, s122 – just and equitable order for winding-up

11.4 Questions and suggested solutions

QUESTION ONE

Oak Ltd is involved with the film industry as production and recruitment consultants. Pat holds 51 per cent of its issued share capital and Quinn holds the remaining 49 per cent. The articles of association of the company are in the form of the 1985 Table A. Ria is the managing director and both she and the other directors are famous names in the film industry worldwide. For many years Pat and Quinn, who dislike each other intensely, have allowed the board to run the company without themselves becoming involved for they have no personal expertise and under the highly skilled management of the directors the company has prospered, yielding a rich harvest of dividends. The directors too have done well, receiving large salaries under very long-term service contracts.

In February 1994 Pat discovered that Shanti Ltd had broken its contract with Oak Ltd but that the directors of Oak Ltd were taking no action even though the litigation was potentially highly lucrative for Oak Ltd. Pat suspects that this is because Ria has been having an affair with the managing director of Shanti Ltd but he has no evidence of this. In March 1994 Pat himself commenced an action in the name of Oak Ltd against Shanti Ltd.

In April 1994 Quinn received anonymously through the post unequivocal evidence that Tim, one of the directors of Oak Ltd, was running his own private consulting business 'on the side' and was taking clients who would otherwise have become clients of Oak Ltd. He raised this with the other directors and with Pat but no-one wanted to do anything about it since Tim was one of the biggest names they had. In May 1994 Quinn commenced an action in the name of Oak Ltd against Tim.

The board of directors of Oak Ltd has now applied to strike out both actions and both applications have been consolidated into one hearing.

Discuss.

University of London LLB Examination
(for External Students) Company Law June 1994 Q7

General Comment

This question covers a number of areas. It requires a discussion on the relationship between the board of directors and the general meeting. In particular, it raises the important issue of who controls corporate litigation. Linked to this is the rule in *Foss v Harbottle* (1843) 2 Hare 461. Directors' service contracts, together with the possibility of removing the directors, also need to be considered.

Skeleton Solution

Relationship between the board of directors and the general meeting – art 70 Table A – the control of corporate litigation – the rule in *Foss v Harbottle* and the fraud on the minority exception – removal of a director under s303 – directors' service contracts: ss318 and 319 – s459 unfairly prejudicial conduct.

Suggested Solution

Commencement of litigation by Pat

A company acts through two bodies. One is the company in general meeting, that is the shareholders. The other is the board of directors, who are appointed by the shareholders and to whom the management of the company is entrusted. The relationship between the board and the general meeting is a contractual one and depends upon the articles: *Automatic Self-Cleansing Filter Syndicate Co Ltd v Cunninghame* [1906] 2 Ch 34.

Oak Ltd has articles in the form of the current Table A, art 70 of which provides that:

> 'Subject to the provisions of the Act, the memorandum and the article and to any directions given by special resolution, the business of the company shall be managed by the directors who may exercise all the powers of the company.'

The day-to-day management of the company then rests with the board of directors. Shareholder interference will only be allowed if a sufficient majority of the shareholders (75 per cent) either change the articles or give 'directions' to the directors.

The decision to litigate in the name of the company rests with the board of directors. It is a management decision: *Shaw & Sons (Salford) Ltd v Shaw* [1935] 2 KB 113. Exceptionally, litigation has been allowed to commence by an ordinary resolution of the members but such cases represent a minority view and were decided on the basis of the older version of art 70, contained in the 1948 Table A: *Marshall's Valve Gear Co Ltd v Manning, Wardle & Co Ltd* [1909] 1 Ch 267. There is probably no point in pressing for this minority view any longer following its rejection by Harman J in *Breckland Group Holdings Ltd v London & Suffolk Properties Ltd* [1989] BCLC 100. Here, an injunction was granted to prevent a 51 per cent shareholder from continuing litigation which he had commenced in the name of the company.

Following the case of *Danish Mercantile Co Ltd v Beaumont* [1951] Ch 680, the court appears to have developed a practice whereby whenever there is a dispute as to authority to litigate, the case is adjourned so that the matter can be referred back to the general meeting. This practice now seems outdated where, as in this case, art 70 makes it clear that interference by the general meeting can only be by a special resolution.

The court is likely, therefore, to discontinue the proceedings in the name of the company against Oak Ltd, because according to art 70 this is a matter for the board of directors. As Pat is only a 51 per cent shareholder, he does not have enough votes to influence the directors' refusal to commence litigation.

Linked with the issue about who controls corporate litigation is the rule in *Foss* v *Harbottle* (1843) 2 Hare 461. This rule states that the proper plaintiff, where directors in are in breach of duty, is the company itself. The company, acting through the board of directors, must bring the action.

It could be argued that by deciding to refuse to litigate the directors are exercising their powers for an improper purpose in breach of their fiduciary duty. A mala fide abuse amounts to a fraud on the minority: *Cook* v *Deeks* [1916] 1 AC 554. As such, it is an exception to the rule in *Foss* v *Harbottle* and Pat will have locus standi to sue in the name of the company. The difficulty here is that it will be very difficult for Pat to establish fraud. He has no real proof as to why the directors are refusing to sue Shanti Ltd for breach of contract, only a suspicion, which is not enough. It is very doubtful that Pat will be able to continue the litigation in the company's name.

An alternative course of action is for Pat to threaten the board of directors with removal under the procedure laid down in s303 Companies Act (CA) 1985. This only requires an ordinary resolution which Pat would be able to secure. This may put pressure on the directors to act. If they do not, then they may be removed and new directors appointed.

One drawback to removing the directors, however, is that they are receiving large salaries under very long-term service contracts. Removal under s303 will probably result in Oak Ltd having to pay a large amount in damages for breach of contract.

Pat should also enquire about the length of the directors' service contracts. As a member, he can inspect these under s318 CA 1985. Where such contracts cannot be terminated by the company by notice, or they can only be terminated in specified circumstances, then they must not be for more than five years, unless agreed to by the general meeting: s319 CA 1985. A breach of this section allows the company to terminate the contract on giving reasonable notice. The contract is also void to the extent that it exceeds five years.

Commencement of litigation by Quinn

What has been said about the control of corporate litigation in relation to Pat applies equally to Quinn. It is normally for the board of directors to commence litigation in the name of the company.

Tim is in breach of his fiduciary duties to Oak Ltd, as he has diverted customers away from Oak Ltd to a business which he has set up 'on the side'.

Quinn may be able to establish locus standi if he can establish one of the exceptions to the rule in *Foss* v *Harbottle* (1843) 2 Hare 461. The most likely one is the fraud on the minority exception. Here, Quinn will have to show that there has been a fraud on the minority, and that the only reason why the company itself will not bring an action is because the wrongdoers are in numerical or de facto control of the company: *Prudential Assurance Co Ltd* v *Newman Industries Ltd (No 2)* [1982] Ch 204. In such circumstances he can bring a derivative action in the name of the company: *Cook* v *Deeks* [1916] 1 AC 554. In a derivative action, Quinn will not get the benefit of any judgment, which will go to the company, for in reality it is the company that is being defrauded.

A 50 per cent shareholder has been held to be a minority shareholder for the purposes of the exceptions to the rule in *Foss* v *Harbottle*: *Barrett* v *Duckett and Others* [1995] BCC 362, and so Quinn, who holds 49 per cent of the shares, is a minority shareholder.

Even if Quinn can establish fraud and wrongdoer control, the court may seek the views of the majority of shareholders independent of Tim, the wrongdoer. In *Smith* v *Croft (No 2)* [1988] Ch 114, for example, a minority shareholder was denied locus standi, where a majority of the shareholders who were independent of the wrongdoers did not wish proceedings to continue. This was because the defendants were the main assets of the company and to sue them might result in their leaving the company, thereby reducing the value of the shares.

This is very similar to the case of Oak Ltd. Pat, the majority shareholder, and the other directors do not want to do anything about Tim's activities, as Tim is one of the biggest names in the film industry. Despite the criticism which *Smith* v *Croft* has attracted, it remains to be seen whether it will be followed.

The problems of bringing a derivative action should not be underestimated. Quinn will have to consider the time, inconvenience and the disruption in management it will cause. Cost is also an enormous obstacle to an action, as legal aid is not available. A costs order under *Wallersteiner* v *Moir (No 2)* [1975] 1 All ER 849 may, however, be available whereby the company has to pay the plaintiff's costs. The court must, however, be satisfied that it would have been reasonable for an independent board of directors to bring the action. In *Smith* v *Croft* [1986] 1 WLR 580 Walton J held that this condition was not satisfied where the company's largest independent shareholder was opposed to the action and where the company was dependent on the services of the defendants, which outweighed suing them.

It is by no means certain that the court will refuse to strike out the action commenced by Quinn. An alternative course of action might be for Quinn to consider a petition under s459 CA 1985 on the grounds that the affairs of the company are being conducted in a manner which is unfairly prejudicial to the interests of the shareholders.

This is a much more flexible remedy, for which legal aid is available. Unfairly prejudicial conduct has been held to cover diverting business away from the company in circumstances similar to those of Oak Ltd: *Re Cumana Ltd* (1986) 2 BCC 99 and *Re London School of Electronics Ltd* [1986] Ch 211.

Where unfairly prejudicial conduct is proved, the court may make a number of orders set out in s461. These include an order that the petitioner's shares be purchased by other members or the company itself. The court may also authorise civil proceedings to be brought in the name of the company and on behalf of the company. This latter order conveniently side-steps the rule in *Foss* v *Harbottle* (1843) 2 Hare 461.

The alternative remedy in s459 would appear to be a much more attractive proposition for Quinn.

QUESTION TWO

Jumbo Limited ('the company') was formed to run the business formerly carried on in partnership by Arthur, Basil, and Charles, each of whom was appointed as a director of the company. Each owns 100 of the 300 issued shares. The articles of association of the company contain, among other provisions, the following regulations:

> '28A Where any shareholder wishes to transfer his shares, he shall offer them for sale to the other shareholders who shall purchase them at an agreed or an arbitrated price.

> 80A A resolution for the dismissal of any director of the company will not be passed unless Arthur votes in favour of such resolution.'

After a number of years, a difference of opinion grew up between Arthur, on the one hand, and Basil and Charles on the other. The latter wished to expand the company's business, but Arthur was opposed to their plans.

The assets of the company were recently valued at £3m and Arthur has called on Basil and Charles to purchase his shares for £1m. They have refused and have proposed a resolution for the dismissal of Arthur from the board of directors of the company.

Discuss.

University of London LLB Examination
(for External Students) Company Law June 1991 Q4

General Comment

The question deals with a number of areas, the rules on transfer of shares and pre-emption rights, as well as minority protection under Companies Act (CA) 1985, s459 and s122 of the Insolvency Act (IA) 1986. The issue of removing Arthur where under the articles he has enhanced voting rights, there is a need to consider *Bushell* v *Faith* [1970] AC 1099, and if this clause can be changed under s9 CA 1985.

Skeleton Solution

Company is a quasi-partnership, therefore members must deal fairly with each other – Arthur may petition under CA 1985, s459 for his shares to be bought at a proper value or he may also petition for a winding-up order under s122 Insolvency Act 1986, but this is a drastic measure – courts reluctant to wind-up a running and viable business – Basil and Charles may wish to change the clause giving Arthur weighted voting rights but such a change must be bona fide for the benefit of the company.

Suggested Solution

Arthur, Basil and Charles have formed a company from what was previously a partnership. Prima facie the company has the characteristics of a quasi-partnership and in *Ebrahimi* v *Westbourne Galleries Ltd* [1973] AC 360 Lord Wilberforce explained 'that such partnerships were formed on the basis of a personal relationship between the participants, and that there is an understanding that each of the participants will be concerned in the management of the business'. Where the relationship of trust has broken down, as seems to be the case here, it may be appropriate to make a winding-up order under 'just and equitable' grounds by virtue of s122 Insolvency Act (IA) 1986. Success for Arthur is not guaranteed for the courts are reluctant to order the drastic remedy of winding-up a solvent and viable company.

A less drastic and perhaps more attractive 'alternative' would be for Arthur to seek an order under s459 Companies Act (CA) 1985 for the majority to buy out his shareholding. In order to be eligible for this, Arthur would have to show that the affairs of the company were being conducted in a manner unfairly prejudicial to himself as he is part of the membership. Case law on this area seems to indicate that in cases of this kind the court may well be prepared to make a s459 order.

Further, s303 CA 1985 allows a company to remove a director from its board by means of an ordinary resolution of the company in a general meeting; however the articles here contain a weighted voting clause in Arthur's favour. Such clauses were approved by the House of Lords in *Bushell* v *Faith* [1970] AC 1099. Although such clauses appear to contravene the principle that a director is always removable by ordinary resolution, the House of Lords in *Bushell* v *Faith* said that the clause merely affected the way in which the votes were counted on such a resolution, and therefore the likelihood of its being passed did not infringe the rule that such a resolution would be effective if passed. This seems a rather subtle distinction, but nevertheless the decision is still regarded as good law.

An alternative solution which Basil and Charles have considered is to seek to remove the *Bushell* v *Faith* clause and s9 CA 1985 allows a company to alter its articles by special resolution. Basil and Charles could command the necessary majority. Arthur, as shareholder will presumably challenge the alteration as not being made bona fide in the best interests for the company. As in *Greenhalgh* v *Arderne Cinemas Ltd* [1946] 1 All ER 512, the question to ask is whether the change benefits the aggrieved member. These authorities go to show that at least in a small company, the majority have to show due regard to the interests of the minority. Although on the face of it this seems a convincing solution, the difficulty here is that the company was set up on the basis that the directors would be protected from removal and the position is a finely balanced one Basil and Charles are by no means certain to succeed in their action.

The last possibility is an issue of further shares so as to reduce Arthur's holding to a level where the *Bushell* v *Faith* [1970] AC 1099 clause would no longer protect him. However, ss89–96 CA 1985 including pre-emption rights to existing shareholders have to be considered. Arthur will be able to exercise these rights to defeat any scheme to dilute his shareholding. Basil and Charles may try allotting non-cash consideration, or may choose to ignore the pre-emption rights. However, s92 CA 1985 will give Arthur the right to compensation for any loss, damage or expenses resulting from such a breach and a further challenge can be made that such an allocation was for an improper purpose: *Hogg* v *Cramphorn* [1967] Ch 254. In such cases the court is likely to refer the matter to a general meeting to decide whether the shares have been properly allotted.

Basil and Charles, therefore, should consider buying Arthur's shares and can refer the purchase price to arbitration in order to fix a fair price, as it seems probable that Arthur will succeed in blocking their attempts to have him removed.

QUESTION THREE

The Law Commission has recommended in its report on Shareholder Remedies (1997, Law Com No 246) that there should be a new derivative action with modern, flexible and accessible criteria for determining whether a shareholder can pursue an action.

Consider and contrast the Law Commission's proposals with the existing law on derivative actions by companies.

University of London LLB Examination
(for External Students) Company Law June 1999 Q2

General Comment

Candidates should avoid writing a general answer on the rule in *Foss* v *Harbottle* (1843) 2 Hare 461. The question requires consideration of the law as it stands regarding the derivative action and its relationship with the rule in *Foss* v *Harbottle*. The second part of the answer should then consider the proposals for reform analyse the differences.

Skeleton Solution

Rule in *Foss* v *Harbottle* states that where a wrong is done to a company then the company is the proper plaintiff in any proceedings – exception: action can be brought in the name of one of the shareholders of the company – this is a derivative action and is brought by the member in a representative capacity – the Law Commission has proposed that reform should be given statutory basis and should be available as relief only where an act or omission involves negligence, default, breach of duty or breach of trust by a director of a company, or where the director's personal interests conflict with duties to the company.

Suggested Solution

The rule in *Foss* v *Harbottle* (1843) 2 Hare 461 states that where a wrong is done to a company it is the company that is the proper plaintiff in any proceedings. However, this rule can cause hardship to the minority shareholder where the company decides not to sue and the decision operates as a fraud on the minority. An obvious example of this is where the directors are the people who are to be sued, but use their power, possibly in the form of a majority shareholding, to prevent any action being taken. A derivative action is therefore an exception to the rule in *Foss* v *Harbottle* and the situations in which such actions are permitted have been set down at common law.

The derivative action

This is a representative action by shareholders to enforce corporate rights by way of damages for the corporation. The action is derived from the corporation's right of action. A derivative action can be brought under the fraud on the minority exception or ultra vires exception to the rule in *Foss* v *Harbottle* where a minority shareholder seeks to recover damages for breach of duty from directors or the restitution of property for the company.

In the case of *Menier* v *Hooper's Telegraph Works* (1874) LR 9 Ch App 350, which was a case involving the misappropriation of company assets, there was held to be a fraud on the minority and the minority shareholders were permitted to bring a derivative action.

Lord Davey in *Burland* v *Earle* [1902] AC 83 stated that a derivative action could be brought where there were acts 'of a fraudulent character or beyond the powers of the company'.

A derivative action was not allowed in the case of *Pavlides* v *Jensen* [1956] 2 All ER 518 where the directors sold a mine at an undervalue. The minority shareholder alleged that the act was negligent and the court held that negligence did not constitute a fraud on the minority and that the company was entitled to make a legitimate decision not to sue in a general meeting. However, it is important to note that the directors did not have control of the voting. By way of contrast in the case of *Daniels* v *Daniels* [1978] Ch 406 the court held that an act of gross negligence was tantamount to fraud on the minority. Here the directors sold company assets to one of their number at a gross undervalue and this quite clearly benefited that director.

In *Estmanco (Kilner House) Ltd* v *Greater London Council* [1982] 1 All ER 437, the court expressed the opinion that fraud on the minority was not confined to common law fraud but could also include equitable fraud, abuse of power or discrimination.

The difficulties in drawing the boundaries of what constitute fraud in these circumstances have continued. In *Prudential Assurance Co Ltd* v *Newman Industries Ltd* *(No 2)* [1982] Ch 204 the court held that directors could still be guilty of a fraud even though they believed they were doing nothing wrong if they misappropriate the company's property. Moreover, the case of *Farrow* v *Registrar of Building Societies* [1991] 2 VR 589 seems to have extended the boundaries even further by stating that a derivative action may be available where there is an allegation of wrongdoing amounting to unlawfulness.

Proposed reform

Because of the lack of clarity in the law as it stands, and because of the drive to further codify company law, the Law Commission has proposed the replacement of the common law by statutory rules covering a derivative action in cases where there has been an alleged breach of directors' duties.

The proposal states that a derivative claim may only be brought if:

'... the cause of action arises as a result of an actual or proposed act or commission involving –

a) negligence, default, breach of duty or breach of trust by a director of the company, or

b) a director putting himself in a position where his personal interests conflict with his duties to the company.'

The proposed statutory provisions state that the derivative action must arise out of an act or omission by a director, but can be brought against anyone. The term director is used in its widest context and will include shadow directors. These proposals reflect the way that the common law has developed over the years.

These proposed rules have the benefit of stopping litigation on what exactly constitutes a fraud and would bring situations of negligence such as the one discussed in *Pavlides* v *Jensen* [1956] 2 All ER 518 within the category of the derivative action. It would, however, exclude situations such as arose in *Estmanco (Kilner House) Ltd* v *Greater London Council* [1982] 1 All ER 437, because the action was taken by a majority shareholder and the proposals clearly refer to acts or omissions by directors. By way of critical comment it has been stated that although there are benefits in setting out the basis for a derivative action in statutory form, the actual proposals themselves are somewhat restrictive.

Finally, the proposal that an action can be taken against anyone means that, if property has been transferred, the person bringing the derivative action will still be able to recover it or relevant damages.

QUESTION FOUR

Wheels Ltd was formed five years ago to provide lorry transport facilities to the computer industry. It has an issued share capital of £500 divided into 300 'A' shares of £1 each and 400 'B' shares of 50 pence each. Alf, Bob, and Colin are the directors of the company. Alf and Bob each hold half the 'A' shares and Colin holds all the 'B' shares. The articles of association of the company provide that:

a) the 'A' shares carry two votes each and the 'B' shares carry one vote each;

b) Colin is to be a director of the company at a salary of £20,000 per year.

Until 1993 the three directors worked well together and the company prospered. However, at a board meeting in August of that year, Alf and Bob disagreed with Colin over a fundamental matter of business policy and the meeting ended abruptly when Colin hit Alf. Colin was later fined £50 for assault by local magistrates. Since then Alf and Bob have continued to run the company but the business policy pursued after the meeting in August 1993 has clearly proved unsuccessful and, although the company is still solvent, it has made no profits since then. Colin continued to received his salary after the August meeting but has attended no board meetings since then, even though Alf and Bob have periodically invited him to do so.

Three months ago Alf and Bob stopped payment of Colin's salary. Colin is now saying that he will attend the next board meeting as he intends to 'make one last effort to lick the company into shape'. Alf and Bob do not want him back and want to run the company without him.

Advise Alf and Bob, and Colin.

University of London LLB Examination
(for External Students) Company Law June 1996 Q4

General Comment

The question calls for examination of the principles governing the 'closely-held' company and the exclusion of members from participation in such companies. Some discussion of the enforceability of rights provided by the articles of association is needed and a general appreciation of the law on minority protection is necessary. A range of remedies is available and, within time constraints, should be dealt with.

Skeleton Solution

The nature of the company: closely held companies – quasi-partnership – unfair prejudice, the principle of majority control and s459 CA 1985 – provision (b) of the articles, s14 CA 1985 – remedies open to Alf and Bob – remedies open to Colin.

Suggested Solution

Wheels Ltd is a private company of the 'closely-held' or 'quasi partnership' variety and this point must be considered in advising the parties here. The essence of this type of company is that it is usually formed by and controlled by a small number of persons acting as the directors of the company. The aim usually is for a far greater involvement by the participators than mere investment. The leading case on this type of company and situation is *Ebrahimi v Westbourne Galleries Ltd* [1973] AC 360 where Lord Wilberforce made the point that the fact of a company being small and private is not, by itself, enough to justify applying equitable principles to the normal questions of company majority control and management. There is also a need to illustrate that other features are present such as evidence that the company was formed or continues to rest upon the basis of personal and mutual trust, indications of agreements that members have and should continue to have participation in management and, usually, some restrictions upon the member withdrawing his membership and capital by transferring it.

If these factors, or some of them, are present the approach of the courts to disagreements between the members goes quite a long way towards recognising a relationship analogous to a fiduciary one between the parties. If the problem cannot be resolved in any other way the court may order a winding-up of the company on the 'just and equitable' ground in s122(1)(g) Insolvency Act (IA) 1986 as happened in *Ebrahimi* v *Westbourne Galleries Ltd* [1973] AC 360 itself (under the equivalent statutory provision at that time). This is similar to the old quasi-partnership agreement used to justify winding-up in the old but well known case of *Re Yenidje Tobacco Co* [1916] 2 Ch 426.

The modern remedy which has been most frequently applied to situations such as this is provided by s459 Companies Act (CA) 1985 (as amended by CA 1989), which is designed to offer a range of solutions to situations where it is alleged that the affairs of the company are being conducted in a manner which is unfairly prejudicial to the interests of all or part of the membership which includes the petitioner. The nature of the remedy offered here is essentially equitable because, in many situations considered under the section, the petitioner is being subjected to majority control which is the general principle underlying English company law. The idea under lying this section is that, so far as possible, the company should not be wound up but the successful petitioner should achieve redress from his prejudiced situation. The jurisdiction to grant relief under this section is amazingly wide but the one area that seems to be clearly outside of the remedy is the situation where the court is expected to consider questions of the business or management policies of the company: *Re Macro (Ipswich) Ltd* v *Anor* [1994] BCC 781. This is, of course, entirely consistent with the court's approach in supporting the majority rule and delegated director powers principles. This is subject to the caveat, in all cases, that directors should make decisions bona fide in the interests of the company as a whole, ie the corporators as a body. This can be seen in cases on alterations to the company constitution as in *Greenhalgh* v *Arderne Cinemas Ltd* [1951] Ch 286 or in situations affecting the reduction or dilution of controlling interests as in *Howard Smith Ltd* v *Ampol Petroleum Ltd* [1974] AC 821 and innumerable other cases.

A point that should be considered is whether the provision in the articles concerning Colin's directorship can be enforced in any way by reliance upon the statutorily implied contract, provided by s14 CA 1985, between the company and its members inter se, on the basis of the memorandum and articles. The short answer is that it does not. This section can only assist the member in his capacity qua member and not in respect of rights given in any other capacity such as director or secretary etc: *Hickman* v *Kent or Romney Marsh Sheepbreeders' Association* [1915] 1 Ch 881.

The remedy that Alf and Bob really are seeking is that of excluding Colin from control and management of the company. Colin is a director and a holder of 40 per cent of the voting rights. Procedurally, s303 CA 1985 allows the company by ordinary resolution to remove a director notwithstanding anything in the articles. Alf and Bob can achieve the ordinary resolution, the question is whether Colin could rely upon the *Ebrahimi* v *Westbourne Galleries Ltd* [1973] AC 360 principle, or s459 to prevent this. This is, in truth a position of irretrievable breakdown between Colin and the other pair and Colin refuses to attend Board meetings to resolve the matter. The cases seem to show that it is not unfairly prejudicial for the majority shareholding directors in a quasi-partnership to openly arrange a general meeting and vote for dismissal: *Re A Company* [1987] 1 WLR 102; and to invoke provisions in the articles allowing the majority to buy out the minority at a fair price. We do not know whether it is easy or difficult for Colin to get clear of the company with his capital reasonably intact. Much would depend upon this and the one thing that Alf and Bob could not do is to force him to sell his shares at an unfair price, the principles being well explained in *Re Bird Precision Bellows Ltd* [1986] Ch 658.

Colin would not be able to use s459 to interfere with the policies pursued by Alf and Bob as the Court will not look into such matters. The question of a winding-up under *Ebrahimi* and s122(1)(g) IA 1986 looks very unlikely as there appears to have been no disagreements at all other than over business policy and no deception or fraud has been practiced by Alf or Bob. As Colin is still a director until such time as the other pair resolve to dismiss him under s303, he is entitled to his contractual remuneration and to attend Board meetings if he so wishes. He would not necessarily be in breach of his duties if he did not attend as his duty is owed to the company itself and it is only a duty to act honestly, with reasonable care having regard to knowledge and experience, for the benefit of the company. The company will be in breach if he is not paid or notified of meetings.

If Bob and Alf decide to remove Colin as a director, they will need to alter the articles of association. Section 303 will override the effect of the existing article and although a special resolution is required under s9 CA 1985 to alter the articles, the court will have the power on a s459 petition (which would almost certainly occur) to authorise alterations to the company's memorandum or articles: s461(4) CA 1985.

QUESTION FIVE

Asa owns 99 of the 100 shares of Cafe Blue Ltd ('the company') which owns the restaurant business that Asa established 20 years ago. Last year Asa agreed to the takeover of the company by the sale of 75 shares to Eat-u-like plc. As part of the takeover deal it was agreed that Asa would be the sole director and managing director of the company for five years at an annual salary of £100,000. The articles of association of the company were also amended so as to include the following regulation:

> '72A Asa shall be the managing director of the company for five years at an annual salary of £100,000 adjusted for inflation in accordance with the retail price index. No resolution of the company shall be taken as passed unless the votes of Asa are cast in favour.'

Asa was duly elected and assumed office as managing director. Management tensions between Asa and Eat-u-like plc soon erupted. Asa wanted the company to maintain the existing market whereas Eat-u-like plc wanted the company to increase business substantially by entering the lucrative lunch market. Asa suspects that Eat-u-like plc are trying to kill-off the company because they have refused additional capital to further develop the company until Asa considers their proposals. Eat-u-like plc are on record as saying that Asa is refusing to co-operate in the company's audit procedures and refusing to consider the views of Eat-u-like plc.

Eat-u-like plc has now requisitioned an EGM and cast its votes at that meeting to pass two resolutions: the first, to delete art 72A by special resolution and the second, to remove Asa as a director of the company by ordinary resolution.

Advise Asa.

University of London LLB Examination
(for External Students) Company Law June 1995 Q4

General Comment

This problem involves the question of validity of art 72A and of the two resolutions at the EGM in the light of a struggle for control of the company. It is necessary to look at the foundation of the capital structure and to see whether there are opportunities to seek the aid of the court to impose inequitable principles in assisting Asa.

Skeleton Solution

Validity of art 72A – common law limitations on powers to alter articles – validity of the two resolutions – effect upon Asa's contractual position – *Ebrahimi* principle – s122(1)(g) – s459 – conclusion.

Suggested Solution

The essence of the question is the validity of the alteration of the articles by art 72A and the validity of the two resolutions.

The validity of article 72A

The effect of this article is to prevent the passing of any resolution unless Asa votes for it, effectively giving Asa absolute control of the company as he is also sole and managing director. There is nothing to stop anyone buying shares without obtaining influence over the company (as with non-voting shares) but it is a very curious takeover arrangement where no control at all is obtained. Asa has attempted here to create a controlling class of shares for himself and he will need to consider, initially, whether he used the appropriate mode of alteration by special resolution: s9(1) Companies Act (CA) 1985 and *Bushell v Faith* [1970] AC 1099. He must then consider whether the alteration has created any conflict with any provision in the memorandum because, if so, to the extent of the conflict, the alteration will be void: *Ashbury v Watson* (1885) 30 Ch D 376. This sounds a distinct possibility here, considering the range of matters which might be covered in the memorandum. If Asa surmounts these obstacles he must then consider the common law limitations upon the power to alter articles that the courts have developed to prevent perceived abuses of company control. Probably the most important is that seen in *Allen v Gold Reefs of West Africa* [1900] 1 Ch 656, that the power must be exercised bona fide for the benefit of the company as a whole. Much depends upon what 'the company as a whole' means. Obviously, when Asa was the only or possibly the major shareholder he would have met the description set out in *Greenhalgh v Arderne Cinemas Ltd* [1951] Ch 286, of 'the corporators as a general body' but the article could not be said to benefit the whole company if Eat-u-like plc is included. The view of the courts since *Greenhalgh* seems to be that the company's future prospects and, indeed, future members have to be considered, and the test is very much an objective one.

There is little doubt that an alteration which greatly increases or decreases the power of the majority shareholders can, in an appropriate case, be for the benefit of the company as a whole, as in *Rights and Issues Investment Trust Ltd* v *Stylo Shoes Ltd* [1965] Ch 250, but one which so completely excludes participation in control in the way that art 72A does would be likely to fail this test and the court, consequently, would strike it down.

The validity of the two resolutions

Clearly, if art 72A has validity, neither of the two resolutions would be valid. Assuming the article to be invalid, Asa will be greatly damaged in two respects here. He loses his ability to prevent any type of resolution of the general meeting and he loses his directorship. His voting control, if based upon an invalid article, was without foundation and he has, in truth, lost nothing. He still has his 24 shares and the attached voting rights. To this extent, the special resolution is unexceptionable and to the extent that deletion will remove the article providing the power to appoint Asa, similarly, little will be lost as he is already appointed and, presumably, has a contract on the basis of the article. The lack of capacity to employ him, if art 72A is invalid, will not affect the validity of the contract: s35(1) Companies Act (CA) 1985. The problem is that there is the ordinary resolution to remove Asa and, provided that special notice had been given of this resolution (s303(2) CA 1985), this seems to have been properly done within s303. Asa will, of course, have an action for breach of contract if there is breach but it does seem that he is in an awkward position.

All may not be lost for Asa because there was, undoubtedly, some mutual contemplation that he would have substantial involvement in the day-to-day management of the company and he might be said to have a legitimate expectation of this continuing throughout at least the five years. Cases such as *Ebrahimi v Westbourne Galleries Ltd* [1973] AC 360 and provisions such as s459 CA 1985 and s122(1)(g) Insolvency Act (IA) 1986 clearly illustrate that the law will, in appropriate cases, apply equitable principles to the exercise of legal rights where unconscionable or unfairly prejudicial behaviour would otherwise succeed. Even if there is some degree of inequitable conduct by the petitioner or plaintiff, this will not always bar relief as in *Re London School of Electronics Ltd* [1986] Ch 211 but there must be clear evidence: that both parties contemplated participation in control by the excluded party (*Re Tottenham Hotspur plc* [1994] 1 BCLC 655); and that the agreement originated in some relationship of trust and confidence; and that some restriction exists upon a proper realisation of the party's interest in the event of a split.

It does seem that the real battle here is about the direction that the company's future development should take and the court may view this as more a test of who controls than one of minority oppression. Whatever view the court takes, the reality is of a quasi-partnership that has gone badly wrong, with little prospect of a reconciliation of views. There are various possibilities. On the basis that the company had proceeded from the equivalent of a partnership, it may be possible to achieve a winding-up on the 'just and equitable' ground in s122(1)(g) Insolvency Act (IA) 1986. In *Re Yenidje Tobacco Co* [1916] 2 Ch 426 the deteriorating relationship between the two principal director/ shareholders in a very profitable company made continuation impossible so the court ordered winding-up. It might prove more difficult to persuade the court that the assertion of a controlling interest so as to pursue legitimate business policies is a matter within s122(1)(g) IA 1986 or that it is a matter within s459 CA 1985. Several cases under s459 involve removal and exclusion from control and office as in *Re Bird Precision Bellows Ltd* [1986] Ch 658 and *Re London School of Electronics Ltd* [1986] Ch 211, but there has to be something more than an honest difference of opinion on policy to constitute unfair prejudice. An irreconcilable breakdown between a minor shareholder/director and the majority director which led to exclusion from office did not constitute unfair prejudice in *Re A Company (No 004377 of 1986)* [1987] 1 WLR 102. The courts are not eager to consider competing views on company policies in these petitions or, indeed, in applications to set aside resolutions aimed at altering articles to further the interests of the majority shareholders: *Re Blue Arrow plc* [1987] BCLC 585. Possibly, the best that Asa could hope for here is for the court to exercise its discretion under s461(2)(d) CA 1985, to order the purchase of his interest without discount for his minority position, as in *Re Bird Precision Bellows*. It is hard to see what else the court could do that would not create more problems than it solves.

Chapter 12

Corporate Rescue

12.1 Introduction

12.2 Key points

12.3 Key cases and statutes

12.4 Question and suggested solution

12.1 Introduction

The concept of corporate rescue is a relatively modern one. Prior to the Insolvency Act 1985 the emphasis when dealing with companies in financial difficulties was on winding-up as a means of protecting creditors. The more modern notion is that greater efforts should be made to rescue the company so that it can continue in business. The Insolvency Act 1986 introduced into English law the concept of the administration order, which lies at the heart of the scheme of corporate rescue which is considered in this chapter. The Insolvency Act 2000 has tried to improve the operation of the voluntary arrangement procedure when proposed by the company's directors by introducing the use of a moratorium, but this is only available to small companies.

12.2 Key points

Context

The notion of corporate rescue arises in cases where companies are in some financial difficulty, but it is thought that there is still a reasonable prospect of saving them from total collapse. The introduction of the administration order regime reflects a change in attitude in the direction of saving companies wherever possible.

Obtaining an order

Directors, creditors or the company may petition for an administration order. The order will be made if it appears that the company is unable to pay its debts and the court is of opinion that the purpose of the order, namely securing the continuance of the business as a going concern, can be achieved.

Alternatively an order may be made for the purpose of enabling a voluntary composition with creditors or in order to effect a more advantageous realisation of the company's assets than could be achieved on a winding-up.

The effect of the order

Once an order has been made no winding-up petition may be presented (and any existing petition will be dismissed). No security may be enforced against the company without the leave of the court.

The administrator

The administrator must be a qualified insolvency practitioner. He is appointed by the court and is at all times under the direction of the court.

The administrator has extensive powers, including the removal of directors and the conduct of the company's business. He is the agent of the company.

The administrator has three months from the date of his appointment in which to formulate proposals for ensuring the survival of the company. These proposals will be sent to the Registrar of Companies, and must also be laid before a meeting of the creditors. Before any scheme can be implemented it must be approved both by the creditors and by the administrator.

One possible defect in the administration order regime is that chargees are still entitled to appoint their own receivers, and chargees will retain their existing place in the order of creditors. So far as the unsecured creditors are concerned this may well mean that the success of the new system will depend upon the co-operation and goodwill of those holding fixed or floating charges.

12.3 Key cases and statutes

* *Atlantic Computer Systems plc (No 1), Re* [1992] 1 All ER 476
  Looks at administrator's obligations on long term leases, but also contains an in-depth discussion on the workings of the IA 1986

* *Bristol Airport plc* v *Powdrill* [1990] BCLC 585
  This case considers the statutory provisions creating a moratorium on enforcement of debts in relation to liens

* *Harris Simons Construction Ltd, Re* [1989] 1 WLR 368
  When seeking to obtain an administration order the applicant must show that there is a real prospect of achieving one of the purposes set out in s8(1)(b) IA 1986

* *Inland Revenue Commissioner* v *Adam and Partners Ltd* [2001] 1 BCLC 222
  On an approval of a proposal for a voluntary arrangement as with administration orders, no proposal can go forward without the consent of the holders of the floating charges over the company's property

* *Powdrill & Another* v *Watson & Another* [1995] 2 AC 394
  Considers the administrator's liability for salaries and wages of a company in administration

- Insolvency Act 1986 – this is still in existence and the procedure has not been used to great effect

- Insolvency Act 2000 – enacted provisions for a company voluntary arrangement moratorium which is available to 'eligible companies', which are small companies as defined in the Companies Act 1985, s247(3). The other main thrust of the IA 2000 relates to the disqualification of directors and enables the Secretary of State to accept an undertaking from a director not to act as a director for an agreed period of up to 15 years

12.4 Question and suggested solution

'The regime of Administration was introduced on the recommendations of the Cork Committee to enable an insolvent company with the potential for partial or total recovery to avoid the destructive effects of liquidation.'

Assess the effectiveness of the means by which the legislation empowers the regime of Administration to achieve this end. To the extent that you believe that the regime fails in its purpose, what changes would you recommend?

University of London LLB Examination
(for External Students) Company Law June 1991 Q3

General Comment

This question deals with the concept of corporate rescue due to changes introduced by the Insolvency Act (IA) 1986. A general review of this new system of administration orders should be made and reference has to be made to previous law. There is however little authority and case law in this area and it is necessary therefore to concentrate on statutory provisions.

Skeleton Solution

Provisions under Insolvency Act 1986 force a company to consider insolvency earlier in order to try and rescue the company and keep it as a going concern – the role of the administrator to try and achieve this – application made by company, director or creditor – other proceedings stayed to allow administrator to make proposals – procedure relatively untested; success dependent on goodwill of creditors and chargees.

Suggested Solution

Administration is a procedure recommended by the Cork Report 'The Report of the Review Committee on Insolvency and Practice 1982' as an alternative to receivership by way of corporate rescue. The basic purpose of an administrative order is to freeze the debts of the company in financial difficulty in order to assist an administrator to save the company or at least achieve a better realisation of its assets. It is not a procedure designed for creditors to try to enforce their security. In *Re Consumer and Industrial Press Ltd* [1988] BCLC 177, Peter Gibson J said that the court had to be satisfied that it was more probable than not that one of the specified purposes would be achieved. This test was adopted in *Re Manlon Trading Co* (1988) The Times 14 June, where on balance the courts refused to make an administration order.

The Insolvency Act (IA) 1986 therefore forces directors to assess the company's financial situation much earlier in order to benefit from this form of corporate rescue, as it may bring about a more satisfactory result for members and creditors alike. The IA 1986 also introduced other provisions to ensure that directors do assess the company's financial position in good time under ss213 and 214 IA 1986, which deals with fraudulent and wrongful trading and imposes personal liability on directors contravening these provisions. Moreover, the Company Directors Disqualification Act 1986 provides further statutory provisions for mandatory disqualification of directors by the courts if these provisions are contravened.

A receiver on the other hand will take a charge over all the company's assets and will concentrate on paying off the company's debts, firstly to preferential creditors and he is not under a duty to rescue the company, whereas an administrator will try to salvage the company's business as a going concern.

Before making an order the court must be satisfied that the company is unlikely to be able to pay its debts and such an order will be likely to achieve the survival of the whole or part of the business as a going concern, as this order would provide a more advantageous realisation of the assets than would be effected on a winding-up order. The other possible purpose for an order would be the approving of a voluntary arrangement under Pt I of the Insolvency Act 1986 or sanctioning of a compromise or arrangement under the Companies Act (CA) 1985, s425.

If satisfied that a realisation can be achieved the court will grant the order under IA 1986, s123. The company, directors or creditors can make an application for such an order under IA 1986, s9. Notice of this petition must be given to any person entitled to appoint a receiver as he must consent to such an order. The effect of the application is that the company cannot be wound up, no charge, hire purchase or retention of title clauses can be enforced against the company, without consent of the court and this also applies to any proceedings commenced against the company.

The making of such an order will automatically dismiss any outstanding winding-up petition and any existing administrative receiver will have to vacate his office.

The administrator must be a qualified insolvency practitioner and his powers include management of the affairs, property and business of the company. He can deal with charged property, remove directors and require information from the officers and employees of the company, and, in exercising his powers, the administrator is deemed to be an agent of the company.

Within three months of the order, he must send to the registrar, the creditors and members a statement of his proposals for achieving the purpose of the administration. A meeting of creditors is then convened to approve these proposals: s23 IA 1986.

This meeting is an important feature of administration, as these proposals must be approved before implementation: *Re Consumer and Industrial Press Ltd (No 2)* (1987) 4 BCC 72. However, this committee is much weaker than the committee of creditors in a liquidation, since it has no powers to give directions to administrators, and its consent is not necessary in his discharging his duties as administrator.

However, where there is a receiver in place, the person who appointed the receiver must consent to the appointment of the administrator. This is the main failing of corporate rescue as any creditor or member may apply to the court for an order that the company is or has been managed by the administrator in a manner unfairly prejudicial to him, and the court can then make any order it thinks fit: s27 IA 1986. This provision is very similar to s459 CA 1985, and unsatisfied creditors have the opportunity to veto the appointment of an administrator.

The Cork Committee made its recommendations after studying various procedures in a number of countries including France, Australia and United States. Its observations were twofold. Firstly, whether administration will work depends on the goodwill of chargees as they can block the procedure by appointing a receiver and then vetoing the appointment of the administrator. This is because it takes a long time between applying for an order and obtaining it and this leaves time for chargees to appoint a receiver. Secondly, when a company is in financial difficulties and an administrator is appointed, the company's business may continue to suffer in that people may be reluctant to trade with the company, as they will be worried that the company may not be able to meet its financial obligations.

Therefore, although the administrator's role is geared towards rescuing a company, his task can be hindered, and his success is very much dependent on the goodwill of chargees.

Chapter 13

Liquidations

13.1 Introduction

This chapter deals with some of the problems which arise when a company goes into liquidation. As these problems can be spread over a wide spectrum of company law, there is a certain amount of cross-referencing.

13.2 Key points

Types of liquidation

If a company is solvent it may commence a members' voluntary liquidation (winding-up) by special resolution passed at a general meeting and the directors must make a statutory declaration of solvency. If the company is insolvent, it must pass an extraordinary resolution and call a creditors' meeting and the liquidation will be a creditors' voluntary winding-up. In each case the date of commencement of the winding-up (which is an important calculation date for a number of statutory sections) will be the date the resolution was passed.

Application may also be made to the court on one of seven grounds in s122 Insolvency Act (IA) 1986, the most usual of which is that the company is unable to pay its debts (s122(1)(f)). This may be proved by showing that notice has been served on the company requiring repayment of a debt of £750 or more and the company has for 21 days neglected to pay. If the petition is granted, the date of commencement of the winding-up is the date of the petition (not the date of the order).

Role of liquidator

When a company goes into liquidation, whether voluntary or compulsory, it is the duty of the liquidator to collect in all debts due to the company and to settle, in so far as the assets permit, all debts owed by the company. Three major types of problem arise. The first is that of establishing which claims on the company are valid. The second is establishing the priority of valid claims. It is likely that some creditors will seek to have their claim classified in a higher category than that to which it properly belongs. The liquidator will have to deal with attempts of this kind. The third type of problem concerns the examination of the conduct of directors and other officers and employees of the company. If there has been misconduct, then it may become the duty of the liquidator to take action against the individuals who are in default.

Validity of claims

The major area of difficulty here arises in connection with retention of title clauses. These are clauses contained in contracts for the sale of goods which purport to reserve title in the goods to the seller until the goods are paid for in full. A more extreme variant of these clauses is found where the parties deal on the basis of a rolling account. In such cases the clause may provide that no title to any goods supplied is to pass unless the account is entirely clear. The effect of this can be to prevent the passage of title even to goods which have been fully paid for.

The validity in principle of retention of title clauses was accepted by the Court of Appeal in *Aluminium Industrie Vaassen BV* v *Romalpa Aluminium Ltd* [1976] 2 All ER 552. Subsequent cases have, however, severely restricted the ambit of the principle, holding that the right to reclaim the goods can be lost if they are irretrievably mixed with other goods, and that in any event the right created in favour of the seller may well amount to a charge on the goods such as requires to be registered under s395 Companies Act (CA) 1985 and is void in the absence of such registration: *Borden (UK) Ltd* v *Scottish Timber Products Ltd* [1981] Ch 25; *Re Bond Worth Ltd* [1980] Ch 228; *Re Peachdart Ltd* [1984] Ch 131; and *Re Weldtech Equipment* [1991] BCC 16. At the present day it is fair to say that the courts look with disfavour on retention of title clauses, and will often find some way of rendering them ineffective if not actually void.

Order of priority

The Companies Act (CA) 1985 provides that the first charge in a liquidation is the costs and expenses of the liquidation, followed by satisfaction of the fixed charges, then preferential creditors (including employees up to four months wages or £800, the Inland Revenue and the Customs and Excise for one year's arrears). Next come the holders of floating charges, then the unsecured creditors. The final creditors are the deferred creditors, after which any surplus is distributed to the members.

Because of the above order of priorities it may be important to know whether a particular charge is valid. This may depend upon whether it has been duly registered at the Companies Registry under s398 CA 1985. There may also be questions about the date at which a charge crystallised.

Misconduct

As a general rule shareholders and officers of a company are not liable for the company's losses beyond, in the case of the shareholders, the paid-up amount of the share capital. This principle may not apply where there has been misconduct. The most blatant form of this arises where the company's funds have been fraudulently misappropriated. In such cases it may be necessary to consider criminal as well as civil proceedings. Misconduct may also take the form of wrongfully authorising payments to a director or to a person or company connected with a director, and here there may be civil proceedings for the recovery of the money. Finally, the questions of wrongful and/or fraudulent trading under ss213–214 IA 1986 may arise. Wrongful trading occurs where the directors carry on business knowing that the company is unable to meet its debts. Fraudulent trading means carrying on business for the purpose of defrauding creditors. It is a criminal offence and liability may be incurred by anyone who is party to it, not just by the directors of the company.

13.3 Key cases and statutes

* *Aluminium Industrie Vaassen BV* v *Romalpa Aluminium Ltd* [1976] 2 All ER 552
  Acceptance of retention of title clause

* *Arrows Ltd (No 4), Re* [1994] BCC 641
  Admission of private examinations under s236 IA 1986 in criminal proceedings

* *Borden (UK) Ltd* v *Scottish Timber Products Ltd* [1981] Ch 25; *Bond Worth Ltd, Re* [1980] Ch 228; *Peachdart Ltd, Re* [1984] Ch 131; *Weldtech Equipment, Re* [1991] BCC 16
  All of which restrict the ambit of retention of title clauses

* *Cranley Mansions Ltd, Re* [1994] 1 WLR 1610
  Meaning of 'agrees' in r1.17(3) of Insolvency Rules – voluntary arrangements

* *Sherborne Associates Ltd, Re* [1995] BCC 40
  Wrongful trading, survival of claim after death of director

* Companies Act 1985, s398 – registration of charge

* Insolvency Act 1986

  * s122 – contains seven grounds for winding-up a company

  * ss213 to 214 – wrongful and fraudulent trading

13.4 Questions and suggested solutions

QUESTION ONE

In May 1989 Pop Ltd agreed to buy Cherry's shares in Orange Ltd for £250,000. The following events then happened in the order listed.

Orange Ltd sold machinery parts, surplus to its requirements, to Pop Ltd for £40,000. Pop Ltd re-sold them for £60,000.

Pop Ltd borrowed £70,000 from a bank.

Cherry transferred her shares in Orange Ltd to Pop Ltd for £150,000 in cash; she also resigned as a director of Orange Ltd. At the same time she was paid by Orange Ltd £40,000 in 'compensation for loss of office' and was appointed a consultant to the company for two years at £30,000 per annum.

Orange Ltd paid £70,000 from its distributable profits to the bank in discharge of Pop Ltd's indebtedness.

Orange Ltd has just gone into insolvent liquidation. Advise the liquidator.

Written by the Editor

General Comment

This is a very mixed question, containing a number of different points which are likely to concern the liquidator.

Skeleton Solution

Sale of machinery may be misfeasance – £40,000 compensation recoverable from Cherry unless approved by company in General Meeting – consultancy fee proper only if Cherry actually works for the company – payment of £70,000 almost certainly improper – may be recovered from directors or payee – note generally IA 1986, ss213 and 214 on fraudulent/wrongful trading.

Suggested Solution

The question suggests that the machinery parts may have been sold at an undervalue of some £20,000. This could possibly amount to misfeasance by the directors of Orange Ltd, and is a matter which the liquidator ought to investigate. In the absence of a proper explanation, he should consider taking action against the directors. In this context Cherry's position is particularly open to question. One interpretation of the facts given would be that Cherry was seeking to benefit Pop Ltd in return for their agreement to buy her shares. It is also to be observed that Pop Ltd ultimately does not pay in full the agreed purchase price of the shares. Although this is not directly relevant to the liquidation, since it is a matter between Cherry and Pop Ltd, it may be seen as further evidence of wrongdoing by Cherry.

On resigning her directorship Cherry received £40,000 compensation. Companies Act (CA) 1985, s312 requires that details of such compensation be disclosed to the company and approved by it. It is unclear whether this was done in the present case. If not, it is suggested that the liquidator may be able to recover the money from Cherry.

As regards the appointment as consultant, this does not appear to be subject to the s319 requirement of approval by the general meeting, since it is not an appointment to a directorship. Nevertheless, the liquidator would do well to investigate the circumstances of the appointment, and in particular to check whether Cherry has in fact been working as a consultant.

The payment of the £70,000 in discharge of Pop Ltd's indebtedness also looks extremely suspicious. It is very hard to understand how the making of this payment can have been in the best interests of Orange Ltd, and the liquidator should certainly investigate the circumstances in which it came to be made. There is a distinct possibility that the directors of Orange Ltd can be made personally liable for this wrongful dissipation of the company's assets, or that the money can be recovered from Pop Ltd: *Aveling Barford Ltd* v *Perion Ltd* (1989) 5 BCC 677.

A more general question which arises from any insolvent liquidation is whether the directors have carried on business knowing that the company was unable to meet its debts (in which case they can be made personally liable for wrongful trading – Insolvency Act (IA) 1986, s213) or whether they have sought to defraud any of the creditors by carrying on business knowing of the insolvency, in which case they may be criminally liable for fraudulent trading – IA 1986, s214.

In summary, the liquidator should be advised to investigate very carefully the circumstances of and justification for all these transactions. If not satisfied by the explanations which he receives, he should consider taking action against the directors of Orange Ltd (especially Cherry) and/or against Pop Ltd for recovery of sums wrongfully paid.

QUESTION TWO

In 1986, Helen, then aged 24, qualified as a chartered accountant. In 1987 she formed Pear Ltd and its wholly-owned subsidiary, Sub Ltd. Helen holds all the shares in Pear Ltd except one, which is held by a nominee for her. Pear Ltd holds all the shares in Sub Ltd, except one, which is similarly held by a nominee for Pear Ltd. Helen is the only director of both companies and neither company has filed any accounts with the Registrar for the last three years. Other than her shares in Pear Ltd, Helen has virtually no assets.

Since 1987 Pear Ltd has made telephone answering machines and has flourished so that it now has assets of over £1 million and employs 40 people. Sub Ltd however, is mainly engaged in supplying Pear Ltd with components and is not run primarily with a view to making a profit on its own, although for the first two years, 1988 and 1989, Sub Ltd made profits of £8,000 and £3,000 respectively. However in 1990 it made a loss of £38,000; in 1991 a loss of £23,000 and in 1992 a loss of £11,000.

In September 1991 Big Bank plc was pressing for a reduction of Sub Ltd's overdraft of £40,000. Helen then paid £20,000 of her own money into the account, taking in return a debenture from Sub Ltd for £20,000 and a floating charge to secure both that £20,000 and an earlier loan by her to the company of £15,000.

On 2 April 1993 a creditor presented a petition for the winding-up of Sub Ltd and a winding-up order was made on 14 May 1993. The assets of Sub Ltd fall short of its liabilities by £60,000.

Advise Helen as to her potential liabilities, if any, and her position generally.

University of London LLB Examination
(for External Students) Company Law June 1993 Q5

General Comment

A fairly straightforward question requiring an understanding of the remedies available to liquidators of insolvent companies.

Skeleton Solution

Avoidance of floating charges: 'connected persons' – wrongful trading: parent companies as shadow directors; relevance of Helen's qualification as an accountant – Company Directors Disqualification Act 1986.

Suggested Solution

The issues are: (a) is the floating charge taken by Helen totally or partially void (b) could Helen have incurred liability for wrongful trading, and (c) is Helen likely to be disqualified as a director?

a) Section 245(2)(a) Insolvency Act (IA) 1986 enables the liquidator of an insolvent company in certain circumstances to avoid floating charges. It provides in essence that a floating charge created at the relevant time will be invalid except to the extent of the aggregate of the fresh consideration supplied to the company at the same time as or after the creation of the charge. The relevant time for the above purposes is defined in s245(3)(a) as being two years in the case of a charge created in favour of a person connected with the company, beginning with the onset of the insolvency.

   From the facts of the instant case it can be seen that in September 1991, Helen in return for her cash injection of £20,000 took a debenture secured by a floating charge to the value of £35,000. As a director of Sub Ltd, Helen is a connected person and so the floating charge (since it was created less than two years before the winding-up order made in May 1993) is potentially liable to challenge from the liquidator. The question is whether Helen has provided fresh consideration. Section 245 IA 1986 aims to prevent the substitution of a secured debt for an unsecured debt. Provided the payment is for the benefit of the company the court will treat it as fresh consideration, *Re Matthew Ellis Ltd* [1933] Ch 458. As per the wording of the statute the consideration provided in return for the charge is £20,000. Helen's security is therefore likely to be valid only to the value of £20,000. She may seek to prove as an ordinary unsecured creditor for the balance of £15,000 but in view of the £60,000 shortfall of assets over liabilities will receive nothing.

b) Is Helen liable for wrongful trading? In order to hold a director liable for wrongful trading the court must be satisfied that at some time before the commencement of the winding-up, the director knew or ought to have concluded that there was no reasonable prospect of the company avoiding going into insolvent liquidation: s214 IA 1986. Section 214(4) IA 1986 provides that the facts of which the director will be taken to know will be judged according to: the general knowledge, skill and experience that may reasonably be expected of a person carrying out the same functions of that director, and the general knowledge, skill and experience that that director has. Helen's conduct will therefore be judged according to both objective and subjective standards. It should be noted that the standard is almost certainly therefore higher than that required to be exhibited by directors in the discharge of their common law duties of care and skill: per Romer J in *Re City Equitable Fire Insurance Co Ltd* [1925] Ch 407. It is significant therefore that Helen is a qualified accountant, as a consequence of which her decision to continue to trade will be measured against the likely decision of a similarly qualified 'reasonable' accountant.

We are told that Helen has not caused Sub Ltd to produce any annually audited accounts for the last three years. Helen's failure mirrors that of the directors in *Re Produce Marketing Consortium (No 2)* [1989] BCLC 520. In this case Knox J found that the directors could not rely on their own failure to keep proper accounts as a defence to the contention that they knew or ought to have known that the company would enter an insolvent liquidation. The only defence available to Helen is that once the inevitability of an insolvent liquidation occurred to her, she took every step with a view to minimising loss to creditors that she ought reasonably to have taken: s214(3) IA 1986. Thus far Helen is prima facie liable for wrongful trading.

Helen might seek to take solace in the fact that Pear Ltd, whilst the parent of Sub Ltd, is a different company and accordingly should logically remain unaffected by the demise of its subsidiary. She should be advised however that liability for wrongful trading applies to 'shadow directors' as it does to formally appointed directors. The term is defined in s251 as 'a person in accordance with whose directions or instructions the directors of the company are accustomed to act'. The Court of Appeal considered the definition of a shadow director in the case of *Secretary of State for Trade and Industry* v *Deverall* [2001] Ch 340. In order to establish that a person is a shadow director, it is not necessary to show that the person gives directions or instructions on every matter on which directors act, but it must be shown that the person has a real influence on the company's corporate affairs. The person can act quite openly in this role. The court will determine whether any communication should be classed as a direction or instruction. It is not necessary to show that the directors adopted a subservient role or surrendered their discretion to this person. We are told that Sub Ltd exists mainly for the purpose of supplying Pear Ltd with components. It is not therefore inconceivable that because of the high degree of connection between the two companies, Pear Ltd may be regarded by the court as a shadow director of Sub Ltd. Thus the assets of Pear Ltd may ultimately be used to satisfy the £60,000 shortfall.

c) Is Helen likely to be disqualified as a director pursuant to the Company Directors Disqualification Act (CDDA) 1986? The 1986 Act provides numerous grounds upon which Helen may be disqualified. By virtue of ss3, 6, and 11 she may be disqualified on the following grounds respectively; for persistent breach of companies legislation (failure to deliver accounts and annual return); duty of court to disqualify unfit directors of insolvent companies; disqualification for participation in wrongful trading. In relation to 'unfitness', Pts I and II of Sch 1 to the Act list the factors that are to be considered by the court in determining fitness. As to the behaviour warranting disqualification it will require at the very least a lack of commercial probity as opposed to ordinary misjudgment: *Re Lino Electric Motors Ltd* [1988] 4 Ch 477.

QUESTION THREE

Ace Ltd manufacturers and distributes Zapgrow, a combination of insecticide and fertiliser for use in crop spraying. Zapgrow has two ingredients, a highly toxic and volatile insecticide called Lethol and a powerful fertiliser called Ferti.

In 1991 Ace Ltd purchased a factory in order to ensure an adequate supply of Lethol for its manufacturing processes. In 1992, acting on advice from its legal department as to possible liability in the event of accidents at the factory, the board of directors of Ace Ltd decided to 'devolve' the manufacture of Lethol. In pursuance of this policy the factory was sold to Fay, a cousin of Cal. Cal is a director of Ace Ltd. Fay then sold it to Greed Ltd which had an issued share capital of two £1 shares which were vested in her brother Harry. Greed Ltd then entered into an agreement with Act Ltd whereby it undertook to supply to Ace Ltd, 500 gallons of Lethol per month. On 20 February 1994 when the factory was shut down for the weekend, chemicals stored there exploded, severely injuring 20 people living in houses nearby. Experts' reports put it beyond doubt that Greed Ltd was negligent in the manner in which the chemicals were stored. On its latest balance sheet Greed Ltd is shown to have a surplus of assets over liabilities of £1,500.

Sub Ltd is a subsidiary of Ace Ltd and has been manufacturing Ferti which it has then supplied to Ace Ltd. Ann and Bob are directors of Ace Ltd and Den and Ern are directors of Sub Ltd. Ern was appointed managing director of Sub Ltd last year. As well as being a director of Ace Ltd, Cal is also a director of Sub Ltd. The two boards have been meeting together once a year to co-ordinate group policy. On 25 March 1994, after receiving an order form signed by Ern 'on behalf of Sub', Ian supplied 200 tons of nitrates to Sub Ltd at a price of £25 per ton. On 9 May 1994 Sub Ltd went into insolvent liquidation with substantial liabilities and virtually no assets and without having paid Ian. It now transpires that it had been in financial difficulties for several years.

Advise Ian and advise Jon (who was one of those injured in the explosion).

University of London LLB Examination
(for External Students) Company Law June 1994 Q4

General Comment

This is a fairly difficult question. Attention to detail is an absolute necessity if students are to distil the legal issues from the morass of factual detail.

Skeleton Solution

Personal liability of directors for improper use of company name and for wrongful trading pursuant to s214 Insolvency Act 1986 – lifting the veil

Suggested Solution

Ian is an unpaid creditor of Sub Ltd which has gone into an insolvent liquidation. Sub Ltd has no assets and it is therefore unlikely that Ian will ever receive payment from Sub Ltd. It is significant that the contract was made by Ern 'on behalf of Sub'.

Pursuant to s349(1) Companies Act (CA) 1985, every company is obliged to have its name mentioned in all business letters and orders for goods purportedly made on behalf of the company. Pursuant to s349(4) of the Act, any director who orders goods on behalf of the company but who fails to mention the company's name pursuant to subs(1) (above) will be liable to a fine. More importantly, he will be personally liable to the creditor unless the creditor is paid by the company. Can Ian use s349 to his advantage and hold Ern personally liable for payment in respect of the 200 tons of nitrates supplied to Sub Ltd?

Ern might argue that Ian cannot have been misled simply by the omission of the word 'Ltd' from the written order and/or that the company's name (ie Sub Ltd's) name was correctly given, notwithstanding this omission. Ern will almost certainly fail on both counts. In *Atkins* v *Wardle* (1889) 58 LJ QB 337 it was held that directors were personally liable even though the word 'Ltd' appeared at one place in the document but not in another. Where a director omits the word 'Ltd' he has no locus standi to seek rectification of the document so as to escape liability: see *Blum* v *OCP Repartition SA* (1968) 4 BCC 771. It matters not whether or not Ian was misled by the omission of the word 'Ltd' unless Ian was himself responsible for the error: see *Scottish and Newcastle Breweries Ltd* v *Blair* 1967 SLT 72.

Ian therefore has no options. He may attempt to prove in the insolvent liquidation of Sub Ltd, or alternatively, he may sue Ern directly. It is worth mentioning briefly that the liquidator of Sub Ltd may seek to impose personal liability on the directors of Sub Ltd for wrongful trading, pursuant to s214 Insolvency Act (IA) 1986. There is insufficient information to advise confidently that liability will be imposed. However, in view of that fact that Sub Ltd has been in financial difficulties for years, it may possibly be worthy of investigation by the liquidator.

Jon will probably be less fortunate that Ian. We are told that Greed limited has an excess of assets over liabilities amounting to £1,500. This may or may not be sufficient to satisfy any judgment that he obtains against Greed Ltd. In the event that it is not,

Jon may ask whether there are any other potential defendants that might be sued. In view of the fact that Greed Ltd manufactured 'Lethol' for use by Ace Ltd, he may ask whether Ace Ltd can be made liable. Any such argument will very likely fail.

Ace Ltd disposed of the 'Lethol' factory precisely to avoid liability for the type of accident which has, in fact, occurred. Crucially, there is no proprietary relationship between Greed Ltd and Ace Ltd, in the sense that Ace Ltd does not own any shares in Greed Limited. The relationship between the companies is tenuous. Greed Limited is owned by Harry, who happens to be a cousin of Cal, who is a director of Ace Ltd. If the facts were different in that Greed Limited was a subsidiary of Ace Limited, or both companies had common owners, Jon might have argued that the 'veil of incorporation' could be lifted so as to make Ace Ltd liable. This would be an 'uphill struggle' for Jon, following the decision of the Court of Appeal in *Adams* v *Cape Industries plc* [1991] 1 All ER 929. In *Adams*, the Court of Appeal expressly recognised that it was a proper use of the corporate structure for groups to organise their affairs so that liability fell upon one company in the group rather than another. Such a scenario is to be distinguished from those cases where the veil is lifted to prevent evasion of a pre-existing obligation.

Chapter 14

Company Investigations

14.1 Introduction

14.2 Key points

14.3 Key cases, statute and report

14.4 Questions and suggested solutions

14.1 Introduction

To some extent this topic can be seen as overlapping with that of minority protection, since seeking an investigation into the company's affairs is one of the ways in which a disaffected minority can protect itself. Investigations are, however, a relatively minor part of that topic, since minorities now have more effective means of protection available to them. Further, investigations arise in circumstances other than that of a disaffected minority, and are worthy of independent treatment.

14.2 Key points

The Companies Act (CA) 1985 (as amended by the CA 1989) gives the Secretary of State a number of powers (note that these are not duties) to investigate the affairs of companies and ownership of their shares. The principal provisions to note are as follows.

a) Section 431 CA 1985 gives power to appoint an inspector on the application of members of the company or the company itself. In the case of a company with a share capital, the minimum number of members is 200 holding not less than one-tenth of the issued shares. The application must be supported by sufficient evidence and the applicants may have to give security for costs.

b) Section 432(2) CA 1985 gives power to appoint an inspector if there are circumstances suggesting one or more of the following grounds:

   i) conduct with intent to defraud creditors or unfairly prejudicial to some part of the membership;

   ii) an act or proposed act or omission of the company which would be so prejudicial, or the company has been formed for a fraudulent or unlawful purpose;

iii) persons concerned with the formation or management of the company have been guilty in connection with it of fraud, misfeasance or other misconduct towards the company or its members;

iv) the members have not been given all the information with respect to the company's affairs that they might reasonably expect.

c) Section 447(1)–(3) CA 1985 give the Secretary of State power at any time if he thinks there is good reason to require the company to produce documents at a specific time or place, or to produce them to his duly appointed officer (who will usually attend at the company's offices without prior notice). This is the most used power, for obvious reasons, and there are criminal sanctions for non-compliance. A person charged with such an offence may have a defence if the documents are not in his possession or it is not reasonably practicable to produce them.

d) Section 448 CA 1985 provides that a warrant may be obtained from a Justice of the Peace (JP) for the police to search the company's premises for documents. Usually a s447 demand must already have been made, but the CA 1989 amended the provision by adding subs(2), so that a warrant may nevertheless be issued if the JP is satisfied that:

i) there are reasonable grounds for thinking an indictable offence has been committed and there are documents on the premises relating to it;

ii) the applicant has the power to require production; and

iii) there are reasonable grounds for believing that if production were required, the demand would not be complied with and the documents would be removed, hidden, tampered with or destroyed.

e) Sections 442–446 CA 1985 contain powers relating to the appointment of inspectors to investigate the ownership of shares in a company. Section 446 CA 1985 sanctions investigations into suspected improper dealings by a director or a person connected with a director of the company.

14.3 Key cases, statute and report

- *Fayed* v *United Kingdom (Case No 28/1993/423/502)* (1994) The Times 11 November (European Court of Human Rights)
  Inspectors' reports did not violate art 6(1) European Convention on Human Rights

- *Norwest Holst Ltd* v *Department of Trade* [1978] 3 All ER 280
  Secretary of State is not required to observe rules of natural justice when deciding whether to make an investigation

- *Pergamon Press Ltd, Re* [1971] Ch 388
  Inspectors are masters of their own procedure

- *Westminster Property Management Ltd, Re* [2001] BCC 121
  Interaction of human rights legislation in area of self-incrimination

- *Companies in 1994–95*
  A report by the DTI revealing a record number of company investigations mainly for fraudulent trading and theft. There were 529 directors disqualified in this period

- Companies Act 1985

  - s431 – power to appoint inspector

  - s432(2) – further power to appoint an inspector

  - ss442 to 446 – power to appoint inspector to investigate ownership of shares

  - ss447(1) to (3) – power of Secretary of State

14.4 Questions and suggested solutions

The two questions which have been set on this topic are printed below. It can be seen that both run along very much the same lines, asking about two matters, the adequacy of the powers in a legal sense and the strength of the political will to use those powers. The suggested essay which appears below the questions would do equally well for either question and, it is thought, for any other essay question on this topic which is likely to appear. It may be observed in passing that students who are not well versed in the relevant legislation would be well advised to steer clear of this topic if at all possible – this is not an area in which intelligent students can bluff their way through.

QUESTIONS

'Although the investigative powers of the Department of Trade have been substantially extended by recent legislation, that Department still lacks both the powers and the will to act as a watchdog for minority shareholders.'

Discuss.

University of London LLB Examination
(for External Students) Company Law June 1984 Q3

'Statute has now provided sufficient machinery for any type of corporate investigation which may be necessary. What is lacking is the will to use that machinery.'

Discuss.

University of London LLB Examination
(for External Students) Company Law June 1987 Q1(a)

General Comment

This is part of a much wider area of maladministration and the remedies that are available. The other aspects of this area are considered under chapters dealing with minority protection and directors. The area of DTI investigations is somewhat specialised and is therefore not a common choice for examination questions.

Skeleton Solution

Powers contained in CA 1985, Pt XIV – appointments of inspectors to investigate and report: Secretary of State may act on their report – investigations into company ownership and dealings in shares: petitions to wind-up company – powers are extensive – major problem seems to be reluctance to use them in practice.

Suggested Solution

One of the duties of the Secretary of State is to ensure that companies conduct their affairs in an appropriate manner and that the interests of creditors are properly protected. Part XIV Companies Act (CA) 1985 gives the Secretary of State considerable investigative and regulatory powers to assist him in carrying out this duty. Amendments to Pt XIV by CA 1989 have strengthened the Secretary of State's powers.

Under s431 of the Act the Secretary of State can appoint one or more inspectors to investigate the affairs of a company. This may be done on the application of certain interested parties or on the application of the company itself. The Secretary of State must be satisfied that there are good reasons for making the application, though the statute does not define what these reasons may include.

Under s432 the Secretary of State may appoint inspectors without the need for any application if he suspects that the company's affairs are being conducted in a manner prejudicial to the interests of creditors or if he suspects fraud. He is not subject to the rules of natural justice in deciding whether to appoint inspectors under this provision: *Norwest Holst Ltd* v *Department of Trade* [1978] 3 All ER 280. Section 432 also allows the court to require the Secretary of State to appoint inspectors.

Once appointed, inspectors are given certain powers by the Act. They may require the production of documents and may take statements under oath from officers and others concerned with the running of the company. They may make interim reports to the Secretary of State and must make a final report. It is a contempt of court to obstruct the inspectors in their enquiries. There is no privilege against self incrimination when required by inspectors to answer relevant questions. See, for example, *Bishopsgate Investment Management Ltd* v *Maxwell* [1992] 2 All ER 856. Once the report is made the Secretary of State may take civil proceedings on behalf of the company if he judges it expedient to do so – s438.

In addition to the above the Secretary of State has the power to order investigations into company ownership (s442) and into dealings in the shares of a company (s449). These powers are supplemented by powers to enter and search premises (s448) and require production of documents (s447). It is a criminal offence to destroy relevant documents in such cases (s450).

In practice the inspector has to work on his own initiative, and the success of the investigation will depend heavily on the energy and perseverance which he brings to his task – see, for example, *Re Pergamon Press Ltd* [1971] Ch 388 and *Maxwell* v *Department of Trade* [1974] 2 WLR 338.

Finally, the Secretary of State may petition for the winding-up of the company under the Insolvency Act 1986, s122 on the just and equitable ground and can apply for a disqualification order against a director or shadow director of a company under s8 and Sch 1, Company Directors Disqualification Act 1986.

The above clearly indicates that a wide range of powers is available, and recent years have seen an increased willingness to exercise those powers, especially in cases such as the Guinness scandal, which attract considerable public interest. The major difficulty seems to be that there is a reluctance to take legal proceedings against those involved in running the company, even when the inspector's report points clearly to serious wrongdoing. It is at this latter point that the regulatory system seems to break down; no change in the law can remedy this, since it is a political issue rather than a legal one.

Chapter 15

External Influences: the EC, Corporate Governance and Human Rights

15.1   Introduction

15.2   Key points

15.3   Key cases and materials

15.4   Questions and suggested solutions

15.1 Introduction

Not all influences on company law come from statute and case law. In recent years, thinking about the structure and management of companies has been affected by outside influences, notably the European Community's harmonisation programme and the increasing pressure for good corporate governance. Both of these topical issues have appeared in fairly recent London papers, and it is convenient to deal with them together here.

15.2 Key points

Company law directives

A number of directives have been issued by the EC in connection with its programme of harmonising the company laws in the Member States of the European Community in order to achieve the aims of the EC Treaty. A directive is not incorporated directly into the law of the Member State but requires the Member State to change its law to conform with the provisions of the directive. Since Britain's accession to the EC there have been some 12 company law directives, although some are still in the draft stage, and not all of those issued have yet been complied with. When considering the provisions of an EC directive, it is worth remembering that most of the Member States do not have a common law jurisdiction, and many favour a different way of dealing with certain corporate problems than has been favoured in England and Wales.

Of the directives, the most important have been the following.

a) The First – which became the notorious s9 European Communities Act 1972 (see Chapter 2: *The Memorandum of Association and Legal Capacity*), and was finally translated into ss35 and 35A Companies Act (CA) 1985.

b) The Second and Fourth – which led to the more detailed regulation of public companies and directors originally contained in the Companies Acts 1980 and 1981.

c) The Twelfth – on single member private companies, which was implemented by Statutory Instrument.

d) The Directive on Insider Dealing – implemented by Pt V Criminal Justice Act 1993 (see Chapter 10: *Insider Dealing*).

Still proceeding are the Thirteenth Directive on Takeovers, the Draft Fifth Directive (two-tier boards) and the Draft Ninth Directive (groups). Of these, the Fifth is perhaps the most fertile ground for questions. The vexed question in relation to the Fifth, which is highly controversial at least so far as Britain is concerned, is 'co-determination'. In Germany, where the concept of supervisory boards (which oversee the operation of the managerial board) originated, worker-directors (or employee-directors) play an important role on those boards. In the late 1970s, the idea of worker-directors gained some popularity in Britain with the publication of the Bullock Report (Report of the Committee of Inquiry into Industrial Democracy (Cmnd 6706)) which recommended employee representation in the decision-making process, although not necessarily at board level. There is, however, a great deal of opposition to the idea from British industrialists. Their views are supported by the current Government and have prevailed to the present day, thus the recommendations in the Report have never been implemented.

Although, as the Fifth Directive is presently drafted, it is thought that the English idea of a unitary board with majority non-executive director representation will be sufficient compliance, the Directive undoubtedly requires a significant employee representation in the decision-making process (even if only in a consultative role) and it is to this that the present Government policy is opposed, hence the delay in adopting the Directive.

Corporate governance

'Corporate governance' is not a legal term of art but a convenient label which has been attached to problems concerning the way in which a company is managed and, in particular, abuse by public company directors of their position.

The Cadbury Report

The takeover fever of the 1980s led to 'scandals' involving directors and senior employees of certain public companies being investigated or put on trial in connection with alleged criminal offences. These included Guinness plc, County NatWest (a subsidiary of National Westminster Bank), Queens Moat Houses plc, Brent Walker plc, Polly Peck plc, and the Robert Maxwell group of companies. Not just directors, but well-known City professionals came under public scrutiny and the City, led by the Stock Exchange, was required to bring in self-regulatory measures in an attempt to prevent a recurrence.

The Committee of Inquiry into the Financial Aspects of Corporate Governance was set up under the chairmanship of Sir Adrian Cadbury, and published its Report (known as the Cadbury Report) and Code of Best Practice in 1993. The Report made a large number of recommendations concerning accounting practices and the management of public companies. Most important for company law purposes are the provisions of the Code which recommend significant non-executive director representation on boards for supervisory purposes. It also recommends the establishment of audit and remuneration committees and the separation of the roles of chairman and chief executive.

Compliance with the Code is not mandatory, but companies have to state in their annual report whether or not they comply with it. Most now do. The main problems with this approach, however, are that it is hard, given the relatively small pool of suitable persons and the interlocking nature of board membership in large public companies, to find suitably independent non-executive directors (indeed there may be no incentive to try), and there are signs that some of these directors resent having to occupy a monitoring role within the company.

The Greenbury Report

Despite the Cadbury recommendations concerning remuneration committees, there was a recent public outcry over the remuneration packages awarded to directors in public utility companies. The Greenbury Committee was set up to look into this and published its recommendations early in 1995. One of these, that share option schemes should be taxed, was implemented immediately and then withdrawn by the Government when it was seen to affect employees other than directors. Changes have also been made to the Stock Exchange Listing Rules to secure prior shareholder approval of long-term incentive schemes and the publication of a company policy statement on share options and incentive schemes.

Self-regulation

This topic may be approached from the point of view of asking whether self-regulatory systems can ever be effective. It may then be combined with the regulation of takeovers and mergers, which is supervised by the Takeover Panel of the Stock Exchange. In favour of self-regulation, it is said that Government and the courts should not interfere too much in the conduct of business, such interference causes delay and is bad for business confidence. Against, it may be argued that self-regulation provides no effective sanctions and that, in the present business climate, something stronger than the disapproval of their peers is required by those prepared to act unethically in order to make a profit.

Human rights

Although these rights are thought of as individual rights, it seems that companies may benefit from them too: see *R v Broadcasting Standards Commission, ex parte BBC* [2000] 3

All ER 989, where the Court of Appeal held that under the Broadcasting Act 1996 a company can complain to the Broadcasting Standards Commission that there has been an unwarranted infringement of its privacy in connection with obtaining material included in broadcast programmes.

15.3 Key cases and materials

- *Centros Ltd* v *Ertvervs-og Selskabsstyrelsen* Case C–212/97 [2000] 2 WLR 1048
  Two Danish citizens registered a company in the UK intending that it would not trade in the UK but through a branch in Denmark, taking advantage of a lack of minimum capital requirement in the UK – Denmark's refusal to register the branch contravened art 43 EC Treaty which prohibits restrictions on freedom of establishment

- Anyone interested in this topic is recommended to read the Cadbury and Greenbury Reports and also the newspaper accounts of company collapses and trials in the latter half of the 1980s. Relevant cases are *Guinness plc* v *Saunders and Anor* [1988] 2 All ER 940; *R* v *Seelig*; *R* v *Spens* [1991] 1 WLR 624; and *R* v *Maxwell* (1996) (unreported)

15.4 Questions and suggested solutions

QUESTION ONE

'The effect of our entry into the EEC has had, and will continue to have, an almost entirely malign effect on the overall development of English company law.'

Discuss.

University of London LLB Examination
(for External Students) Company Law June 1993 Q2

General Comment

A fairly simple question provided that the candidate has a sufficient working knowledge of the underlying subject matter. A good opportunity for candidates to illustrate that they have their finger on the pulse.

Skeleton Solution

Impact of Community law upon UK company law: aims of secondary legislation; difficulties – examples of secondary legislation translated into Companies Acts: are the difficulties with the implementation conceptual or practical?; has the UK achieved the aims of the secondary legislation? – the future: proposals for increased worker participation; a supervisory board for the plc.

Suggested Solution

That Community law has already had a tremendous impact on English company law cannot be doubted. To maintain that its effect upon English company law is and will continue to be entirely malign is demonstrably inaccurate. Such inadequacies as have appeared to date may be properly attributed to our own parliamentary draftsmen who experience difficulties in expressing secondary legislation in terms appropriate to the domestic canvas. Hence many Community reforms were introduced in the Companies Act (CA) 1985, but have only been properly implemented 'second time around' by virtue of CA 1989. That the problems are not conceptual is best illustrated by considering some of the principal (and almost entirely beneficial) changes that have been made to our domestic law.

Perhaps the most significant changes to domestic law can be seen in the form of the new ss35, 35A, 35B as implemented by s108 CA 1989. In its original unamended form s35 CA 1985 represented the codification of art 9 of the First Directive on Company Law of 1968. Its greatest flaw was that s35 attempted to deal in an instant with the doctrine of ultra vires but without distinguishing between ultra vires and directors' want of authority. This and the wording of the section itself led to difficulties of interpretation, for example, when does a person 'deal' with a company? What was meant by 'good faith'? Did the transaction have to be expressly approved by all of the directors? Lawson J's judgment in *International Sales & Agencies Ltd v Marcus* [1982] 3 All ER 551 is famous for providing answers to some at least of these questions. But it is more significant for present purposes to note that the directive itself made no mention of 'dealing' or 'good faith'. These constructions were the product of our own draftsmen. Thus the fault lay not with the aim of the Commission but with our implementation of the Directive.

These problems were largely ironed out by s108 CA 1989 which noticeably avoids any reference to 'dealing' and provides guidance as to the meaning of 'good faith'.

The beneficial effects of Community intervention may also be seen in the area of consolidated accounts and in particular the obligations imposed by virtue of the Seventh Directive (Pt VII and Sch 4A CA 1985). By virtue of these amendments there is a new (and more stringent) definition of parent and subsidiary and there is also an obligation on companies to include unincorporated subsidiary 'undertakings' (eg, partnerships) owned by the group in the accounts. The value of this practice is that companies are now less likely to be able to borrow massive amounts via subsidiaries but to keep the subsidiary and therefore also the subsidiary's borrowing off the group balance sheet. The effect is entirely beneficial since the investing public is less likely to be misled into investing in a group that appears to be more solvent than it in fact is.

The above Directives represent a fraction of the law that has passed into our statute books in the area of company law. If there is to be a complaint about the impact of Community law then it must be largely centred around the piecemeal approach of the Commission to reform. Thus as directives are issued the national states make legislation without knowing (with any certainty) whether a further directive will require alteration of the legislation based upon the preceding directive.

Before concluding we must ask whether there are likely to be any future malign consequences of our membership of the EEC. Again, because of the piecemeal approach (referred to above) little more can be done than to consider briefly some of the proposed changes that may or may not become law.

The draft Fifth Directive provides for more effective monitoring of management in the case of public limited companies by making a division between directors responsible for management and those responsible for their supervision, the two tier board. Especially significant is the proposal that directors are to be jointly and severally liable except to the extent that the individual director can prove that no fault is personally attributable to him. If implemented such a proposal can only serve to better managerial standards and hopefully go some way towards preventing the reoccurrence of commercial catastrophes like the Maxwell and/or Polly Peck sagas.

Secondly, the Fifth Directive contains proposals to increase worker participation, possibly by guaranteed representation at board level. The precise degree of participation afforded to workers is a matter for debate, but it cannot be doubted but that an informed and well represented workforce is likely to be more productive. Present thinking in the UK favours the consultation model, which is one of the four possible options presently on the table.

QUESTION TWO

'It is quite pointless to think that we can discuss any questions of "policy" [in law reform] in the abstract ... when the reality of the matter is that it is Europe that has loomed largest in the minds of everyone who has been concerned with companies legislation in recent years ... For we have to accept that, so long as we are in Europe, there will be pressure for changes in company law, and this pressure will not go away.' (Sealy)

Discuss.

Is there a need for clearer policy in company law reform?

University of London LLB Examination
(for External Students) Company Law June 1994 Q1

General Comment

A fairly difficult question requiring a critical appreciation of the impact of European Community law upon our domestic company law.

Skeleton Solution

Need for domestic reform: hitherto impact of European Community law on domestic company law – domestic legislation: potential conflict with Community law; need for clearer policy – likely ambit of domestic and Community legislation: continuing need for formulation of policy.

Suggested Solution

Taken at face value, Sealy appears to be suggesting that accession to the European Community has paralysed domestic reform of company law and, moreover, that it has rendered both the consideration of reform and the adoption of policy a sterile exercise. At any rate from a domestic view point. There is indeed a need for clearer policy in company law reform. While it cannot be doubted that simple domestic reforms may have a very limited shelf life, in so far as they may be rendered superfluous by Community law, it will always be necessary to formulate policy at domestic level. Only then can the United Kingdom address the challenge of taking a more active role in the preparatory stages of Community legislation.

Since 1972, the major changes to domestic companies' legislation have been underpinned by numerous directives, eg the First, Second, Third, Fourth, Sixth, Seventh and Eighth Directives. The impact of the Directives has been almost entirely beneficial; for example, the substantial abolition of ultra vires, the general liability of promoters upon pre-incorporation contracts and the new rules governing the preparation of group accounts. However, with company law, as with other areas of law, the legal translation of directives into domestic legislation has not proved altogether smooth, eg see s35 Companies Act (CA) 1985 (unamended).

The possibility of domestic legislation being superseded by Community directives is a real one. It has the consequence that the legislature is likely only to pass consequential or amending legislation, without tackling some of the fundamental and perennial problems which face the courts regularly, eg should parent companies be liable for the debts of wholly owned subsidiaries? Professor Gower in *Principles of Modern Company Law* (5th ed, p70) puts it thus:

> '... the reaction has been to add to the existing framework without ever re-examining its foundations to ensure that they are sufficiently sound to bear the weight of the expanding superstructure.'

It should also be borne in mind that Community law will be enacted only in so far as it is necessary to 'harmonise' the domestic laws of Member States. The Companies Division of the Department of Trade and Industry produces an annual report entitled 'Harmonisation of Company Law and Related Law in the European Community: Progress of Draft Directives and Proposals'. A cursory glance at the report reveals the array of proposals which may or may not eventually become Community law. Against this background of potential Community law it is almost impossible for domestic legislation to be formulated (or at least implemented) in any lasting or meaningful way.

Domestic reforms are therefore likely to be of a very technical nature without any attempt being made to address fundamental problems, except to the extent that harmonisation requires that they be addressed. There is, however, a tendency to forget that Community law is decided upon collectively by Member States. Logically, the way forward should be for much-needed domestic policies and proposed reforms to be pursued into the European arena.

QUESTION THREE

'In spite of the growth in the number of superficial legal restrictions imposed on them in recent years, directors are in fact as free as ever to misuse their powers. The self-regulatory approach advocated in the Cadbury Report merely serves to underline the government's abdication of responsibility for providing a suitable legal framework.'

Discuss.

University of London LLB Examination
(for External Students) Company Law June 1995 Q3

General Comment

The proposition can be dealt with by examining the foundations of directors' power and the rationale for the freedoms that lead to abuse. This raises consideration of whether the abuses can be ended without reducing the discretion given to directors to act in the best interests of the company. The question requires an overview of directors' powers and duties, and the consequences of a directors' powers regime based upon other foundations.

Skeleton Solution

Legal rationale of English director law – directors' powers, origin, purpose, scope for setting limits – wide or narrow scope of powers – significance of director/shareholders – concept of director as fiduciary – duty owed to company – alternative basis of powers likely to remove discretions and fiduciary basis – existing safeguards – conclusion.

Suggested Solution

The proposition suggests the possibility of a legislative framework of controls which would prevent, as distinct from punishing, the misuse of directors' powers. Such controls would necessarily have to operate without substantial restrictions upon the management of the company's affairs. It is submitted that the proposition fails to take into account the legal rationale of directors' powers, and the great importance of individual and collective freedoms and discretions that are given to directors in managing the affairs of the company so as to achieve the fullest potential of the corporate form in providing benefits to company, director, member, employee, creditor and society generally. It is necessary to consider the origin and nature of directors' powers in order to assess whether any alternative regime would be as effective, overall, as the present one.

Directors' powers

A company as a legal, non-natural person, cannot act for itself but must necessarily act through the agency of the Board or the General Meeting. The powers of the Board are determined largely by the memorandum and the articles which, subject to the Companies Act (CA) 1985, divide powers and functions of the company between either the Board or the members in General Meeting. Table A art 70, allows for the Board management of the company's business and the exercise of all the company's powers subject only to the 1985 Act, the memorandum, the articles and the special resolution of the General Meeting. From this, it follows that the extent of the Board's powers is initially determined by the purposes of the founders of the company and, subsequently, by its controllers. The appointment, remuneration, retirement, circumstances of dismissal and even the regulation of directors' proceedings such as Board meetings can be prescribed by the articles: see Table A CA 1985 arts 64–98. The obvious consequence of this is that the width of directors' powers can range between the case of one who exercises little power at all to another who is almost omnipotent and is, in reality, subject only to the power of the courts in applying the companies legislation. The problems of potential width of powers are amplified by the possibility that the directors may also be shareholders and may well be responsible qua member for the scope of their own powers as directors. This is where the real potential for abuse lies and it is hard to see what legislation can do to remedy the problem of controllers giving to directors such powers as they think appropriate. The only possible way to deal with the near-infinite permutations of company control and management is by a clear and well-established doctrine of directors' duties which the courts can apply to all company directors, irrespective of the width of powers that they exercise, coupled with a wide range of sanctions for breach of the duty. The flexibility of the directors' duty concept lies in the principle that the duty is one of good faith and that it is owed to the company itself, generally to the exclusion of, or in priority to, duties owed to others. Thus, even the owner of most of the shares in a company, if he is a director, will owe duties to the company which he ignores at his peril.

Directors' duties

Directors' duties are of a fiduciary nature and really come down to the necessity for each director to act honestly, carefully and with such skill as he possesses in the best interests of the company as a whole. This has to be seen in the context of the business world, where speculation and some risk-taking is often necessary, so that the duties are somewhat different to those of a trustee or an agent as regards discretion to act. A clear illustration of the flexible but effective use of duty as a check upon abuses is seen in the cases concerning claims that the directors owe duties to persons other than the company. These cases all show that the powers must be exercised for the benefit of the company itself, that is the members collectively rather than for: the directors themselves (*Regal (Hastings) Ltd v Gulliver* [1967] 2 AC 134n); or company officers or employees (*Parke v Daily News* [1962] Ch 927); or the company's subsidiary or holding company (*Charterbridge Corporation v Lloyds Bank* [1970] Ch 62); or a section of the membership

(*Multinational Gas & Petrochemical Co Ltd* v *Multinational Gas and Petrochemical Services Ltd* [1983] Ch 258).

It does not follow from this general rule that no duties at all are owed to others by the directors. There are circumstances where the directors will be found to owe fiduciary duties to members as illustrated by *Allen* v *Hyatt* (1914) 30 TLR 444 and *Dawson International* v *Coats Paton plc* [1989] BCLC 233 and, of course, there can be liability towards members on a *Hedley Byrne* basis (*Hedley Byrne & Co* v *Heller and Partners* [1964] AC 465) for negligent misstatement: see *Caparo Industries plc* v *Dickman* [1990] 2 WLR 358. The general rule remains that the duties are to protect the good of the company as a whole. Even the statutory duty owed by directors in performing their functions (to have regard to the interests of employees) is owed to the company alone: s309 CA 1985.

It can be seen that the English law view of the director as a fiduciary justifies the width of powers that may be given to him at the instance of the incorporators, provided breaches are remediable. Any attempt to replace this system with a statutory code, breach of which would be punishable according to the statutory penalties, would almost certainly lead to many directors being unwilling to continue upon such a basis, as their freedom to act would be considerably compromised. The existing investigative and punitive safeguards under CA 1985, Insolvency Act 1986 and Company Directors Disqualification Act 1986, the growing use of minority oppression petitions under s459 CA 1985 combined with the wide and comprehensive case law on directors' duties should be found capable of containing abuses to a publicly acceptable level for the foreseeable future. This depends upon sufficient political will and funding to enforce regulatory and disqualification proceedings. The safeguards upon any insolvency involving abusive directors will continue to be used with vigour by the wide and increasingly experienced body of insolvency practitioners, and it is submitted that the existing legal framework is perfectly adequate and should be used to maximum effect rather than trying to replace it with something which may damage the corporate form considerably.

Chapter 16

Corporate Crime

16.1   Introduction

16.2   Key points

16.3   Key cases and statutes

16.4   Question and suggested solution

16.1 Introduction

The expression 'corporate crime' relates to the question of the company's possible liability for criminal and/or tortious acts carried out on its behalf by its agents.

16.2 Key points

Criminal liability

The principal difficulty of fixing a company with criminal liability is the problem of imputing mens rea. This problem is circumvented in the case of offences relating specifically to corporations by making them crimes of strict liability, which do not require mens rea. However, this leaves other offences where it is indisputable that the acts which constitute the actus reus have been committed in the name or in the course of the business of the company.

English law, therefore, identifies the company with its 'organs' (organic theory), the leading case in the area being *Tesco Supermarkets Ltd* v *Nattrass* [1972] AC 153. Here, the actual perpetrator of the offence was the manager of one of the many supermarkets belonging to the company, and the House of Lords held that the company could not be held responsible. For there to be corporate liability, the commission of the offence had to be by an organ of the company – individuals who are part of the 'directing mind and will' of the company – which effectively means the board. However, in the earlier case of *R* v *ICR Haulage* [1944] KB 551 it was held that the company could be liable for a managing director's acts, even when he was acting outside the normal scope of his duties.

Because of the mandatory sentence of life imprisonment, it is assumed that a company cannot be charged with murder. However, in recent years, interest has focused on attempts to make corporations liable for manslaughter, highlighted in the unreported prosecutions brought against *PLO* (1990) and *OLL Ltd* (1994) as a result of disasters in which members of the public lost their lives. In these cases, at least, the courts remained faithful to the principles enunciated in *Tesco Supermarkets Ltd* v *Nattrass* [1972] AC 153.

However, some commentators claim to have detected a recognition by the courts in other cases of the limitations of the *Tesco* concept of liability, where the offence in question was statutory and liability turned on an interpretation of the statute. In *Re Supply of Ready Mixed Concrete (No 2)* [1995] 1 AC 456; *Tesco Stores Ltd* v *Brent London Borough Council* [1993] 1 WLR 1037; and *Meridian Global Funds Management Asia Ltd* v *Securities Commission* [1995] 3 All ER 918 the House of Lords, the Divisional Court and the Privy Council respectively inclined towards a more direct application of the principles of vicarious liability (see below). In *Seaboard Offshore Ltd* v *Secretary of State for Transport* [1994] 2 All ER 99, where the House of Lords had to consider the application of a new statutory offence created in response to the *Herald of Free Enterprise* disaster, the Lords refused (on a construction of the statute) to impose vicarious liability for all the ship's employees but suggested it may be possible to establish liability by showing that the company failed to establish a safe system. On this basis, it has been suggested that the law may be moving towards a 'systems and procedures' approach.

Tortious liability

The law of tort has long imposed liability on employers for the tortious acts of their employees committed in the scope of their duties (vicarious liability), and companies are no different from any other employer in this regard. It is necessary to establish that the tortfeasor was an employee of the company, and that he acted within the scope of his employment. The company has a right of indemnity against the employee who committed the tort. *Lennard's Carrying Co* v *Asiatic Petroleum* [1915] AC 705 is perhaps the leading tort case where it was held that a company could be liable for the default of its managing director. There are many other cases where companies have been held vicariously liable for torts committed by employees but, as this topic falls within the ambit of the law of tort, it is highly unlikely that a candidate would be expected to analyse them in a company law paper.

It will rarely be the case nowadays that an executive director of the company who commits a tort is not an employee, but if this should be the case, the company may be held liable on agency principles if the tort was committed within the scope of the director's authority.

16.3 Key cases and reports

- *El Ajou* v *Dolar Land Holdings plc & Another* [1994] BCC 143
  Non-executive director who was also the company's chairman was also the directing mind and will of the company

- *Meridian Global Funds Management Asia Ltd* v *Securities Commission* [1995] 3 All ER 918
  In deciding what acts are to be attributed to the company the court may choose to apply either the 'directing mind and will' theory or the wider principles of agency

- *R* v *P & O European Ferries (Dover) Ltd* (1990) 93 Cr App R 72
  A company could be indicted for manslaughter

- *Seaboard Offshore Ltd* v *Secretary of State for Transport* [1994] 2 All ER 99
  The company was not convicted

- *Tesco Stores Ltd* v *Brent London Borough Council* [1993] 1 WLR 1037
  Directing mind and will defence rejected

- *Tesco Supermarkets Ltd* v *Nattrass* [1972] AC 153
  Directing mind and will of the company

- *Williams* v *Natural Life Health Foods Ltd* [1998] 1 WLR 830
  Director can avoid personal liability in tort it there is no personal responsibility

Note: in an unreported case (*OLL* (1995)), a company was convicted of manslaughter and the managing director was sentenced to imprisonment.

- Law Commission Involuntary Manslaughter (Consultation Paper No 135) 1994

- Law Commission Legislating the Criminal Code: Involuntary Manslaughter (Consultation Paper No 237) 1996

16.4 Question and suggested solution

To what extent can (a) tortious and (b) criminal liability be imposed on companies?

University of London LLB Examination
(for External Students) Company Law June 1985 Q3

General Comment

This question requires examination of both the major problem areas – tort and crime.

Skeleton Solution

Tort: vicarious liability for acts of employees within scope of their employment – also for acts of directors/managers acting in that capacity – ultra vires acts can also be the basis of liability – Crime: general principle is that acts of 'directing mind' of company are company's own acts – this is question of fact – company may escape if act is through 'default of another'.

Suggested Solution

It is clear that a company, like an individual, is vicariously liable for torts committed by its employees when they are acting within the scope of their employment, even if the tort includes wilful malice: *Citizens' Life Assurance Co v Brown* [1904] AC 423. The same principle applies to criminal liability if the statute creating the liability imposes liability on employer as well as employee and the employer is a company.

In some cases the court has interpreted a statute as imposing liability on the company when the offence was committed by an officer of the company acting within the scope of his employment: *DPP v Kent and Sussex Contractors Ltd* [1944] KB 146. More recently, though, there has been some reluctance to impose such liability unless the persons who generally manage the company have actively participated in the crime. In *Tesco Supermarkets Ltd v Nattrass* [1972] AC 153 the company was charged under s11(2) Trades Descriptions Act 1968 with advertising goods at a lower price than that at which they were sold. The situation arose because the manager of the particular Tesco store had failed in his duty to ensure that the goods advertised were in fact available. The company had a sophisticated supervisory system designed to prevent this sort of thing from happening, but it had broken down on this occasion. Tesco pleaded that the offence was due to the default of another (the manager) and that they had taken all reasonable care. This defence is specifically allowed under the 1968 Act. The defence succeeded: Lord Reid pointed out that a company must act through living persons; in some circumstances that person is the embodiment of the company rather than its agent, and no question of vicarious liability can arise. However, it was the board of directors here which was the embodiment of the company, and its authority had not been delegated to the store manager, who was therefore to be treated as a separate person.

This case requires to be treated with some caution, for the 'default of another' defence was contained within the 1968 Act, but is not generally available to companies charged with criminal wrongdoing. The case does illustrate, however, that not every act by every junior employee will be considered to be the act of the company for the purposes of the criminal law.

Two major areas of difficulty have arisen here, and these have not so far been explored in any detail by the courts. First, for what acts of the board of directors is the company to be held responsible? So far as tort is concerned the company is responsible for the tortious acts/omissions of those who manage the company when they are acting in that capacity. In *Lennard's Carrying Co v Asiatic Petroleum* [1915] AC 705 the company was held liable for the default of a single managing director who ought to have known that a particular ship was unseaworthy. It was said that the managing director was the directing mind and will of the company (or, as it is sometimes expressed, the company was his alter ego).

The search for the directing mind and will of the company is not restricted to looking at the formal provisions of the memorandum and articles; rather, this is a question of fact to be determined in all the circumstances. This is so equally in criminal cases, and if the company is to be convicted it must be proved that the (natural) person in question controlled the management of the company: *R v Andrews Weatherfoil Ltd* [1972] 1 WLR

118. A difficulty arises here where a sole director is charged with conspiring with the company: conspiracy necessarily requires two independent minds, and these cannot be found if it is established that the company has no mind or intelligence independent of the will of the sole director: *R v McDonnell* [1966] 1 QB 233.

In *R v ICR Haulage* [1944] KB 551 it was held that the company could be criminally liable for the wrongful act of its managing director even though the act was outside the normal ambit of his duties. *Lennard's Carrying Co v Asiatic Petroleum* [1915] AC 705 suggests that the position would be the same in tort.

Other criminal cases (eg *Re Supply of Ready Mixed Concrete (No 2)* [1995] 1 AC 456) have turned on the question of whether, on an interpretation of the statute in question, vicarious liability could be attributed to the company. In one case, however, the House of Lords has suggested that a company could be held liable for failing to establish a safe system (*Seaboard Offshore Ltd v Secretary of State for Transport* [1994] 2 All ER 99). Again the case concerned interpretation of a particular statute and it remains to be seen whether the courts are prepared to develop that approach.

It may be noted finally that one effect of the 'alter ego' doctrine is to circumvent the problem of imposing liability for offences which require a specific intent; even if the company cannot form the intent, its alter ego presumably can, and this is enough to found liability.

Law Update 2003 edition – due March 2003

An annual review of the most recent developments in specific legal subject areas, useful for law students at degree and professional levels, others with law elements in their courses and also practitioners seeking a quick update.

Published around March every year, the Law Update summarises the major legal developments during the course of the previous year. In conjunction with Old Bailey Press textbooks it gives the student a significant advantage when revising for examinations.

Contents

Administrative Law • Civil and Criminal Procedure • Commercial Law • Company Law • Conflict of Laws • Constitutional Law • Contract Law • Conveyancing • Criminal Law • Criminology • English and European Legal Systems • Equity and Trusts • European Union Law • Evidence • Family Law • Jurisprudence • Land Law • Law of International Trade • Public International Law • Revenue Law • Succession • Tort

For further information on contents or to place an order, please contact:

Mail Order
Old Bailey Press
at Holborn College
Woolwich Road
Charlton
London
SE7 8LN

Telephone No: 020 7381 7407
Fax No: 020 7386 0952
Website: www.oldbaileypress.co.uk

ISBN 1 85836 477 9
Soft cover 246 x 175 mm
450 pages approx
£10.95
Due March 2003

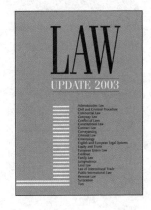

Unannotated Cracknell's Statutes for use in Examinations

New Editions of Cracknell's Statutes

£11.95 due 2002

Cracknell's Statutes provide a comprehensive series of essential statutory provisions for each subject. Amendments are consolidated, avoiding the need to cross-refer to amending legislation. Unannotated, they are suitable for use in examinations, and provide the precise wording of vital Acts of Parliament for the diligent student.

Commercial Law
ISBN: 1 85836 472 8

European Community Legislation
ISBN: 1 85836 470 1

Conflict of Laws
ISBN: 1 85836 473 6

Family Law
ISBN: 1 85836 471 X

Criminal Law
ISBN: 1 85836 474 4

Public International Law
ISBN: 1 85836 476 0

Employment Law
ISBN: 1 85836 475 2

For further information on contents or to place an order, please contact:

Mail Order
Old Bailey Press
at Holborn College
Woolwich Road
Charlton
London
SE7 8LN

Telephone No: 020 7381 7407
Fax No: 020 7386 0952
Website: www.oldbaileypress.co.uk

Suggested Solutions to Past Examination Questions 2000–2001

The Suggested Solutions series provides examples of full answers to the questions regularly set by examiners. Each suggested solution has been broken down into three stages: general comment, skeleton solution and suggested solution. The examination questions included within the text are taken from past examination papers set by the London University. The full opinion answers will undoubtedly assist you with your research and further your understanding and appreciation of the subject in question.

Only £6.95 Due December 2002

Constitutional Law
ISBN: 1 85836 478 7

Jurisprudence and Legal Theory
ISBN: 1 85836 484 1

Criminal Law
ISBN: 1 85836 479 5

Land Law
ISBN: 1 85836 481 7

English Legal System
ISBN: 1 85836 482 5

Law of Tort
ISBN: 1 85836 483 3

Elements of the Law of Contract
ISBN: 1 85836 480 9

For further information on contents or to place an order, please contact:

Mail Order
Old Bailey Press
at Holborn College
Woolwich Road
Charlton
London
SE7 8LN

Telephone No: 020 7381 7407
Fax No: 020 7386 0952
Website: www.oldbaileypress.co.uk

Old Bailey Press

The Old Bailey Press integrated student law library is tailor-made to help you at every stage of your studies from the preliminaries of each subject through to the final examination. The series of Textbooks, Revision WorkBooks, 150 Leading Cases and Cracknell's Statutes are interrelated to provide you with a comprehensive set of study materials.

You can buy Old Bailey Press books from your University Bookshop, your local Bookshop, direct using this form, or you can order a free catalogue of our titles from the address shown overleaf.

The following subjects each have a Textbook, 150 Leading Cases/Casebook, Revision WorkBook and Cracknell's Statutes unless otherwise stated.

Administrative Law
Commercial Law
Company Law
Conflict of Laws
Constitutional Law
Conveyancing (Textbook and 150 Leading Cases)
Criminal Law
Criminology (Textbook and Sourcebook)
Employment Law (Textbook and Cracknell's Statutes)
English and European Legal Systems
Equity and Trusts
Evidence
Family Law
Jurisprudence: The Philosophy of Law (Textbook, Sourcebook and
    Revision WorkBook)
Land: The Law of Real Property
Law of International Trade
Law of the European Union
Legal Skills and System
    (Textbook)
Obligations: Contract Law
Obligations: The Law of Tort
Public International Law
Revenue Law (Textbook,
    Revision WorkBook and
    Cracknell's Statutes)
Succession

Mail order prices:	
Textbook	£14.95
150 Leading Cases	£11.95
Revision WorkBook	£9.95
Cracknell's Statutes	£11.95
Suggested Solutions 1998–1999	£6.95
Suggested Solutions 1999–2000	£6.95
Suggested Solutions 2000–2001	£6.95
Law Update 2002	£9.95
Law Update 2003	£10.95

Please note details and prices are subject to alteration.

To complete your order, please fill in the form below:

Module	Books required	Quantity	Price	Cost
		Postage		
		TOTAL		

For Europe, add 15% postage and packing (£20 maximum).
For the rest of the world, add 40% for airmail.

ORDERING

By telephone to Mail Order at 020 7381 7407, with your credit card to hand.

By fax to 020 7386 0952 (giving your credit card details).

Website: www.oldbaileypress.co.uk

By post to: Mail Order, Old Bailey Press at Holborn College, Woolwich Road, Charlton, London, SE7 8LN.

When ordering by post, please enclose full payment by cheque or banker's draft, or complete the credit card details below. You may also order a free catalogue of our complete range of titles from this address.

We aim to despatch your books within 3 working days of receiving your order.

Name

Address

Postcode   Telephone

Total value of order, including postage: £

I enclose a cheque/banker's draft for the above sum, or

charge my   ☐ Access/Mastercard   ☐ Visa   ☐ American Express
Card number

☐☐☐☐ ☐☐☐☐ ☐☐☐☐ ☐☐☐☐

Expiry date   ☐☐☐☐

Signature: ....Date: ....